THE WALLS CAME TUMBLING DOWN

Sourcebooks in Negro History

MARY WHITE OVINGTON

The Walls Came Tumbling Down

With a New Introduction by
CHARLES FLINT KELLOGG

SCHOCKEN BOOKS • NEW YORK

FOREWORD

ALTHOUGH I have searched diligently for the most descriptive phrase to cause you to know Mary White Ovington as we have worked with her many years, I can think of none more precise than "Fighting Saint." Born of a family of culture and means, she might have been secure in conforming to the prejudices and conditions of her society. Instead she threw herself into the most difficult social problem in America—the Negro Question. She did so with full awareness, despite her modest disclaimers to the contrary, of the scorn, insult, and even physical danger her espousal of ex-slaves and their descendants would bring down on her. She has marched serenely ahead armed with the assurance that the fight she was making was as much, in the words of the late James Weldon Johnson, to save white America's soul as it was to save black America's body.

Belonging to the great majority of readers who never read prefaces, I content myself with urging you to read Miss Ovington's beautifully simple story of a gallant fight for one of the most fundamental of the principles of democracy. She has been most fortunate in having voluntarily enriched her life by being in the words of Whittier, "part of a noble and unpopular cause." Unlike most pioneers, however, she has lived to see enormous changes as a direct result of her own efforts. But being the perfectionist she is, she will never be content until she sees the complete attainment of her goal—the abolition of the color line in democracy. Having read her book, the actual story told from the inside, it is up to you and me to do our share in the attainment of that goal.

WALTER WHITE
Secretary of the NAACP

PREFACE

In the old days when Booker T. Washington was at the height of his popularity, he drew many visitors to Tuskegee: diplomats, legislators, governors, presidents. Washington would lead the visitor of the day to the rostrum, seat him, and a pageant would begin. To the sound of stirring music, the students would march into the room. Boys and girls wearing their uniforms, two by two came up the aisle, past the rostrum, and then down to their seats. The procession was unhalting, seemingly endless. When the visitor at length arose to make his speech, he was likely to say what the visitor of the day before had said. Likening himself to the Queen of Sheba, he had come to visit the famed Solomon and had learned that all he had heard was true; that indeed "the half had not been told."

I have been fortunate that the pageantry of the Negro race has passed before me for some forty years. I cannot report the half of what I have heard and seen. My sins of omission are heavy, but after all, it is the march that counts.

The chronicling of thanks is always difficult. I must first recall a few early publications by *The Survey* (then *Charities and the Commons*), *The Independent*, *The Century* and *The New York Evening Post*. Oswald Garrison Villard, then editor and owner of *The Post*, was most generous in printing my stories. This was contrary to the general opinion of editors of the day, who published little that did not concern Negro industrial education—though the then new firm of Harcourt, Brace and Howe printed a novel of mine on the Negro in 1920. Today, Negro material is accepted rather on the basis of its literary value. This has come from the genius of the Negro writer himself.

In 1932, I published my "Reminiscences" in Mr. Carl Murphy's excellent paper, *The Afro-American*. With his knowledge and his good wishes, some of the events there related have been used again here. I wish to express to him my warm gratitude for his generosity and continued interest in my work.

I am indebted to the *Haldeman-Julius Monthly* for its excellent story of the Sweet Trial.

Walter White, NAACP Secretary, made available all the records of the Association, and to him and to all the Association's staff I would express my warmest thanks.

Arthur B. Spingarn, now President of the Association, was kind enough to read and annotate the manuscript. Arna Bontemps of Fisk University Library, was helpful and hopeful. Others who read the manuscript were the Reverend John Haynes Holmes, Dr. Louis T. Wright, Mrs. Daisy E. Lampkin, and Miss Julia Baxter. My secretary, Carrie B. Overton, has typed and prepared this manuscript, improved it, and kept me from discouragement. "For this relief, much thanks." As other prefacers before me have said, the faults of the book are my own.

MARY WHITE OVINGTON.

New York

CONTENTS

Foreword by WALTER WHITE   vii

Preface   ix

Introduction by CHARLES FLINT KELLOGG   xiii

Chapter I.   THE OPENING SCENE   3

Chapter II.   THE NORTH   13

Chapter III. THE SOUTH   53

Chapter IV.   THE NAACP BEGINS   100

Chapter V   JOHN R. SHILLADY, WHO PUT OUR
                HOUSE IN ORDER   147

Chapter VI.   JAMES WELDON JOHNSON; WE MEET
                THE NATION   176

Chapter VII. WALTER WHITE; WE MEET THE
                WORLD   244

Chapter VIII. THE WALLS CAME TUMBLING DOWN   283

Appendix   300
Index   301

INTRODUCTION TO THE
1970 EDITION

MARY WHITE OVINGTON, whom scholar–philanthropist Joel E. Spingarn termed "the rebel saint," was unique among her contemporaries. She was a rebel in turning away from the comfortable, liberal, upper-middle-class way of life of Brooklyn Heights into which she was born in 1865. Educated at private schools and at Radcliffe College, for a time she tried the social life of a debutante. But this kind of life was not for Mary White Ovington. While a student at Radcliffe her interest in labor problems and in socialism had been aroused, and she finally determined upon a career as a social worker.

Many persons mellow and turn conservative with age, but Miss Ovington was a rebel and a radical until the end. At the age of seventy-five she wrote her pastor, John Haynes Holmes, that twice in her lifetime she had witnessed the middle class turn against the working class when the latter had almost achieved success. It seemed to her that middle-class liberals, in spite of their avowed sympathy with the workingman, brought about reforms in a way that left themselves in power. Mary White Ovington, observing the Europe of 1940, was convinced that the workers alone could bring about prosperity and lasting peace. "Of course they will be violent," she wrote, "this is a violent world."

Holmes, a fellow Board member of the National Association for the Advancement of Colored People, agreed that the hope of the world lay with the workers, for they alone, he wrote, "could reproduce what we are now losing, and build again what is now collapsing." To him there was no other hope "save religion's vision of the Spirit." To Miss Ovington the intellectual class was of value to the working class only by exposing evil conditions. After that the intellectuals were more likely to hinder the reform movement than to promote it. She compared the intellectual to the abolitionist who exposed slavery and then opposed the compromise measures that in the end had brought about its abolition. Likewise, the Girondists of the French Revolution were revolutionists until they found that their interests would be destroyed by the success of the workers. Miss Ovington was convinced that the class to which she and Holmes belonged had failed. She maintained that the two great World Wars showed an enormous lack of intelligence. Her hope for the future lay in a worker's government, though she admitted such a government, at its worst, already existed in the Soviet Union. Nevertheless, she wrote Holmes, "I am profoundly a Communist, though I know a communist state would destroy the basis of the civilization under which I live and under which I have had an unusually happy life."

Holmes agreed that Communism as a philosophy of life was sound and that it was the cooperative principle essential to Christianity. But as it had developed in Russia, Communism was abhorrent to him as a spiritual interpretation of life. It meant tyranny and terror, force and violence, materialism and atheism, and the justification of any means by the ends. "Yes, I am a Communist," said Holmes, "as the early Christians were, as Robert Owen was, as the Brook Farm people were, and as Gandhi is in his program for village life in India. But I am not a Communist as Stalin and the Bolsheviks are." He warned Miss Ovington that she should make this distinction clear and suggested that she use the word "Collectivist" instead of "Communist" to avoid the connotations which in the beginning had never been intended or foreseen. Holmes thought "Collectivist" was a better term because it better expressed Mary White Ovington's philosophy and removed any misunderstanding about her belief.

In her religious thinking Miss Ovington was also a rebel and a radical. She went even further than Holmes, who had left Unitarianism, which was considered radical, and had sought to revolutionize religion by creating a "Community Church" dedicated to the spiritual values of all mankind. Miss Ovington, who had been reared as a Unitarian, confessed to Holmes that she was no longer "religious" as she would define the religion of her childhood. She no longer believed in "a power not of ourselves that makes for righteousness." But she was not dogmatic, and she thought it foolish to be didactic about the mortality of man. She believed that man is on earth to better conditions before leaving it; that man has two intense urges, sex and acquisitiveness; that he could never create a Utopia; that there is no absolute good; and that the physical conditions under which men live—in wealth or poverty —make different sets of values. She believed that those who live in security, unless they have "amazing imaginations," never comprehend the values of those who live in insecurity. Her idealism was that of one who in her early days had been "drenched in romance," and this may also have affected her decision not to marry, "fairy princes being few in number." But she had no regret at not marrying, because her career was all important.

It was natural that as a rebel, a radical, and a protagonist Miss Ovington should have a close affinity with, and ally herself to, the other members of the Board of Directors of the NAACP who shared her feelings and beliefs—William English Walling, John Haynes Holmes, Charles Edward Russell, and William Edward Burghardt Du Bois—rather than with more conservative members such as Walter Sachs, Thomas Ewing, Jr., Moorfield Storey, and Oswald Garrison Villard. The skill and quiet determination with which she championed racial and economic justice, woman's suffrage, pacifism, and other reforms led Walter White to dub her the "Fighting Saint."

All of her co-workers in the NAACP thought well of her. She received high praise from Du Bois, who was extremely sensitive to any hint of racism, for in her personal relationships with black people she was without the faintest trace of prejudice or bias. She was one who truly loved mankind. She was admired likewise by Villard, who belonged to the conservatives in the NAACP and who was very critical of his associates and co-workers. Joel Spingarn he called a "firebrand"; Walling and Russell he wrote of as "contemptible" and given to "vituperation"; Du Bois he held to be "dangerous, mistaken, and mean spirited." He held Rabbi Stephen S. Wise in the highest contempt for "that fanfare of publicity which surrounds his every move." In spite of Miss Ovington's sympathy with the radical group, Villard had only praise for her, though she frequently disagreed with his policies as chairman of the Board. Villard considered Miss Ovington the perfect administrator, always unperturbed, "a most ladylike, refined and cultivated person." Nearly three decades later, in his memoirs, he recalled that Mary White Ovington was "in herself the personification of lovely and spiritual womanhood."

To some it might seem that a radical who was largely responsible for the founding of a radical organization dedicated to the achievement of full equality for a despised minority could be none other than a fanatic or bitter partisan. However, Miss Ovington's personal and professional relationships were never marred by pettiness or carping criticism. She remained above and strove to prevent factional strife within the organization.

Miss Ovington was also unique in that she was the first professionally trained social worker in the United States to devote her career and personal fortune to the cause of the Negro. To social workers Florence Kelley, Sophonisba P. Breckinridge, Lillian Wald, and Jane Addams, the plight of the Negro was secondary. Their chief interests lay with protection of women and children, consumers' leagues, factory legislation, political reform, and the predicament of immigrants and slum dwellers. Among the women prominent in the reform movements of the progressive era, Anna Howard Shaw of the National American Woman's Suffrage Association, Alice Paul of the National Women's Party, and the leadership of the Young Women's Christian Association were antagonistic to the aspirations of the NAACP and the National Association of Colored Women. Some notable exceptions were Fanny Garrison Villard, daughter of the abolitionist William Lloyd Garrison and mother of Oswald Garrison Villard, Mrs.

John E. Milholland, and her daughter, Inez Milholland Boissevain, but in general white reformers and philanthropists ignored the race problem and, when approached by the NAACP leaders, were found to be indifferent or hostile. On the other hand, Mary White Ovington chose a career in social work that dealt with black–white relationships, the most pressing, difficult, and neglected social problem in America. She too realized, with Du Bois, that the color problem was worldwide and must be attacked on a world-wide front. In the face of considerable opposition from some of her colleagues on the NAACP Board of Directors, Miss Ovington supported Du Bois in his program of Pan-Africanism, and she was primarily responsible for the Association's sponsoring and financing of the 1919 Pan-African Congress held in Paris at the close of the Great War.

In preparation for assuming the full responsibility of implementing racial justice, she set about acquainting herself with the problem by becoming (in 1904) a fellow at Greenwich House, a settlement founded by another fighting crusader, Mary Kingsbury Simkhovitch. Among her associates there were two young men who were later to join in the founding of the NAACP. One was Paul Kennaday, "a young man of fastidious tastes, but great moral passion," who gave up the practice of law to engage in social work. The other was Romanian-born Henry Moskowitz, who as a youth had grown up on the lower East Side, and after graduate study at the University of Berlin also became active in social work and campaigned for factory and labor legislation.

It is interesting to note that the members of the Greenwich House Committee on Social Investigations, which awarded Miss Ovington her fellowship, were all on the faculty of Columbia University. Edwin R. A. Seligman, the chairman, and Vladimir G. Simkhovitch, the secretary, were economic historians, while Franz Boas and Livingston Farrand were anthropologists. Henry R. Seager, Miss Ovington's supervisor, was an economist, Franklin H. Giddings, a sociologist, and Edward T. Divine, general secretary of the Charity Organization Society and director of the New York School of Philanthropy (later known as the New York School of Social Work), was a professor of political economy. Professors Boas and Farrand together with philosopher John Dewey, who was chairman of the Greenwich House Committee on Education, were recruited by Miss Ovington to speak at the National Negro Conference in 1910, out of which the NAACP evolved. Dewey and Seligman also served on the NAACP's General Committee.

During the period of her fellowship at Greenwich House she made two trips to the South to observe conditions that were bringing about the migration of Negroes to Northern urban centers, and she lived for a year in a model tenement for Negroes in New York City. Here she came to know black men and women of the working class. Through W. E. B. Du Bois and her contacts in the Social Reform Club and the Cosmopolitan Club, she came in contact with Negro professional people.

By 1907 social-service agencies were paying more attention to the Negro, who was migrating to New York in ever increasing numbers. Lillian Wald's Henry Street Settlement, originally founded to minister to Jewish immigrants, extended its nursing service to the Negro district, while sociologist Frances Keller started work to protect Negro girls arriving from the South. Miss Keller's project grew into the National

League for the Protection of Colored Women. Miss Ovington was one of the founders of this group and helped to establish (in 1905) the Committee for Improving Industrial
Conditions of Negroes in New York. Her interest in this organization stemmed from her concern for the working classes
and their economic problems. These two groups merged in
1911 with a third to form the National Urban League, but
by this time her complete attention was centered on the
NAACP.

All these associations and experiences contributed to Miss
Ovington's expanding knowledge of conditions among Negroes. In 1911 she published her findings in *Half a Man: The
Status of the Negro in New York*. Again she was unique in
that she was the first white person to make such a survey. In
1899 Du Bois had published *The Philadelphia Negro: A Social Study*, but John Daniels, a free-lance writer and lecturer,
did not bring out *In Freedom's Birthplace: A Study of the
Boston Negroes* until 1914.

Miss Ovington began her writing on the Negro in 1904
with articles and poems in *Outlook* and in Villard's *New
York Evening Post*. Her last effort on behalf of the Negro,
The Walls Came Tumbling Down, originally appeared
in 1947. In the meantime her writing included articles in the
Crisis and in the liberal periodicals on racial justice, the Atlanta
riots, social work among colored children in New York, the
Russian Revolution, and the relations between the United
States and Puerto Rico. As early as 1906 she wrote an article
on the Negro and the trade unions in New York for one of
the learned periodicals (*The Annals of the American Academy
of Political and Social Science*). In 1926 she wrote about the
founding of the NAACP for the *Journal of Negro History*.

Mary White Ovington was also the first white person to realize that there were no books to satisfy the longings of black boys and girls for stories of their own people. The pioneer work in this field was *Hazel: The Story of a Little Colored Girl* (1913). Since white publishers felt there was no market for stories of Negro life, the book was issued by the Crisis Publishing Company, Du Bois' short-lived venture to seek an outlet for material on the Negro which ordinarily would be rejected by the established publishing houses. *Hazel* received scant notice in the white press, but its author was pleased that over two thousand copies were sold.

Hazel was followed by *The Upward Path* (1920), compiled in collaboration with Myron Thomas Prichard, editor of several educational journals. This was the first anthology of sketches, poems, addresses, and stories by black writers collected for Negro children in which were mirrored the traditions and aspirations of their people, and which revealed the richness of Negro literature just coming into flower in the Negro renaissance of the 1920's. Again, the pieces were chosen not only to give pleasure but to foster racial pride through illustrations of accomplishments. The following year, Du Bois endeavored to establish a children's magazine, the *Brownies' Book,* to provide reading material presented from the black point of view, but the venture was not a success.

Zeke (1931), Mary White Ovington's third book for Negro children, was, like the other two, not concerned with the race problem but was the story of a boy and his adjustment to the pattern of living and studying in a large vocational school. By the time *The Upward Path* and *Zeke* were issued, a different climate of opinion prevailed in the publishing field.

Not only were they accepted for publication by a reputable publisher, but their appearance evoked favorable comment by reviewers.

Miss Ovington wrote two race plays, *The Awakening* (1923) and *Phillis Wheatley* (1932), which were suitable for presentation by NAACP youth groups, who until this time had no material written especially for them. She also produced a novel, *The Shadow* (1920), combining her two great interests, the labor movement and the race problem. It, too, was a pioneer work in opening up new possibilities in American literature, for it gave the black and white characters the same human attributes rather than conforming to the traditional literary racist stereotypes.

Portraits in Color (1927) is a collection of sketches of the lives of twenty interesting black men and women. In a very real sense this book is a brief for the Negro, free from argument and propaganda. Its aim is to combat self-hate and to instill pride of race in Negro readers, young and old.

The Walls Came Tumbling Down was completed in 1947, when Mary White Ovington was eighty-two years of age. The final chapter had been interrupted by illness and depression, and the year after the book's appearance she became ill again. She died three years later on July 15, 1951, at the age of eighty-six.

In spite of her illness and advanced age, *The Walls Came Tumbling Down* is a remarkable piece of work, recording as it does the mores and shifting temper of the first half of the twentieth century. There are numerous errors of detail, which one might expect from a person of her advanced age, but the over-all story is accurate. Her recollections of the coming of Joel E. Spingarn and John R. Shillady to the NAACP are blurred, but these are matters which are of no particular concern to the general reader.

The first part of the book through to the founding of the NAACP is largely autobiographical. It is to be regretted that the rebel and fighting saint, after sketching her part in the founding of the Association, does not record more of her very considerable role in its future growth and development until her retirement in 1947. Instead, with her characteristic modesty and self-effacement, she writes of the effectiveness of others. One would scarcely guess that she was a major force in molding the Association's character and in influencing its philosophy and direction. She held every important office in the NAACP—secretary, treasurer, director of branches, and chairman of the Board of Directors. For forty years she was its inspiration and leading spirit, a humble, cultured gentlewoman who battled fiercely to arouse the conscience of America.

The Walls Came Tumbling Down is the dramatic, compelling, and moving story of the National Association for the Advancement of Colored People, told with Mary White Ovington's usual effective restraint. It reveals how a little band of men and women, black and white, were welded together to form the most powerful and successful agency to work for the eradication of the "shame of America," the prejudicial, discriminatory, and unjust treatment of the Negroes of America.

CHARLES FLINT KELLOGG

Dickinson College
Carlisle, Pennsylvania
January 1970

The research for this Introduction was done under grants from the Penrose Fund of The American Philosophical Society, and the Division of Research and Publication of the National Endowment for the Humanities.

C. F. K.

Joshua fit de battle of Jericho,
Jericho, Jericho.
Joshua fit de battle of Jericho,
And de walls came tumbling down.

THE WALLS CAME TUMBLING DOWN

CHAPTER I

THE OPENING SCENE

EVERY IMAGINATIVE child who has access to books or who hears tales of a romantic past—and the past grows romantic in the telling—has a gallery of heroes upon which he loves to brood. The exiled king, the soldier, the pioneer, furnish portraits of courage and daring. I had my gallery where Robert Bruce dwelt and Erling the Bold; but the pictures that stirred me most and that I turned to oftenest were those of fugitive slaves. I saw Eliza crossing the ice on the last lap in her course to freedom; Box Brown arising from the trunk in which he had been tossed about for days, Anthony Burns incredibly escaping to Boston to be incredibly returned to slavery; and Frederick Douglass—most dramatic because he wrote his own story—questioned by the conductor on the train through Maryland and accepted on a false card of identity, seeing recognition in the eyes of a white man on the boat crossing the river to Philadelphia, praying blessings on the man when he turned away, at last stepping onto Pennsylvania's free ground, from slavery to freedom. These were true tales (Mrs. Stowe verified her fiction), but I liked best to make up my own.

We spent a number of summers at Chesterfield in western Massachusetts, and on quiet starlit nights I would go out on the road where few teams passed, and study the constella-

3

tions. Here was the full dome of the heavens. I loved Emerson's "If the stars should appear for one night in a thousand years how men would worship and adore and preserve for generations the memory of the city of God that had been shown!" I would keep my eyes on the ground as I walked along the road, and imagine looking up to nothing, only emptiness! But they were all here: Vega bright overhead, the long line of the milky way, Sagittarius on the horizon.

The star that most excited my imagination was in the North, the lower line of the Dipper pointing to it. The others moved from month to month, but this remained in its place—the North Star that led the slave to freedom. It was insignificant, but it pointed the way. When clouds obscured it, the slave must remain in the swamp, bitten by mosquitoes, shaking with fever, or lie hidden in a cabin where some friend courageously gave him shelter. My hero went through intense peril as, helped by the underground railroad, he slowly found his way to British territory where no man might be held as a slave. He would be wounded, his black skin dripping with sweat, but I saw to it that he always reached Canada. There I left him, without a thought as to how he might be able to live in that new and chilly land.

I did not get all the material for my dreams from books. My mother's mother, who lived with us, came from Brooklyn, Connecticut. As a young girl she listened to the sermons of Samuel J. May, Unitarian and ardent abolitionist, and became herself an abolitionist.

Brooklyn, in the northeast corner of Connecticut, received its culture from Boston and Providence, not from the orthodox Connecticut of New Haven. One of Brooklyn's dramatic moments was the imprisonment of Prudence Crandall in its county jail. Prudence Crandall—there is a beautiful picture of her at Cornell—was a young teacher in the neighboring town of Canterbury, who took a colored girl into her select school for young ladies. When the white young ladies were removed from school by their outraged parents, Prudence filled their places with colored girls, and for this was sent to jail.

Carrying her abhorrence of slavery with her to Brooklyn, New York, my grandmother went to abolition meetings, and enjoyed, when it was over and well in the past, telling the story of Isaiah Rynder and his mob who broke up a meeting she attended, dragging Charles Burleigh, a non-resistant, about the stage by his beard.

My father and mother sang naturally well. On their wedding journey they found themselves inside a lumbering coach on their way to the Catskill Mountain House. It was raining hard, the passengers were crowded inside, and the young couple began to sing. They were loudly applauded and continued to sing the melodious, sentimental songs of the day. But one Stephen Foster song met with silence. A last verse, which my father had written, went like this:

> Now harken white folk all
> And listen to the call
> Your heavenly father is proclaiming.
> Break every yoke,
> Release every slave,
> Way down in their old cabin homes.

The young couple learned the next morning that they had been singing to a party of South Carolinians.

With mention that my father left Plymouth Church because Beecher approved of giving money to the American

Board of Foreign Missions, an obscure issue now but a real one then, my background should be sufficiently described to account for my intensity of sympathy for a race that I felt had been diabolically brought in slave ships to this country, and after arrival systematically wronged by enslavement.

This was the world of the Negro as I knew it. Of actual contacts I had none. We did not have colored servants, and in no other way would I be likely in my home on Brooklyn Heights to speak to a colored person. I did go once or twice to a West Indian dressmaker, but though her face was dark, I was assured positively that she was not a Negro. An old, blind colored man, led by a little boy, came to our church once a year to ask for money for the Howard Orphan Asylum. Oddly, neither at my own (Unitarian) church nor at Plymouth which my grandfather attended, did I happen to hear any appeal for colored teachers in the South. Had I come under Armstrong's influence, I might have gone to Hampton Institute where my ignorance of housework should have had me thrown out, while Booker T. Washington won his entrance by dusting a room four times!

Reconstruction silenced the ex-slave holder, but in the eighties, Thomas Nelson Page, in the *Century Magazine*, began to write of the faithful uncle or mammy who settled wisely important problems in the lives of the whites. We devoured these stories at home, making frightful gulps at the dialect. The *Century* also introduced us to Harry Still-ward Edwards, Joel Chandler Harris, and others. They interested me. I was surprised at the familiarity between master and servant, but they taught me little. The servant who is wholeheartedly sympathetic with the children in a household, I took for granted. I loved our Irish servants devotedly, and thought, and still think, their stories of Johnny and Kate, of leprechauns and the pot of gold as good as Br'er Rabbit. But I recognized class lines. I wanted to meet the upper class of Negroes, the descendants, spiritually at least, of the fugitive slaves. I wanted to talk over my favorite books with them, to learn their tastes. But I was as little likely to meet one of these people in my small world as to find Queen Victoria ringing my door bell.

While I met no educated Negroes, I saw and heard Frederick Douglass. He was speaking in Plymouth Church, and I asked the young man of the moment to be my escort. You needed an escort when the streets were dark with only an occasional gas jet on a tall lamp post. Inevitably we discussed Douglass's marriage to a white woman. Douglass himself said to a mixed audience in Atlanta, "My father was white, my mother was black. My first wife was black, my second wife is white. I have paid my respects to both my parents." This failed to satisfy my escort whose roots were in Baltimore. He kept repeating, "How could she do it! How could she do it!" Reaching Plymouth Church, we sat in the front row of the balcony at the far end where we looked directly onto the platform. Douglass entered. My first impression was of power, of a dominating personality. His skin was bronze with an undertone of yellow, his features massive. His bushy white hair standing out from his head gave him extraordinary dignity. I heard my companion gasp. Then he turned to whisper, "I don't wonder she married him. He looks like Aesop!"

Once I just missed a friendly contact with a colored student. My leisurely education at private schools ended with two years at Radcliffe, then known as the Harvard Annex.

Returning the next year to visit an old friend, I saw a colored girl, her books under her arm, walking down the lovely stairway at Fay House. She did not notice me, but I stared at her, wondering regretfully why she had not come to college a year sooner. I learned later that she was a resident of Cambridge, and if she had liked me, I might have met her friends and might have entered, without need of debating the color problem, into her social group. I think now that the debate would have come early in our acquaintance, for the race problem is in the front of the Negro's mind. At any rate she would have introduced it, not myself.

W. E. Burghardt Du Bois was at Harvard when I was at Radcliffe, but our paths did not cross. One of my fellow students in history told me excitedly that while walking from her history seminar with a Negro (if she said his name I did not note it,) she had been cut by a southern student. I was bitter at my loss of opportunity. If he had treated me that way, I would have used my every social and academic and imaginary influence to have him ground in the dust. To dare to do such a thing in Cambridge! In years to come I was to be given opportunity to smite the southern Philistine, but with little success. Beneath his pleasant manners is the steel-like armor of race righteousness. I have also met the southern rebel against race tradition, the most courageous figure in America today.

After two years at college, I became registrar for a year at Pratt Institute; and then, with the generous help of Frederick B. Pratt and of students in domestic art and domestic science classes, we started the Greenpoint Settlement of the Pratt Institute Neighborship Association. We were housed in a model tenement, the Astral, a solidly built brick building that stands as firmly as ever, overlooking the river at Twenty-third Street in New York. I took up the work half-heartedly for I had little emotional urge. But I knew that Arnold Toynbee, after studying economics at Oxford, decided to see working class conditions at first hand; and while formal economics at college had left me uninterested, two things in history had profoundly impressed me, as they still impress me today.

William J. Ashley had recently been called to Harvard. He gave a course in English Economic History. I took the course at Radcliffe, and did a piece of research on the Peasants' Revolt. Students at Radcliffe were few, and we were given access to the stacks at the Harvard Library. There I read all the source books that I could find on my subject, searching among the shelves. The books were few, and all were written from the landlord's standpoint. Not a word from the peasants themselves! This seemed manifestly unfair but was entirely natural. The landlords had learned to write.

I also had a course in Modern European History with Silas MacVane. We spent a long time over the French Revolution, reading voluminously. When we came to the Reign of Terror, the authors used many pages telling, sometimes tearfully, always with great severity, of the men and women guillotined under the rule of Danton and Robespierre. In a short reference book on the Revolution that I was reviewing for examination, after a long chapter on the Reign of Terror, I turned a page to read, in one paragraph, that more people had been killed in the White Terror following the revolution than in the Red Terror. I can see that paragraph now at the top of the left-hand page. It told nothing in detail of these murdered men, women, and children. Their lives were not worth noting. This neglect of the sufferings of the worker, this continual presentation of facts by historians from the standpoint of the propertied classes was something not to be forgotten. It helped me to decide to see for myself, in my own city, the life of the working class.

I learned a great deal at the settlement in Greenpoint while I was there from 1896 to 1903. I saw unemployment, that nightmare that continues through the days and the months when a man is seeking work. I met the unionist who had tried to improve conditions by going on strike and was now on the black list—an exile from his native city. I learned the time the factory girls, who had been in our gymnasium class the night before, started work, since the seven o'clock whistle woke me from sleep. I learned that children were more nervous when the family was seven in four rooms, than when, like my own family, there were seven in a four-story house. I also saw much happiness, for ours was not really a poor neighborhood except at the northern end of our ward.

During my first two years as a settlement worker, the Negro was non-existent. Then one afternoon we had a dramatic meeting. I took fifteen boys, representing eight nationalities, for an outing to Prospect Park. We went in an open trolley, and the boys were more than ordinarily noisy. I may say that I soon learned at Greenpoint to discount national traits. Whether his parents were born in Ireland, Germany, Denmark, Italy, or a Russian Ghetto, every mother's son became an American, earmarked by the public schools and the street life. They were active, destructive, likable children. As we neared the park, we turned into Gwinnet Street and began to pass by a line of unimproved, wooden houses on whose steps, for it was a hot day, colored women sat and talked to one another. Suddenly, as at a signal, every boy jumped on his feet and yelled, "Nigger, Nigger, Nigger!"

The colored women looked unconcerned, taking it as a part of life, but I was hot with anger. The performance was not repeated on the return trip, not because my speech at the Park on brotherhood had made an impression, but because I was the boss. Yet the boys had no race prejudice. Their yelling was a ritual that they had learned. When the Astral employed a colored janitor, the same boys seriously interfered with his work, so anxious were they to talk with him. He never seemed to me especially amusing, nor did he say anything remarkable, but he had a fascination for the children.

It was not until my last year at the Settlement, in the winter of 1903, that the Negro and his problems came into my life, where they will remain until my death. It happened accidentally, as important things often happen.

At the beginning of this century the Social Reform Club, of which I was a devoted member, had become a unique and interesting gathering place in New York. With a membership made up of professional and working people, it discussed practical and theoretical humanitarianism and did some good civic work. Ernest Howard Crosby, single-taxer, was for years its president, and in its membership were Josephine Shaw Lowell, Charles Stover, Leonora O'Reilly, James Paulding. Charles Spahr, then editor of *The Outlook*, and chairman of the program committee, proposed one evening that the Club give a dinner to Booker T. Washington and his wife. "Up From Slavery" was at this time appearing in *The Outlook*, and was attracting much attention. The Club agreed. I was one of those on the committee of arrangement. Spahr instructed us to devote some of the program to conditions in New York City. "Don't make it purely southern," he said; "let us hear of conditions at our own door."

Washington and Tuskegee of course made the dinner a success, but the New York Negro was not forgotten. We learned of our dark neighbor living around the corner. It was a picture of ramshackle tenements, high infant mortality, and discrimination in employment that made it almost impossible for a Negro to secure work that paid a decent wage. A colored physician testified to this, and assured us that conditions grew worse, not better, as immigrants, in great numbers, entered the city port. We left the meeting, as Spahr intended we should, with a realization that not only in Alabama but in our own New York we had a Negro problem.

The next year I left Greenpoint Settlement and became a fellow of Greenwich House, engaged in a study of the Negro in New York City.

CHAPTER II

THE NORTH

N EW YORK CITY, at the time I began my study, 1904, had a Negro population of 60,000. My objective was to draw a picture of these people, their homes, their churches, their businesses, their professions. The Social Reform Club dinner had fired my imagination. If the Negro in New York was the most neglected element in the population, I wanted to be of some help to this neglected element. Settlement work was my profession, and I at once went to my friend Mary Kingsbury Simkhovitch, headworker at Greenwich House, for advice on how to begin. Mary Simkhovitch had deep sympathy and a clear head. "But you know nothing about the people you want to work with," she said. I assented, and before I left she had planned a Greenwich House fellowship for me. I was to write a survey of the Negro in New York. The fellowship was soon secured by Dr. Simkhovitch of Columbia, and I was put under the guidance of Professor Henry Seager. It was a nominal guidance, for when I went to Seager for advice, he always told me that he knew nothing on the subject. So I went my own way. I did not live at Greenwich House though I was always welcome, and I did some work among the neighborhood's colored children. Of course, the investigation took longer than we expected. I kept taking time for other work among

Negroes. It was not until 1911 that my study was published by Longmans Green under the title *Half a Man: The Status of the Negro in New York*.

For the purpose of starting a settlement, a study of the status of the Negro poor would have been sufficient, but I at once decided to do more than that. I would survey the colored population in its entirety, the rich, the well-to-do, and the poor. Charles B. Spahr had recently brought out his book, *The Present Distribution of Wealth in the United States*. He had found that 10 per cent of the people owned 90 per cent of the wealth, and that the richest one per cent received a larger income than the poorest 50 per cent. How would this compare with the Negro Village, the 60,000 colored in New York? Would they show a one per cent of what we would call real wealth? Of course they would not, but I was surprised to find how small the possessions were of what might be called the possessing class. White friends were already telling me that the Negroes should support their own charities. But good social work costs money. Where should I find the Negro millionaires?

Fortunately for my work, the census for 1900 had a volume on the Negro with definite figures regarding Negro occupations. *Domestic Service* occupied 58 per cent of the workers—more than half. With whites, the figure fell to 18 per cent. This group included caterers and waiters; at one time a few of them had made real money, but foreign immigration, especially Swiss and French, had made the Negro waiter unfashionable in New York. The next largest occupational group was *Trade and Transportation*, 28 per cent colored to 37 per cent white. Highly paid workers in factory, store, and office were in this category. But trade and transportation for the Negro meant jobs such as porter, driver, and expressman; it meant the elevator boy going up and down past floors containing expensive goods sold by white men and women. On the trains the Negro was fireman, but not engineer; Pullman porter, but not conductor.

Some Negroes were in skilled trades, and whether skilled or not, those who were organized received a decent wage. James Wallace, formerly of Virginia, was head of the Asphalt Workers and stood in high esteem at the Central Federated Union. More than half of the workers in his organization were Italians. He was a prominent figure for a time in union councils, but his trade was doomed.

One group under *Trade and Transportation* was important because it was operated by the Government—the United States Post Office. The posts at the top were appointive, but the clerks and the mail carriers were under civil service open to men regardless of color.

Under the third group, *Manufacturing and Mechanical Pursuits,* where the Negro percentage was nine against the thirty-nine for whites, there were no colored superintendents of great plants, only occasionally a stationary engineer and often the janitor.

Looking at each heading, I could not find a modicum of Negro wealth. Of course there were exceptional men. A Negro assistant district attorney and an assistant corporation counsel were earning real money. Later, through introductions, I was to find exceptional men in all these groups. The white philanthropist liked to tell of his Negro printer, or clerk, or mechanic who worked side by side with white men. But such talk always concerned one Negro, and I strongly suspect that when he died his place was taken by a white man.

There were Negro real estate firms—Nail and Parker and Philip Payton, Jr., who were keen enough to take advantage of the exodus to Harlem. I should have met John B. Nail at this time and learned from him about real estate investments, for Nail knew his New York better than any other colored man, but I was not to have that advantage until later. In the main, Negro business was precarious, and the resources of the great capitalists were unknown to the colored. There were people of modest means who bought their own homes, usually in Brooklyn, had leisure and used it pleasantly, and lived on the economic plane of what we call the middle class, the class to which I belonged. A few of these were in the census occupations already given, more were in the professions.

Professional Service was the last census group, and the Negro percentage was encouraging—3.6 to 5.6 among the white. Here were the teachers, the doctors, the lawyers and the clergymen, the musicians and the actors. This was the group I had always wanted to know. My investigation would give me the opportunity of meeting with these men and women who were leaders in their communities.

"Has he white blood?" or "How much white blood has she?" were the usual questions asked me by friends to whom I was introducing new acquaintances. That all Negro success came from white inheritance was a common belief. Booker Washington had a white father, so had Frederick Douglass, and though no one knew who these parents were, all were sure that white intelligence and energy had made these mulattoes famous. "Craniologically and by six thousand years of planet-wide experimentation, the Negro is proved to be markedly inferior to the Caucasian," Professor W. B. Smith of Tulane University, New Orleans, was teaching his classes. Exceptions were pushed aside, and if facts denied this theory of racial inferiority, the facts were altered. I remember seeing an illustrated history in which the Egyptian kings of Negro origin were given Greek faces. Probably it was thought wrong to show a white child a picture of a Negro ruler. White blood meant intellectuality, and black blood savagery. A favorite theme (Edward Sheldon used it in his powerful play, *The Nigger*) was that black blood would out. Behind the deceptively white skin dwelt the savage who any day might spring and rape a white woman.

Among my new acquaintances was Dr. Owen M. Waller, one time of South Carolina, for years a physician in Brooklyn. He helped me in many ways. One evening a small group of people, white and colored, met at his home to hear him give an informal talk. Dr. Waller's features were not heavy, but he was light-brown in color. Knowing that we would be curious regarding the white Negro, he talked about the presence of colored blood among whites, illustrating his facts by photographs. "Here is a family of eight children," he said, "where pigmentation appeared in only four. Of the other four, three of the men are 'passing' and succeeding at work they might not do if they were known to be Negroes. This daughter," he passed us a picture of a strikingly handsome, to all appearances, white woman, "has married a white man and has two beautiful white children."

And so on. When the question of reversion to type arose, we were told that while pigmentation might skip a generation or two to reappear, the black baby of the story book, with kinky hair and Negroid features, born to two seemingly white parents, *was* a story. I think that is about what research on this subject tells us today.

How the people live who go over white, the pull of affection, the open visiting of the one sister who is passing and the covert visiting of another who lives in the colored world, is exciting narrative. One well-authenticated tale that I heard in the West is an illustration.

A man, high in the business world, is at a dinner given in his honor. Speakers shower their praise, and he responds with a graceful speech. At length he is escorted to his hotel, good nights are exchanged, and he goes to his room. A few minutes later he leaves his hotel and makes his way from the well-lighted, finely-paved street to the dark, broken pavement of the Negro quarter. Climbing a wooden stoop, he takes a latchkey from his pocket and enters his childhood home. The story of the return of the wealthy son is familiar enough, but this is a different tale, for the colored mother who goes forward to greet this son is excited, tremulous. She has seen to it that the shades are down. Many of the men and women who are gripping the visitor's hand are dark in color and heavy in feature. He is a million miles away from the hotel guests and the banquet and the speeches. And yet not so far, for his brother, who comes up to josh him, had waited on him at table. He laughs and jokes and feels the relaxation that comes with entrance into a familiar past. When he returns to his hotel in the early morning light, the room clerk, idly wondering where he has been, is incredibly far off in his guess.

No one will give him away. His friends may differ as to where his duty lies, but none questions his right to join the white world. Any deceit he may practice is more than offset by the rotten deal the white world would have given him had his skin been dark.

That a small amount of Negro blood has dribbled and is dribbling into the white race is certain—and unimportant. Had slavery continued a century or two longer, Albert Bushnell Hart used to tell us at Radcliffe, the Negro race would have disappeared through amalgamation. Under freedom, the colored woman, if not respected, is more and more left alone. In some cities, North and South, the mulatto class had a formal social life for light of skin only. Charles Chesnutt, who was writing at the beginning of the century, told amusingly, and pathetically too, of the efforts of a light family to prevent intermarriage with a black family. Had the whites encouraged this, as did the British who established three classes in the West Indies—white, colored, and black—the United States would have had a definite "colored" class. To this class, as in the West Indies, many privileges would doubtless have been granted. In slavery times, some fathers felt responsible for their light offspring. Lincoln University, a college in Pennsylvania, was started by planters who wished to give their colored children an education. But after Reconstruction, the southern states began to account any Negro ancestry, however distant, as establishing Negro status. Our census compilers gave up trying to find a mulatto class fifty years ago. Within the race, success, fame, wealth, compensated for darkness of color, and light women married dark men. The Negro tends toward a medium coloration. This is happening among Caucasians, and blonds are fast disappearing. The white American is growing darker, and the colored American seems to be slowly growing lighter.

But while the upper group in the Negro world was not, as

I saw it, overmuch concerned with pigmentation, its members were deeply concerned with maintaining such privileges as they had painfully gained. I learned of the valiant battles in the past from the Ray sisters, daughters of a Brooklyn clergyman, an old-time Negro abolitionist who was once secretary of the New York State Vigilance Committee of which Gerrit Smith was president. Ray was prominent in underground railroad work, and one of his daughters loved to remember the night they sheltered fourteen Negroes. "Their number seemed endless," she said, "as they came stealthily out of the darkness." The younger of the sisters, Cornelia, had written a volume of verse which The Grafton Press published.

They told me of Maritcha Lyons, a graduate of the city normal school, who in a long battle, won the right to teach in a white school. How entirely she had destroyed official race discrimination I learned when, in my zeal for statistics, I asked the superintendent of education, William Maxwell, for a list of his colored teachers. He told me indignantly that he had no such list and never intended to have one. His teachers were given positions on the ground of ability, not of color.

There were other stories of courageous battles in the past. Even the right to ride in a streetcar had to be won by a woman the conductor threw off into the street. But as I heard these and other incidents, the battle seemed over. The people living in their pleasant houses, while leading a social life distinct from their neighbors, were on bowing acquaintance with them and were satisfied. Their money was as good as other people's money, their vote was sought at election time, and they were proud of their citizenship.

To them, however, came the menace of the influx of
Negroes from the South who had never been to school, whose
ideas on cleanliness were sketchy, and who understood nothing of the conveniences of modern city life. These newcomers
were also violators of the law. They were being arrested for
pilfering, for street fighting, for razor slashing. And they
cast reflection on the whole race.

This was manifestly unfair. The morning paper would
carry two stories: one of a boy who snatched a purse from
a woman as she was crossing the street; the other of a black
boy who snatched a purse from a white woman. One boy was
as bad as the other but the white neighbor, reading this, would
look suspiciously at the next Negro he saw. So thought the
old citizen of colored blood as he folded his paper and wished
to heaven that the southern exodus would stay away from
Brooklyn. The newcomers who belonged to his own class
were welcomed, especially those ministers who had been
called North because of their growing fame as orators. It
was pleasant to welcome congenial newcomers into what was
a small society. But the good had no news value. Only the
bad were written about.

Some of these people knew and feared the South with
its segregated Negro section, where the house of prostitution
might be next to the public school, for all those in authority
cared. They wanted their children to grow up under pleasant
surroundings. They did not ask for intimacy with the whites
but they asked for recognition as law-abiding, intelligent,
wholesome men and women who wanted the best for their
children. Now they might be classed as "niggers," a word
they hated with an undying hatred.

This antagonism to the southern influx was common in

other northern cities, Chicago, Cleveland, and especially in Boston. I speak of Boston because I spent some time there during an agitation regarding a separate YMCA. Old colored Bostonians especially resented this since the white Y had not refused admission to colored applicants. But the applicants were few and the young men recently arrived from the South were many. The realistic Booker Washington element that saw jobs in segregation (and jobs were very necessary) favored a colored Y. The discussion was on.

Against segregation was Adelene Moffat, formerly of Tennessee, Mrs. Quincy Shaw's secretary. Miss Moffat supervised and encouraged a social settlement in Cambridge that had mixed classes and clubs. The Robert Gould Shaw House, with Isabel Eaton as head worker, while started primarily for colored, had a white as well as a colored enrollment. Since white and colored went to the public school together, it was contended that for philanthropy to segregate was contrary to the spirit of Boston.

The Boston Negro was intensely American and proud of his record as an American citizen. He never forgot that Crispus Attucks's was the first blood shed in the American Revolution. On the edge of Boston Common stood the Shaw Memorial, dedicated to Shaw and the Massachusetts Fifty-fourth Regiment. You saw its bronze soldiers marching down Beacon Street, down to the South and war. These determined men had refused all pay until put on an equality with the white soldier, and had fought desperately and well. Boston honored them, and Boston Negroes thought of them as symbolic of their loyalty to the nation and to the state and the city of their choice.

This Boston saw segregation growing more pronounced

with the migration of Negroes from the South. They hated
what they saw. Monroe Trotter, Phi Beta Kappa, Harvard,
voiced this hatred in his paper, the Boston *Guardian*. Trotter
was Boston's most belligerent spirit. He decried every form
of segregated institution except the church. Had it not been
so strongly entrenched he might have decried it also, but
Negro churches like white churches are social as well as religious centers and impervious to attack. Segregated businesses, too, had to be accepted, and many professional men
would have starved but for segregation. But no oppressed
people can be consistent. Trotter rejoiced at the success of
the tailor, Lewis, who made the bell-trouser famous; at the
wig maker, Dr. Grant; but he knew these were exceptions
and that the number of colored men patronized by whites
was few.

One of the pleasantest homes I entered was Butler R.
Wilson's in Boston. He and his beautiful wife were from the
South, but Boston was their adopted home and they loved it
and its history. Wilson was a lawyer with white as well as
colored clients. Moorfield Storey, Boston's great constitutional lawyer, who left college to be Charles Sumner's secretary, at times called upon Wilson in his legal work, and the
two were good friends. Butler Wilson was ready to help any
member of his race in a battle for human rights, but he was
adamant against segregation. He believed that Boston would
degrade itself by putting "colored" on the name of any
institution.

Where this position ultimately led, I found one afternoon
when we two walked together through a poor Negro section
on the south side. Wilson was talking about urging more colored young men to seek entrance in the YMCA. I was listen-

ing, but also noting the shabby, once handsome houses, the lounging boys, the poolroom in the middle of the block, the saloon on the corner. A game of craps was going on almost under our feet.

"These boys," I said, "won't go to white philanthropy. They need a Y of their own, if they are to be persuaded to go to a class or a club. They need their own gymnasium and swimming pool. Of course, you're right about segregation, but after all, here are these young people. What's to become of them?"

"Let them rot," he answered.

This particular issue is now closed. Colored YMCA's are all over the country, even in Boston. But the segregation issue only moves from one subject to another. It is never absent from the mind of the Negro.

Manhattan had acquiesced in the matter of the colored YMCA. Thomas J. Bell was secretary of the one on West Fifty-third Street, and helped me with my statistics, checking up the census figures with a few hundred men in his own group. The difference was slight. Across the street from the Y was St. Mark's Methodist Episcopal Church, open every week-day evening, and on Sunday for twelve hours. It was not institutional as we think of the white institutional church —its activities all carried a religious note—but it provided broad social activity for its members. A spacious church, its white congregation hurried out when the Sixth Avenue elevated ran past its doors. West Fifty-third Street, between Sixth and Eighth Avenues was a pandemonium of noise until the elevated was torn down. Whether it suited what he was saying or not, the minister must shout with each clanging train.

Dr. W. H. Brooks was St. Mark's minister at this time, and remained with the New York congregation until his death. Unlike most of the colored Methodist preachers, he was with the white general assembly which, appreciating the excellence and the importance of his work, kept him in New York. His study was at the rear, a dark room lighted by gas, and in winter with a gas burner that stood on the floor. The yellow light seemed to emphasize the darkness of his face, and his black coat and white collar gave a luminosity to his dark eyes. There was much wisdom in them, as I was to learn as I went to him again and again for advice and encouragement.

One matter I remember on which we disagreed. Booker Washington had recently dined with President Theodore Roosevelt, and the press discussed it in a caste spirit worthy of England in India. I felt that the President had honored Booker Washington and that, of course, Washington should accept the honor. But Brooks thought differently. He believed a Negro could foresee the position in which he was placing the President. He wrote me a letter on the subject in which he said, "Mr. Roosevelt had the right to invite Mr. Washington, and Mr. Washington had the right to accept. But is it the best and highest wisdom or the finest taste to make our friends suffer because it is in our power to do so?"

I recalled this letter later when I traveled in the interests of the NAACP, as I did year after year, in the South. My train was met and I was often entertained by colored people. I had a sense of adventure in literally crossing the color line, but my friends in little ways and in the finest taste saw to it that I should not suffer. A woman, usually light in color, met me at the station. Where prejudice was strong, a woman always sat by me when I rode about to see the city. When I stayed at a hotel with colored service, I was surrounded with consideration. Whether correct or not in the particular incident that called forth his letter, Dr. Brooks voiced the kindly, courteous consideration the Negro gives his white friends.

I met one of Dr. Brooks's workers and asked her what social service the Negro most needed in New York. She answered without hesitation, "A home for delinquent girls committed through the courts. Philanthropy has provided such homes for white girls, but nothing has been done for the Negro." My investigations proved her correct. So did the investigation of the Urban League, which followed mine. And at long length the Katy Ferguson Home came into existence, I hope to the satisfaction of the woman who knew what was wanted all along.

However, I should not decry investigation. One of the annoying things I met with was caused by the white man who, without investigation, pushed forward a colored project. The Negro is a powerful pleader and with the white man's money starts a project that is not well thought out, perhaps not even wanted. I incurred the severe displeasure of one white man who, having raised $50,000 for a Negro doctor who wanted a private hospital, thought, without investigation, that I should help him to raise more. That I should consult colored people or question the need of this private hospital, was picayune. Yet if a white man had come to him with such a project, he would have investigated before asking for money from the public.

✦

In 1907, the Ladies' Garment Workers went on strike, and a few colored girls acted as strikebreakers. I was consulted as to the best tactics to prevent this, and helped the union hold a meeting in the old Bridge Street Church, Brooklyn. William Maley, an organizer among miners, spoke. He dwelt on the loyalty of the Negro miners to their union in Alabama. It was a speech intended to convince the Negro that it was treachery to act as a strikebreaker. He carried his audience with him though "that's the only way we ever get into a trade," someone said from the floor. "The union won't admit us until we're at work. Later it comes around to organize us." This could not be denied, but Maley pleaded with them to fight to enter not only by the back but by the front door. His speech was eloquent of brotherhood. The strike was soon ended, and race conditions remained as they had been.

My investigation of the census headings, *Actors* and *Musicians*, brought me unqualified pleasure. The popularity of the Negro spiritual and the deep appreciation of the Negro singer were to come later. Roland Hayes was then passing through New York unnoticed. One singer had received proper recognition, Harry T. Burleigh. Dr. William Rainsford, rector of St. George's, an Englishman, brought Burleigh into a choir rehearsal one evening and told the choir that he was engaged as baritone. There may have been consternation, but it certainly was not expressed then to Rainsford who was a commander of men. In a short time, Burleigh, by the beauty of his singing and the quiet dignity of his bearing, won acceptance and, later, enthusiastic support. When in 1944, he celebrated the fiftieth anniversary of his engagement at the church, choir and congregation gave him an overwhelming welcome. Burleigh is an accomplished composer and has arranged many of the spirituals. We must not forget, too, that we owe one movement in Dvorak's *New World Symphony* to Burleigh's friendship with the composer.

Many of the Negro musicians counted in the census were on the stage, and actors and singers were often interchangeable, the singer taking an important part, the composer in the conductor's seat, or dancing or singing his new hit. The most popular songs of the day, after Gilbert and Sullivan, were Negro. Some of them have survived: "The Right Church but the Wrong Pew," "Nobody," "Under the Bamboo Tree," "Why Adam Sinned"; Will Marion Cook's fascinating "Rain Song" you may hear any night over the radio. In the old days you heard them at Negro shows. "Why, your chorus has better voices than we hear at the Metropolitan," a musician said to Will Marion Cook after hearing "In Bandanna Land." "Naturally," Cook answered, "we have voices which, if it were not for race prejudice, you would hear at the Metropolitan as soloists, not in the chorus."

But while the music was excellent, what delighted this investigator—and her friends who went to scoff and returned the next night to see it all over again—was the humor, the spontaneous merriment of the play. Whether it was Cole and Johnson (Johnson at the piano; Cole singing "The Congo Love Song" written by James Weldon Johnson) or whether Bert Williams, tall, awkward, joshed by his dandified partner, Walker, singing "Nobody," it was fresh, different. Miller and Lyle revived the old technique years later in "Shuffle Along," but a revival can rarely be as good as a first impression.

Cole and Johnson, Williams and Walker, these were the

best known comedians, but two others were, I thought, equally original and amusing, Ernest Hogan and Sam Dudley. Dudley lived to a good old age and liked, in his comfortable Washington home, to talk of the old times. He alone had been careful of his money. He had had a little donkey that always acted with him. He showed me the manuscript of one of his plays, and I was surprised to see how little was written on it. It told of a down-at-the-heel, shabby Negro barber who dreamed of going to the White House and shaving the President of the United States. He talked to his donkey about it. "You won't find the talk," Dudley said apologetically, "because I had to change it each night to suit the donkey. Folks thought the donkey clever, but I knew better."

Ernest Hogan, in *The Oysterman,* played the part of the rural southern "darkey" opposite the white man who tried to get the oysterman's money. He is importuned to take stock in a land company where the watermelons are as common as potatoes, and chickens thrive like sparrows. Hogan, unlike Bert Williams, was really dark. His black face, as he sat listening to the slick talk, was perplexed, wondering. The curtain went down on a figure altogether too much like life for wholehearted laughter.

And yet the audience did laugh, for it was Negro farce played before a Negro audience, and we can make fun of ourselves endlessly if we do not depict the truth. When comedy holds the mirror up to nature, it is a different matter. The audience had a smattering of whites in the orchestra, but except in New York it was only a smattering. The show was written for Negroes—the gay dancing (dancers with *really* smiling faces) the rhythmic music, and the figure of the

"Innocent," funnier than Mark Twain's *Innocents Abroad*. These shows were often farcical, but always in good taste.

The cinema soon monopolized the modest theaters where *In Dahomey* and Sam Dudley's donkey played, and the Negro show went out of business. Then commercial vaudeville seized upon the black actor, and audiences roared at the white man's conception of black burlesque. "Blackbirds" discovered Florence Mills, Bill Robinson, and other stars, but the old, merry farce was gone. The white producer introduced vulgarity. Some years later, Ridgely Torrence, Paul Greene, Du Bose Heyward, Marc Connelly and, greatest of all, Eugene O'Neill, discovered the Negro actor and gave him a place among the artists. When to the beat of the tom-tom the curtain rose upon Charles Gilpin in *The Emperor Jones*, the Negro presented his consummate genius in one of America's greatest plays.

Census figures placed the majority of Negroes in *Domestic Service*. Some lived with their employers, but many went out to work. Of this I gained daily knowledge as I climbed flight after flight of stairs in an investigation of the Negro tenement. For ten days I went with a tenement house inspector through the old dumb-bell and railroad tenements on West Sixtieth and West Sixty-first Streets between Tenth (West End) and Eleventh Avenues. West Sixtieth Street had a mixed population, and the white homes were singularly depressing. Children and dogs vied with one another as to which could retain the most dirt, and the hallways were the subject of much condemnation by the inspector. Frowsy and tangled hair made ragged women distressing to look at. I felt as though I were with Dickens at Lime House Hole or where Fagan kept his famous school.

Fewer colored than white opened their doors to the inspector. "They were out at work," someone explained, "scrubbing or cooking or washing." Sometimes a girl peeked out and explained her mother's absence. Again, the little flat would be full of steaming clothes, or the clean smell of ironing; and a mother, with a baby on the bed and another at her skirts, would be taking in washing. The husband, a night worker in domestic service, might be asleep in the one other room. These homes were fairly clean, the bed with a bright spread, china on the shelf. But they were poor, very poor. I had seen nothing before of poverty like this.

Once by myself I found an unforgettable Negro home in an old neighborhood in the West Side Thirties, now demolished by the building of the Pennsylvania Station and Hotel. It was a queer spot to find in New York, a shallow street-front with rear houses irregularly placed, New York's nearest approach to the alleys of Philadelphia and Washington. All kinds of people lived in it, and I was warned to stay away at night. Among this clutter of buildings, on some pretext, I turned into a large ground-floor room. Muslin curtains shaded the window, the shining brass bed had a white counterpane, a coal fire was in the open grate, and two valuable engravings hung on the wall. The place was immaculate and, to complete its story-book character, a very old, black Mammy sat before the fire, rocking her body to and fro. In the middle of the room stood an ironing board, sign of the laundress, where a middle-aged woman, not so black, was pressing a thin muslin dress. They both greeted me kindly and the older woman found a chair for me while the younger one resumed her work. We talked a little about New York and then the old Mammy, a rumbling sound in her voice, began to tell all that the other had done for her. "She hunt fer me fur an' wide," she crooned, "fur an' wide, year an' year. Then," briskly, "she done foun' me, an' she brung me up here." She looked around the room proudly, as Padraic Colum's Old Woman of the Roads looked, in imagination, at the "hearth and stool and all." "My daughter brung me here. She make fifty dollar a month." Then, her story told, she looked into the fire and rocked back and forth.

The younger woman walked out with me when I went and said gravely, "I was sold away from my mother when I was two years old. I went down las' year to hunt for her. Things had changed. She's sure she knows her baby," she nodded toward the room, "but me, I ain't so sure."

A new tenement-house law, passed at the beginning of the century, was rapidly changing the living arrangements of multitudes. New York had been built in solid blocks of three-story-and-basement houses, which at this time were used in three ways: as private residences, as tenements housing four or eight families, and as boarding houses. The new law allowed only two families to keep house in one of these residences unless drastic changes were made, chiefly in fireproofing. The landlords for the most part made no changes and took to renting rooms. The boarding house has slowly given way to the lodging house, and New York has become a city of innumerable restaurants. And while this was happening, new-law tenements were built on vacant lots uptown or where old buildings were torn down. In poor sections, the new tenements were walk-ups limited to six stories.

The Negro benefited a little by these changes. He did not

get into new-law tenements, but he began to move into tenements vacated by the whites. His need for housing was desperate when the Pennsylvania Railroad demolished blocks of property, and he had to go uptown. Aided by Negro real estate men, and with the consent and to the profit of the whites, colored families put their possessions on trucks and trekked to Lenox Avenue and 134th and 135th Streets. Every day was moving day, and white tenements were knocked over to Negroes as you knock down a house of cards. It was then, by 1910, that the Negro city of Harlem began.

One evening, when dining at Greenwich House, I heard the residents talking about a recent guest, John E. Milholland. After a long sojourn in London, he had returned to New York with his family. Evidently he had been a good talker, and was greatly enjoyed. "And he knows lots of rich men," a girl said with that eager grasping of the philanthropist for the check book with a big balance. "He knows Henry Phipps," she added turning to me.

Now Henry Phipps, according to a long write-up in the papers, had decided to do something to improve housing conditions among the poor of New York. He had already built one large tenement in a white neighborhood. The tenements were to be operated on a return to the investor of only 4 to 5 per cent. We all decided that if Phipps was interested in housing the poor, it should be brought to his attention that, more than any other element in the population, the Negro needed a decent and reasonably priced place to live. His record as a renter was simple; he paid the most money and he got the worst quarters. It was arranged that I should meet Mr. Milholland as soon as possible. It meant a great deal to me to meet this friend. Wholly sympathetic with what I was doing, he took up the matter of the Negro tenement with great energy. I gave him a statement of the need for decent housing, but he asked for a statement from the most prominent Negroes whom I knew. With this he felt he could convince Phipps of the gravity of the situation. The statement, when secured, was so dignified and so powerful that Henry Phipps was convinced; and the Tuskegee, on Sixty-third Street near Eleventh Avenue, was soon erected. It was a beginning in model housing for Negroes, and Milholland's name should be associated with it.

For nearly three years I had been gathering material, and while my book was not finished, I believed that I had a trustworthy knowledge of the life and occupations of the people among whom I wanted to live, for I still clung to the idea of a settlement among Negroes. The Greenpoint Settlement, where I had worked for seven years in Brooklyn, had been situated in a model tenement built by Charles Pratt of Standard Oil fame. What better place for Negro work than another model tenement—built this time with money made from steel? I resolved to live in the Tuskegee as soon as it was finished.

Compared with the model tenements built today, the Tuskegee looks like an apple tree by the side of a redwood. It was a walk-up six stories high. The rooms were very small except the kitchen. Someone must have told the architect that the poor lived in their kitchens, and he had made this the living room. He failed to reason that the poor lived in the kitchen, not because they liked it but because it was the only warm room they had. Since the Tuskegee was steam-heated, the kitchen should have been small, and a decent living room should have been provided. This was the chief objection to the apartments. They were modern forty years ago, with hot water and baths. Expecting to live alone and needing space to entertain guests, I asked to have no partition between the two front rooms in the second-floor apartment that I had chosen. Even this space, with desk and bookcases, was crowded and my "parties" were small. The bedroom was a cubicle, but it had enough air and light and more than enough noise. The Tuskegee still stands, though many of the tenements about it have been torn down to make room for storage plants and garages.

Except for Hell's Kitchen directly south, no neighborhood had then so unsavory a reputation as San Juan Hill. The name was given either because a few veterans of the Cuban San Juan Hill lived on it, or because it was a New York battleground. It rose from Fifty-ninth Street, reached its height at Sixty-second and dropped at Sixty-third. To the west lived, not Spaniards, but white enemies. Here were boys and young men always ready for a fight; while the New York Central Railroad, with its open tracks, was a neutral, which maimed black and white impartially. The whites on Eleventh Avenue gave the appearance of being even poorer than the Negroes, but they were augmented by white boys from the mixed tenements on West Sixtieth and perhaps from Hell's Kitchen. As they rushed east up the streets, black boys and men, like the San Juan Hill warriors, poured out to meet them. The battling was bloody and furious. But those days, I found from experience, were ending.

There continued the animosity, though back of it, I believe, was a convention such as I had seen when with my Greenpoint boys I had motored through Gwinnett Street. The convention was that any group of Negro children trying to cross a white street was to be attacked. Whether they were little or big apparently did not matter so long as their faces were black.

One of the philanthropies of West Sixty-third Street was the Walton Free Kindergarten with Helena Emerson, a devoted social worker for Negroes, in charge. One day, she and her coworker were to take the children the short walk to Central Park, and I was asked to join them. The children were arranged in couples, no one of them over five, and some three years of age. They started walking quietly two by two on the north side of the street, led by two little girls.

Everything went well at first, and then, as though at a signal, white boys from West End Avenue bore down, and we were in the midst of a raid. Armed with sticks, the boys ran between the lines, striking as they went and yelling "Nigger! Nigger!" From end to end the street rang with the hated epithet. Of course we teachers did our best by command and energetic handling to drive the boys away. But it was one of the little girls in the lead who got the line over West End Avenue and up the quiet residential street where, again as at a signal, the boys dropped away. This girl, not more than four, on the street-side where she was most exposed to attack, held her head high. When her comrade dropped back, she pulled her forward, and I heard her say, "Don't notice 'em. Walk straight ahead."

As children are the most frequent visitors in settlement work, I especially studied conditions among the children on San Juan Hill. Tabulations and first-hand information obtained by visiting, told me what I knew already—that low wages and frequent unemployment crowded families into

the dark unwholesome tenements where tuberculosis always
lurked. If the family was small, the rent was eked out by
the ubiquitous lodger. One square block, north Sixty-first and
south Sixty-second, housed 5,000 persons. That some of the
children looked neat and clean aroused my admiration.
The long hours expected of servants left many others neglected. I asked a public school teacher how the colored children stood in comparison with the white children. "Not so
well," she answered; "often not half so well. They could do
just as well though. It's in them." But where could they
study? Fearing fire, the mother would often lock the door
behind her, and her children, when school was over, would
wander through the street or sit on the stairway. How could
a little child give its attention to the next day's lessons under
such conditions?

I made one study when on the Hill that seemed to me of
lasting importance. I had always heard that Negroes stole;
I was told it as though it were a race trait. African travelers
corroborated this, for their "boys" were always stealing from
the white men. With a deep belief in inheritance as marking
differences between individuals, differences of physical and
intellectual stamina, I had grown increasingly skeptical regarding the inheritance of "race trait." I believed that
Negroes differed among themselves as much as whites did,
but that when the race seemed to have a characteristic, like a
tendency to pilfer, it was the result of environment.

The Children's Court, then recently established, gave me
an opportunity to test my theory. After court hours, I was
allowed to examine the record of each arrest. The child's
address was given and, in the case of the Negro, its race. The
chief offenses were petty larceny, grand larceny, burglary,

robbery, assault, improper guardianship, truancy, and mischief.

A knowledge of the city, its European groups and its economic life, helped to an understanding of the figures. Petty larceny was commonest, not among the Negroes but among the Jews and the Italians who were constantly tempted by the pushcart. The total number of arrests for all forms of theft was 21 per cent, against 19 per cent for the Negroes. The Negroes were less mischievous than the whites, 30 per cent against 38 per cent. Where the colored exceeded the white was in improper guardianship, 31 per cent to 24 per cent. This could be accounted for by the colored mothers going to work. I isolated the tenth and eleventh wards, Russian-Jewish, where I knew the mothers were likely to be at home, and found that improper guardianship there was only 15 per cent. Under the heading *Depraved Girl*, the Negro's percentage was 4.6 against 1.2 for the whites. These were the girls committed through the courts, the girls who Dr. Brooks's social worker said so much needed a detention home since they usually were without home companionship.

The courtroom where I studied the records after hours was a dreary place, but when a case was on trial it might become exciting. One mother, on seeing the judge place her child in the custody of the Children's Aid Society, literally tore her hair, and wailed as in torment. "A bit of hysterics from the East," a policeman remarked to me as he saw her hustled out. I hope she felt relief from expression. The sad-eyed Negro woman I had seen the day before, who quietly saw her child led away, affected me more. Man's cruelty to her was to be expected and borne. But I very occasionally stayed to a session. My time was spent with some young

Junior League debutante, sent me by Mrs. Simkhovitch, who called off the records while I tabulated. My best helper was Ruth Draper who later—with Burbage's "bare boards" for scenery and with a shawl for costume—so unforgettably represented *Three Generations*, Italian grandmother, mother, and daughter. I count her seemingly simple monologues among the greatest drama produced in America.

The Tuskegee apartment was at length finished and I moved in, fervently hoping that, as at Greenpoint, I might build up a settlement in a model tenement. Its tenants, for the most part, were hard working men and women not often appearing before the courts. There was much loose living on the block. The number of men about in the daytime could not all be accounted for by night jobs or unemployment. Some were living on their girls' earnings, but they did not trouble me, an outsider. I attributed my position primarily to the work the school teacher had done before me. She had gone to the children's homes, held mothers' meetings, and had been a friend. The genuine democracy of the public school system, the teachers' readiness to be of service, had made the presence of another "teacher"—as so they called me—natural and to be respected. Then, few people in a well-to-do residential neighborhood realize that when their street is empty at night, it is more dangerous than a crowded tenement neighborhood.

All of us on the Hill owed a great deal to its most important figure, the Reverend George H. Sims, minister of the Union Baptist Church. He was a friend to all social work —the Children's Aid Society, the Hope Day Nursery, the Walton Free Kindergarten. It was he whom Rosalie M.

Jonas found in 1904, and his church has had a tree for colored children ever since "Crowded Out" appeared in the newspapers in December of that year.

> Nobody ain't Christmas shoppin'
> For his stockin'—

Rosalie Jonas wrote, and, behold, toys and clothes and food and money came pouring in for the colored children's Christmas held at the Union Baptist Church on San Juan Hill. Through her verse these children have appealed again and again to New York's generosity, and it has never failed to give them their good time, though now one has to go to Harlem to find the Union Baptist Church.

George H. Sims of Virginia had felt the call, had entered the Baptist ministry, and soon was preaching in New York on San Juan Hill. Here he found Southerners like himself, some of them very recent residents of this new, disturbing city. He gathered them into his congregation and ministered to them. Not involved in doctrine, when he talked of Christ from his pulpit, Jesus became alive, a workman, a carpenter who took off his apron and went out to answer the call to preach. Zebedee lost two good fishermen when his sons, James and John, left him at the call of the Master, but Zebedee should be of good cheer. So Christianity came alive Sunday morning.

There was much shouting, much noisy getting of religion that to the outsider seemed childish and distasteful. In contrast, I went to St. Benedict, the Moore, and saw the Catholic congregation, about evenly divided between white and colored, celebrating reverently the centuries-old Mass. At the Episcopal Church of St. Philip's, the music was as beautiful as I had heard in New York, and the ritual correct, impressive. These congregations in no way differed from the neighboring white congregations. But no white Baptist church was like the Union Baptist, not even at a revival. No Billy Sunday had to stride up and down our platform, arousing religious emotion. It was close to the surface and the Negro sang and cried Amen, not droning his responses, but in a lusty voice. Civilization loves decorum and is forever putting things before our eyes and ears while demanding that we give no answering word. It laughs at the worker who sings at his task. I think a psychiatrist would find something to say in favor of our shouting church—gone now, moved to Harlem. And if the congregation were the sheep in this Baptist pasture, they aspired to be definitely parted from the goats who made their noise in unsavory retreats.

There were a few philanthropies on the Hill, the Walton Free Kindergarten, a Day Nursery, and the Children's Aid Society. As always, the colored churches did much relief work. West of us, daring to go across Columbus Avenue, was the Episcopal Church of St. Cyprian. Many of its congregation were West Indians, seemingly less emotional than the American Negro and with, I was told, business acumen. I organized a committee and did fresh air work that summer, Mary E. Cromwell of Washington coming to take charge. With incredibly little money we sent about a hundred children away for two-week vacations, and some hundreds of mothers with their babies went on day excursions and picnics. Miss Cromwell found our mothers doubtful about trusting their children to strangers, a fear I had not found at Greenpoint. Some hated to receive charity, and many boys and girls lost a good time in the country for want of decent clothing. We had fairly to force a pair of shoes upon a mother whose husband was a porter receiving seven dollars a week. Her rent took a third of this, not an unusual proportion today but unusual then for all but colored. She did not want "charity," she reiterated, as Betty Higdon said in Dickens's England. Had she been in her old southern surroundings, she might have felt differently.

My little room in the Tuskegee had many visitors, children and mothers during the day, men and women eager to discuss the race problem in the evening. One evening visitor was a Negro, a keen observer, who had been sent abroad to get impressions, but was too indolent to write them—or perhaps was unable to. His comments on the English and the French were inimitable. He had been entertained in private homes in both countries, liked the French, but disliked the English whose serene confidence that their way of living was perfect, without flaw, annoyed him. His special aversion was the afternoon teas to which he was continually taken! He claimed to have been engaged to an English girl and to have broken it off, telling her that she had no affection for him, but just wanted a sensation—which was doubtless the truth. He thought that he and I could write a good book, and that if our pictures were taken together, it would have a good sale! Mary Cromwell called him crazy; of course he wasn't. He understood publicity, but he had come to the wrong person for it. Not even having your picture reproduced in the society column was good form at that time on Brooklyn Heights where I spent my week ends.

How did my friends and acquaintances accept my removal to a Negro tenement on Sixty-third Street near the New York Central railroad tracks? Those who knew anything about it thought it natural that a settlement worker, when making a survey, should want to live with her work. Two Brooklyn friends after dining with me at the Tuskegee, called up on returning home to say they believed I was in a dangerous neighborhood and they had felt fearful to leave me there alone.

Was it a dangerous neighborhood? I, whose status was that of teacher, whose work was in the daytime with mothers and children, saw nothing dangerous. After a hard day's work, I was tired enough to go to bed and to sleep at eleven o'clock. The tenements to the east, whose dark stairs I often climbed, might be awake through the night but it was none of my affair. San Juan had a lusty sex life. Its little rooms looked out on dark, narrow courtyards that smelt of garbage. Its chief pleasures were gambling and sex. Infidelity was common, and infrequently some heartbroken wife would tell me about it. I would commiserate with her, then talk of something else. I was there to try to do a little—it could be very little—for her and for her children. No one molested me or questioned my right to be there.

I did achieve notoriety though just when I was moving to San Juan Hill. For a day my name was "news" to the papers all over the country, and I was besieged by reporters. It happened in this way: during my investigations I had met a number of Brooklyn's well-established colored families—the Petersons, Mars, Wibecans, and others. I have spoken of Dr. Waller. Quite spontaneously, a little club grew up calling itself the "Cosmopolitan Club." We met in private homes, usually in Brooklyn, and discussed various phases of the race question. In the spring we planned a larger meeting with guests. I had recently attended a socialist dinner at Peck's restaurant on lower Fulton Street, and suggested that we meet there. I remember the reaction of André Tridon, a Frenchman and our president. Perhaps what happened later makes me believe that I saw a twinkle in his eye when, after a moment's hesitation, he acquiesced enthusiastically in my suggestion. We secured the restaurant, sold tickets, and when the evening came, sat down to a pleasant gathering of quiet, well-dressed people—and to be well dressed in public in those days meant to be inconspicuously dressed.

The races were about evenly divided. The majority of the whites were professional persons—doctors, ministers, social service workers. A number of my old friends came from Greenpoint, among them Dr. Edmund Devol, born with only a river between him and Kentucky, but always a strong supporter of the Negro's rights. Oswald Garrison Villard was with us. He made a moving speech, inspired by the much discussed play, *The Servant in the House*, then on Broadway. Hamilton Holt of *The Independent* spoke, and also John Spargo, a prominent socialist. Dr. Waller presided. The colored speakers were the Reverend Fraser Miller of St. Augustine's Church, Brooklyn, and William Ferris. The talk was overserious, for the Christ character in Kennedy's *The Servant in the House* dominated the meeting. It might have been held in the parlor of some church where the educational work of a colored school was under discussion.

But it wasn't in a church parlor, and when we were about half through, with the connivance of a few club members, reporters came into the room. "What are those men doing here?" Mr. Villard said to me suddenly in a voice I had never heard before. "I don't know," I answered, not appreciating what troubled him; but when I was asked by one of the intruders if he might take a picture, I said "No" emphatically. After gathering some names and addresses, he, with the others, went away.

The meeting ended with pleasant words of good fellowship. I felt elated, but I can still see Villard looking at me intently. He had printed a number of contributions of mine in the *Evening Post*. "Can anyone be so naive," he must have thought, "and not be a fool?"

The storm broke the next morning and poured down anathema, not on the Negroes this time—they were only tools—but on the degenerate whites. The New York papers were deeply displeased, and their editors said so in dignified language. They read us all a lesson and showed especial indignation at the two publicists, Holt and Villard. No paper gave any idea of what the meeting was about or of the almost religious character of the speeches. This had no news value. What was news was that colored and white had sat down together at a public restaurant.

This news, our sitting down and visiting together, while treated without much personal comment in the North, became exciting reading as it moved South. We were reproved even on the floor of Congress and, as we fell below Mason and Dixon's line, our sober dinner became an orgy. Those who wrote it up did not comment on the white man who sat next the Negro woman, but they poured their spleen on the white woman who sat next a colored man. We were described as drinking and making love. "The whole affair," Burleson of Texas said, "was unbelievable, abhorrent, and inconceivable." "We have bitter contempt," the Richmond *Leader* cried, "for the whites that participated in it and illustrated that degeneracy will seek its level;" and the St. Louis *Despatch* declared, "This miscegenation dinner was loathsome enough to consign the whole fraternity of persons who participated in it to undying infamy."

The longest and most picturesque account was Judge Norwood's in the Savannah *News*. Sometimes the Judge was funny. He told of two Desdemonas, on either side of an Othello, who told of his exploits in the Spanish-American War. A woman of seventy was described as leaning amorously against a very black West Indian. Young girls—there was one present with her mother—dropped their heads on black men's shoulders.

"Worst of all was the high priestess, Miss Ovington, whose father is rich and who affiliates five days every week with Negro men and dines with them at her home in Brooklyn, Sundays. She could have had a hundred thousand Negroes at the Bacchanal feast had she waved the bread-tray. But the horror of it is she could take white girls into that den. That is the feature that should arouse and alarm northern society."

The papers had given the Hotel St. George as my address. My mail was unspeakable. It was so bad that I ran away from it to my sister's for a few days. "We expected you to land in jail," my brother-in-law said casually. We laughed, and life again assumed its normal proportions. One letter, from a small Maryland town, that I found on my return, compensated for the rest. "I am a white man," it said, "but I glory in your spunk in standing up for what you believe to be right."

The Cosmopolitan Club Dinner taught me how to read the morning paper. I had been so trustful! Now I realized that a controversial event is reported in accordance with the paper's policy. Some events are simple items like weather reports, but many are controversial. The editorial is not alone in expressing the paper's opinion; the facts reflect it. Not distinctly untruthful, they will be out of focus. To get at the truth, one must read both sides.

Like any other unimportant piece of news, the Cosmopolitan Club Dinner was soon forgotten. And yet not wholly forgotten because in New York the spectacle of white and colored sitting down together was never news again. We had many interracial dinners after this; I remember one at the Café Savarin for Du Bois. When, in 1935, James Weldon Johnson was given a dinner at the Hotel Pennsylvania, among the hundreds of white and colored guests were many people of distinction. "This reads like *Who's Who*," Carl Van Vechten said as he read the names of the sponsors. The dinner over, Villard came up to where I was standing and said triumphantly, "You and I can appreciate this! Remember the Cosmopolitan Club Dinner!"

I went to another dinner about this time, that clinched my determination to devote such ability as I had to the cause of the Negro. It was a dinner given by the Intercollegiate Socialist Society, and the leading speaker was Lucien Sanial, an old man who had stood with the workers during the Paris Commune. His hair and beard were white while his eyes were black, piercing. Later he became blind. He told us something of socialism and of working class conditions. We had eaten well and had opened our program by singing William Morris's "March of the Workers." It is sung to the tune of "John Brown's Body." Well-fed, well-dressed, we stood at our tables and shouted Morris's stirring chorus:

Hark, the rolling of the thunder!
Lo, the sun! and low thereunder
Riseth wrath and hope and wonder
'Tis the people marching on.

We were mostly middle-aged folk, for the students held
their meetings in their colleges. Sanial must have thought of
this song when he stopped in the middle of his talk, and looking down, not at us but through us, said, "Remember, you
can be of no use to the workers, no least use, unless you
repudiate your class, absolutely repudiate it; and even then,"
he stopped to look at us again, "even then, most of you
would be useless."

I went home profoundly disturbed. I believed then as I
do now that the economic problem is civilization's first problem, and that the workers' continued rebellion against their
lot is the most profound fact of history, but I knew that I
was not one of them. I was only cheering and throwing a few
pennies. Very well then, I would cease to work for socialism
and give what strength and ability I had to the problem of
securing for the Negro American those rights and privileges
into which every white American was born. Thus the Negro,
if he willed it, should be able to march with the working
class. This resolution seemed important to me at the time,
and so I put it down here.

My long desired interview with Henry Phipps came and
went, without results. He assured me that, while interested
in housing, he was not interested in the carrying on of social
work within the tenements which he erected. He seemed a
man who knew his own mind; anyway, I had not the ability
to change it. I thought possibly the management of the Tus-

kegee had been against my project. The superintendent of the
Astral Apartments had complained of my work at Greenpoint until he found protests useless. Social work with children is noisy, and since the Tuskegee took in as few children
as possible, I could not hope to win over its management.
I would have to give up my dream, go home, and finish my
book. I was needed there, and I could no longer let my father
support me while giving nothing in return.

San Juan Hill was appealing during those last days. The
weather was mild and the people in great numbers were on
the street. The children sang their songs, some learned at
kindergarten and others their own, like "Sound dem Wedding Bells." They were graceful, engaging. Having lived
among what the unsympathetic Greenpoint visitor called
"tough children," I was always surprised at Negro courtesy.
As a friend and I walked down the street one afternoon, a
little boy, seeing his mother ahead, ran up to her, took her
bundles, and carried them to their door. My friend looked
at him in amazement. "That's not unusual," I said proudly.
"Indeed!" she answered, still amazed; and then, with ready
Irish wit, "You don't need to be accounting to me now for
the high death rate among children!"

On one of my last afternoons, three little girls came to
call. They were in freshly laundered dresses, and immaculate
even to their fingernails. I gratefully took half a peanut that
the smallest one divided for me from her stock of two. They
were shy, not given to talk. From my chair I read them
Peter Rabbit while they sat close together on a long sofa.
Their eyes were bright and shining and they did not fidget.
Later, I visited a woman whom the Charity Organization Society had just saved from public eviction. She was living in

tiny quarters with her daughter Annabel. The woman had worked hard for years, but this last trouble had broken her spirit. She took my going away as one last cross. Annabel, aged ten, walked down the four flights with me when I had finished my sad visit.

"I know what I'm going to be when I grow up," she said as she skipped and jumped down the stairway.

"Yes?" I asked. We had reached the bottom where she twirled engagingly on one foot.

"I'm going to be a dancer!" She made an inimitable gesture, her eyes rolled up, "I'm going to make *money*. Look at my mother, she works and works and she hasn't got a thing. They took her best chair and my bed." Annabel was in earnest. "I'm going to be a dancer. Dancers make money." Then, seeing an acquaintance, she ran out into the street.

The rear-hall door stood open, and I walked into a courtyard. It was small, dirty, but as I turned back, I noticed handwriting on the wall. Experience of handwriting on walls in dirty courtyards led me to expect obscenity. But on this wall, in a well-formed hand, I read,

Unless above himself he can erect himself, how poor a thing is man.

and just below:

No conflict is so severe as his who labors to subdue himself; but in this we must be continually engaged if we would be strengthened in the inner man.

Shakespeare and Thomas à Kempis on San Juan Hill! Sixty-third Street, from West End to Eleventh Avenue was a Hyde Park for propaganda. From the top of the Hill, to the music of a single violin, marched a preacher, a few men and women following. They sang a gospel hymn and then he began his exhortation. "Salvation is so convenient, Brother, it is so convenient." He was a West Indian, speaking with an English accent.

The door of the Union Baptist Church was open, and I slipped in to hear of salvation for this world. "If you want to prevent the contraction of tuberculosis," a business-like woman was saying, "you must lead moral lives. Disease multiplies with frightful rapidity as vice enters." The women, for unfortunately there were no men in the audience, then learned that they should wear heavy flannels in the winter, particularly if they came from the South.

On the corner, dandified-looking men, without words, preached their doctrine of an easy life with a hard-working girl to make life happy.

Down the street, almost to dangerous Eleventh Avenue, beyond the Tuskegee, I heard a spiritual:

> Bye an' bye, bye an' bye
> I's gwine ter lay down dis heaby load.

The voices quavered, for youth does not sing the spirituals. But age understands. There was little here for youth. Possibly, by incessant work and great ability, Annabel might become the dancer of whom she dreamed. Probably the courageous child who led the kindergarten would become a teacher and lead her own people. But for the many there could only be long hours of work away from the hard-earned shelter of a home where children crouched shivering at the door.

A loud laugh came from an open doorway and a girl ran

out followed by a boy. Here was life, a physical expression, a short-lived joy.

The singers of the spiritual moved up the Hill. Their number was augmented. You heard a strong, masculine bass.

Years later, in two lines, Langston Hughes was to tell it all,

> At de feet ob Jesus
> *Sorrow like a sea.*

CHAPTER III

THE SOUTH

A T THE beginning of this century, the Northerner usually was familiar only with the tourist South: the Appalachians, especially around Asheville, Charleston, New Orleans at Mardi Gras. The Negro South was little known. Businessmen visited the cities, but after hours scarcely concerned themselves with the race question. Robert Ogden took parties to Hampton and Tuskegee and occasionally to some other Negro school. Today millions of automobiles have been driven over the South's highways, and millions of soldiers have encamped among its hills or by the sea or in the hot valleys. They have learned much of Negro prejudice, but I doubt if half a dozen have met representative Negroes. One cannot go South and be in both the white and the colored world. With my mother I had visited the tourist South of northern Florida, Charleston, parts of North Carolina, but the Negro had been only a part of the landscape. I was therefore elated when, in the spring of 1904, I was invited by Dr. Du Bois to attend the Atlanta Conference held at Atlanta University. I would be entertained at the University. Would I come? Of course I would!

I must have answered by return mail. The conference would bring me in contact with the colored intelligentsia of Atlanta, perhaps give me a chance to study the Negro's position, the well-to-do and the poor, in a southern city. Best of all, I would meet a writer with whom I had corresponded for some time and who had written *The Souls of Black Folk.*

Du Bois was professor of history and economics at Atlanta, had studied in Germany, and had taken his Ph.D. at Harvard. He had made a survey of the *Philadelphia Negro,* and had written a lengthy and erudite thesis on the *Suppression of the African Slave Trade.* He has since contributed valuable historical and sociological books, including a study of *Black Reconstruction*—of great importance in view of the North's increasing acceptance of the prosperous southern white man's viewpoint of that period—but he was then best known by a volume of sketches, *The Souls of Black Folk.* Some of the sketches appeared first in the *Atlantic Monthly* and were so poignant, so terribly sincere, that McClurg, Chicago publisher, asked Du Bois for a book. *The Souls of Black Folk* has been in print through the years, an integral part of American literature.

I was, then, to meet this man who could write inspired prose and who had dared counter Booker T. Washington; and I was to see Atlanta University that stood unswervingly for higher education.

The first sight of the college was disappointing, but then all of the colleges built during that terrible Victorian period were too high for their breadth, too high-windowed, too indicative of long flights of stairs. But my welcome was warm and heartening. And when at supper I found myself seated next to Du Bois, his head like Shakespeare's done in bronze, my cup of happiness was full. "Miss Ovington thinks that I am weeping all the time," Du Bois said to a teacher opposite him, and proceeded to talk nonsense throughout the meal.

It was a good dinner, eaten in a large dining hall that held both teachers and scholars. This was not usual in colored colleges where the teachers were generally by themselves, but this school invited its young men and women to break bread with them. For this, white Atlanta slammed its doors against the teachers who nevertheless enjoyed themselves.

This meal in common meant much to the students. Though they came from educated homes, they did not know white people, except as they might have worked for them in some servant capacity. Here they learned to talk to them naturally, as equals, an advantage if they went North, a disadvantage if they remained in the South. And also, as an old graduate explained to me later, "It made us accept rigid discipline because we saw that we were elevated by it, that we were expected to grow to be the equals in manners and morals and intellectual power of these white men and women about us. The kindly Southerner forgave us a great deal because he expected little. At college we were not forgiven easily if we broke rules, but then we were not only children of God to these white teachers, we were also heirs to their world."

The conference occupied only a part of my time, and I was able to meet the prosperous people about me. They seemed better off than the same group among my northern friends, probably because one could live better on the same sum of money. One man had the best barbering establishment in the city, catering entirely to whites. Harry Pace was already successful in the insurance business. I was entertained in pleasant homes, and I could always turn to the Du Bois apartment. There, if the Doctor and Mrs. Du Bois were away, I would browse in their excellent library. I met Mrs. White, Walter White's mother, and heard the car conductor, who recognized her, order her to a rear seat though in color she was as light as I.

Complete segregation was comparatively new to Atlanta which, after the Civil War, had been under northern influence, and the older Negroes resented it bitterly. One of the city's oldest and most respected colored men, Dr. Crogman, was president of Clark University, situated on another of Atlanta's hills. (The missionary colleges seemed to occupy all the hills.) He was a man of dignity, who had known the city under the Civil Rights Law—later declared unconstitutional by the Supreme Court—and refused to accept the new city statute that demanded segregation. He would not enter an Atlanta street car. At first he had a horse and buggy, but when the college could no longer afford this he walked, and it was no short walk to the city. Du Bois did the same. I found the young people prepared to accept the inevitable.

In an old-fashioned carryall, Dr. and Mrs. Du Bois took me through the best and the worst parts of Negro Atlanta. The worst were very bad but to a New Yorker, tumble-down shanties look worse than tenements. The tenement conceals its inadequate plumbing, but the shanty with its near-by malodorous outhouse, its unpainted, dirty walls, its sagging porch, proclaims all its ugliness to the passer-by. One section called "Darktown" by everyone, seemed as dangerous as the old Five Points in New York.

I could not have steeled myself to live for eight months in any of Atlanta's congested, working-class neighborhoods as I had lived on San Juan Hill.

Most of the streets in the Negro neighborhoods were paved and lighted, but I was told that it was impossible to keep out the saloon or the house of prostitution. White capital introduced these questionable but profitable enterprises, and the Negroes were powerless. Primary and grammar schools were few, and even when schools had double sessions, colored children played all day untroubled on the streets.

The grievance of which I heard most during this visit was the inadequacy of public schooling. The injustice of constant criticism of Negroes, while failing to give them improving education, exasperated my new friends. And on this particular matter, they had a means of retaliation. At the election of men for city, state, or national office, they were disfranchised—not directly but by the white primary. The white primary nominated the Democratic candidates. Its meetings were stormy and sectional—but the nominee once chosen, the election was over since no Republican was ever elected. But when the city decided to spend more money on education, it resorted to a bond issue at which property owners voted. Here the Negro vote was registered and here, twice, the bond issue was turned down. The Negro was ready and glad to contribute his share of taxation if he could be properly assured that he would get his share of money for his schools. No trustworthy assurance was given and, to show his determination to have his race considered, he voted against the issue.

I spent a pleasant week at the University, and was entertained in various homes where, though we might start talking literature or politics, we always ended with the race problem. Feeling ran unusually high. Labor was scarce, and the courts arrested men who were seen idling and sent them to the chain gang as vagrants. Sometimes they were respectable people from the country seeking work in the city. With them would be the loafers, the drunkards who, too, went to the chain gang. A chain gang was working on one of the streets outside the school while I was there, and their shackles live in my memory. Released from imprisonment, the man would sometimes use his freedom for bestial things. To rape, to murder, would be a natural reaction after the brutality and the coarse companionship experienced for a month or two or three, or perhaps for years. The separation of a man from his normal life is a dangerous thing under the best conditions. Here it was at its worst.

We talked of segregation rather than of crime when we discussed the race problem. Some of these men had had exciting experiences. I learned that Professor Towns, whose wife could pass for white, had been arrested for being out driving with her! A white man who had a grudge against an educated Negro could, literally, corner him. One of the professors had been walking down a street beside a high wall that enclosed a residence, when he saw a white man and woman rapidly walking toward him. The white man was on the curb and as the two parties approached, he pushed the woman toward the wall, planning that she should brush against the Negro when the white man could raise a cry of assault. "I flattened up against that wall," the professor explained to me, "until I was as flat as a pancake, and then slipped by, fast. I didn't look back to see if they were disappointed."

Later I remembered these stories when one of the young Negroes who was making a name for himself in Atlanta, Max Barber, came to the college to take me into the city to have supper with Addie W. Hunton. Barber was editing *The Voice of the Negro* at this time, an outspoken magazine that I had seen in New York, and wondered how such writing could be printed in Atlanta. He was evidently a dare-devil, for, after I had taken my place on the back seat of the carriage he had hired, he sat down, not with the driver, but with me. It was an open carriage and for some miles we rode through the streets, I talking animatedly. "I doubt if you were ever stared at so much before," he said, when we reached our destination. We both enjoyed it, he seeing the danger, I too secure to more than half appreciate it.

Mrs. Hunton told us at supper of her near neighbor, a German by birth, who had recently come into the neighborhood, for Atlanta, like Washington, had its mixed streets. She had been pleasant and friendly, but that day had visited Mrs. Hunton to say that such relations must cease. "I like you and I would like to know you," the white woman said. "I do not sympathize with this prejudice against color, but I find that my children are being persecuted at school. We must live in Atlanta and they must have white friends. You understand?" Mrs. Hunton ended by saying, "I understood her position perfectly and I told her so." This ability to understand another's position did not prevent Mrs. Hunton from being militant. Whether in the South or later at her home in Brooklyn, she spoke unequivocally against all forms of segregation. I found myself looking at her very often that evening, if not openly staring. Deep brown in color with a finely molded mouth, and large unfathomable eyes, she was a nobly beautiful woman. I was not surprised as years went on to find that her work brought her international reputation.

I did not meet white people on this trip. Atlanta University's teachers had long since learned that their social world must be confined, while in the South, to the race which they had come to teach. It was nearly a quarter of a century since Tourgee had published *The Fool's Errand,* a best seller in its time, which portrayed the contempt of the white South for the "nigger" teacher. I had an example of this contempt when, some years later, I went with Mrs. Adams, the wife of the University's president, to ask a favor of a city editor of one of Atlanta's largest newspapers. He knew Mrs. Adams, and thinking me also a teacher of Negroes, kept his hat on. When he learned that I was from New York, he took it off. Such an attitude is unfortunate, for the contempt felt by the Northerner is as great as that of the Southerner.

The following year, I was to see Atlanta again as a correspondent of the New York *Evening Post.* I was to report the proceedings of the National Negro Business League of which Booker Washington was president. I stayed at a hotel and saw nothing of my old friends, for the meetings were lengthy, the city hot, and all my strength was needed for my work.

Booker Washington presided at the meetings. I met New York businessmen, Payton who spoke on real estate, and Wallace who gave a good labor-union talk which some did not like. Northern businesses, however, were insignificant compared with the South. Thirty-two banks were represented, and numbers of builders, contractors, druggists, newspapermen, laundrymen. These businesses, for the most part, were supported by trade within the race. More than once we heard that where prejudice was greatest, one found business opportunity.

Washington was then at the height of his power. The South respected him because he was trying to make the Negro a better workman. The North poured money into his effort. His autobiography, *Up From Slavery,* had told his story to mankind. Few American names are so well known throughout the world. I remember reading a Westerner's account of a visit to India, and of how his host, after a few minutes asked to be excused. They were celebrating the birthday of that great American, Booker T. Washington, he said, and he must be present. Washington's fame is a commentary on man's profound desire to rise from slavery.

As I watched him preside, I thought him like Theodore Roosevelt, then President. Both were bent on practical achievement, and both had a passion for facts. Washington's appearance was in no way unusual, except for the light eyes in his brown face. His mouth was strong, his wit quick and opportune. In his world-famous speech, he had told the people of Atlanta to put down their buckets where they were —and he meant to give them something worth pulling up.

At the hotel I noticed the shiny coats of the Negro waiters and their frayed linen. Evidently they were underpaid. I tipped generously, but I was embarrassed when, at one restaurant, I found an old friend, a minister from New York, waiting on me. He had been dissatisfied with his meager theological training, and had come to Gammon Seminary where he was studying, earning money in the meantime at this restaurant. I did not tip, but it seemed as though I should find some graceful way of giving him what was really a part of his wage. He told me later that the manager wanted to know "who in hell is Mr. Mitchell," when I called him by name.

I was too busy to observe the unrest in the city. Washington felt it, and urged the papers not to publish so much sensational news, some of it false, of Negro rape. But in spite of this, the fear of riot was in the air.

When I returned to New York, Villard asked me to write something on the relations between the races in the South. I wrote an article on a recorder's "Morning in Court" as reported in the Atlanta *Constitution*. It happened that the presiding judge was absent and one of the aldermen was taking up the Negro cases one by one. (I quote from the Atlanta *Constitution*, the city's famous newspaper.)

"They ought not to be at large any more than a mad dog," remarked the alderman, and he gave them thirty days as fast as they came before him. He was facetious and the cases went like this: Rossie Demmie, a small Negro boy, had stole a set of harness and pawned it.

"Thirty days in the stockade," said the recorder. "You stole harness and for thirty days we will lose all trace of you."

George Bailey, a half-witted Negro, who spends eleven months out of every twelve in the stockade, was brought before the alderman on the charge of being a vagrant.

"Thirty days for George," announced the alderman. "He is better off in the stockade than on the streets."

When he reached the door George turned around and "cussed" the acting recorder. The alderman started to enter a fine for contempt of court, but when he was informed that the Negro had been cursing the judge for twenty years, he changed his mind and said:

"I don't care to take away any of the standing prerogatives these people may have."

Mamie Smith, a Negro woman, raised both sand and Cain on Peters Street.

"Thirty days for Mamie," said the acting recorder. Whereupon the remorseful Mamie began to weep.

"If you don't hush that," exclaimed the alderman, "I'll give you another thirty days. I ain't going to have any crying niggers around me."

So it went on. The last case was of a white man who had been found drunk and who said he must hurry back home to milk his cow and feed his little pig. "I'm going to send you right back," the alderman declared. "I don't care so much about you as about making the cow and pig suffer."

John E. Milholland read this article, and liked it so much that he wrote asking me to go South at his expense and write more. I wanted greatly to go South again for a long stay, but I doubted whether I could write what Milholland wanted. I wanted to have a picture of the southern Negro that I could compare with my picture of the New York Negro; while he wanted sharp articles of censure. I accepted an initial check, but soon was going my own way. I should have followed his instructions, for there were plenty of important issues, education, politics, that would have made good reading. Instead, I enjoyed dawdling through the State of Alabama, seeing a good deal but writing little.

My first stop was Atlanta, at the University again, but a different University, for in September 1906, the Atlanta rioters tore through the city and left sorrow and fierce anger in every heart.

A case of rape reported in the evening papers was the immediate cause of the riots. But, of course, it all went back to long before that. Vicious reports of crime had been filling the papers, and reports of assaults that were not crimes at all, but imaginings. A little girl charged the old janitor of her school, who had had many years in service, of assaulting her.

He was innocent, but her mind was inflamed. So the minds of the white people were inflamed while the colored people went about in fear or defiance. What about their women? Their danger was real. A white man's attack on a little colored girl went unpunished. Uproar broke out, and the city went mad. Negroes were hunted out and shot at sight. Ammunition was sold to any white man who came for it. Mobs raced through the streets, and a dark face was a target mark.

Walter White, today secretary of the NAACP, was then a boy of thirteen, living in Atlanta where his father was a mail carrier. He was driving with his father as the father was finishing his work that Friday night. Both were white of face and went unmolested, but the description that he gave me of what he saw that first night conveyed a vivid idea of the riot.

He saw a great crowd rush down a street pursuing a black man, saw a knife flash, and the black man fall dead. . . . He saw seven Negroes killed, one a crippled bootblack whom he knew, a mild hard-working fellow. . . . He also saw, by Grady's Monument, a white man driving an old-fashioned carriage in which crouched two Negroes. The man, high in the driver's seat, held the reins in his left hand, while with his right he slashed at the mob with his whip, cursing them for cowards. Whether he rescued his freight White never knew.

The next day he and his father sat at their window armed, their womenfolk in the back of the room, ready to shoot upon the mob. They heard it come down the street, it stopped and they heard the cry, "Burn the place. It's too good for a nigger!" Then a voice cried, "Darktown," and capriciously the mass of men rushed by and left them unharmed. It is small wonder that the boy, who saw this as a child, has dedicated his manhood to the uprooting of lynching.

The cry, "It's too good for a nigger," led to the destruction of the settlement of Brownsville, near Clark University. The place had been occupied chiefly by working men, among them a number of skilled workers, plasterers, carpenters, and painters. In a study of Negro losses from the riot, I found that thirty families had been forced to leave Brownsville, all of them good workers. Students guarded Atlanta University day and night; the mob drew very near, but it did not attack. Like all mobs, it was at heart cowardly, hunting out the defenseless, even the women.

Darktown, the worst colored section of the city, armed itself and wrote a notice, "Don't send us the militia; we want the mob." And it was from Darktown that defense came. The mob did not like Darktown. "That's the irony of it," Dr. Crogman of Clark said to me. "Here we have worked and prayed and tried to make good men and women of our colored population, and at our very doorstep the whites kill these good men. But the lawless element in our population, the element we have condemned fights back, and it is to these people that we owe our lives."

Surely Thou art not white, O Lord, a pale, bloodless, heartless thing!

So Du Bois cried in his *Litany of Atlanta*, written as he sped back to the city from a trip in the far South. Yolande, his little daughter, had been taught to hide in the closet clad in black, in case the University was stormed. It was a game to her. It was far from a game to those who watched.

The riots sobered Atlanta. White and colored met together, Negro on one side of the room, white on the other, to plan for better relations. Will Alexander, who became the newly formed committee's head, served with tact, understanding, and always with courage. Church women were active, declaring they wanted no such riots in defense of their honor. No one will ever know how much the committee has done, for work of this sort is preventive and would lose its potency if publicized.

I was glad to leave Atlanta University. It was hurt, bitter. It would soon be in stride again, educating its boys and girls who, in turn, would be endangered by this very education. I was absolutely convinced that what they did and how they did it, was right, and the years have shown that their graduates have more than justified the most sanguine expectations. But I wanted to see something different. I journeyed to Montgomery and 20 miles south to a school of which I had heard much in the North, especially in Boston, Calhoun Colored School.

The English who settled New England had a profound belief in the value of education. They had left England to better themselves, and they meant that their children, though living in a wilderness, should be schooled, their minds trained in the learning that was necessary if America was to foster trade and to become a part of the culture of the old world. Their ideas and their curriculum, to a considerable extent exist in the public school of today.

It was natural that the teachers who went South at the end of the war, descendants for the most part of New Englanders, wherever they might then be living, should carry the cultural idea of education into the South. They taught the three R's, the tools by which learning lives, and they introduced the Negro to great literature. Their colleges educated him for the professions. They also taught cleanliness, order, decorum. Their eager scholars studied words and numbers, believing these would lead them to the promised land, as indeed at times they did. But a second problem faced the emancipated slave and his children: What work could he do immediately that would give him enough to live in the decency and the security that all were learning to desire?

Among the people of missionary background who attacked this problem was General Armstrong. His parents had been missionaries in Hawaii, and he had seen the native population there learn to work regularly for wages. He understood the disorganized conditions in the conquered South and he felt that, besides education in books, the Negro should be trained for work. With the purpose of bringing these two forms of education to the Negro, he founded Hampton Institute.

Hampton's most famous graduate of course is Booker T. Washington. Well-known among its former teachers is Charlotte R. Thorne. General Armstrong found Charlotte Thorne leading a happy social life in New Haven, and persuaded her to come to Hampton to teach. She went, and for a time was satisfied. But Booker Washington's penetration into an obscure, ignorant Negro section of Alabama excited her imagination. A fellow teacher, Mabel Dillingham, shared her enthusiasm and to Armstrong's consternation, he found two of his best teachers resolved to start a school of their own.

They wrote Booker Washington for advice as to where to settle. He told them that he had recently visited Calhoun, a few miles south of Montgomery, where he found the Negroes praying for a school. He reasoned if they wanted it that much, it would be a good place to start. So they went to Calhoun.

Miss Thorne said little about their early days of teaching, when they met with many rebuffs. The colored greeted them eagerly, but the whites were hostile. Once their food was poisoned. Mabel Dillingham died under tension, but Charlotte Thorne, who was stronger physically, carried on her work successfully. While never quite accepted by her white neighbors, she grew to be tolerated.

The school founded, literally in answer to prayer, was in a small community where one man ruled with the authority of plantation days. He owned thousands of acres that were tilled by whites and Negroes. The latter were the majority. These workers were in his power, and if they escaped from his plantation, they might be captured and imprisoned. It was peonage under the sharecrop system.

The sharecropper was a natural outgrowth of conditions after emancipation. Whether the Negro was slave or freeman, he was living on a certain piece of land, doing a certain piece of work, and that work had to be continued or he would starve. As the man who had been his master had lost his capital in the war and could not pay wages, the two struck up a bargain: the former master would furnish his former slave with cabin, tools, clothing, food, while in return the Negro would furnish labor, his own and his family's. When the crop was gathered, they would share and share alike.

These terms differed in different localities, but they arose from necessity and became common among white as well as colored. The more intelligent, industrious laborer bought land, which was cheap; but many could not acquire capital. In Calhoun, where the plantation was large, the sharecrop system flourished and became the rule.

The abuses to which it can be put are apparent. The laborer starts with indebtedness. The proprietor, as soon as he accumulates capital, has the laborer in his power. He gets to own the store at which the cropper is advanced goods, he keeps the accounts, he owns the tools with which the cropper works, he owns the scales on which the cotton is weighed. By arranging that the crop, when weighed, shall be worth less than the amount owed, the capitalist can keep his worker continually in debt. If, feeling his position hopeless, the cropper runs off, he can be arrested and either imprisoned or returned to the owner as a criminal. Thus he becomes a peon, a person held for debt.

Although the sharecrop system was in full working order at Calhoun, Miss Thorne never allowed the information to be published, but now it is so far in the past that former conditions may be written of as history. White as well as colored feared the owner of the plantation who worked his tenants hard, his overseers helping him. He was equally severe in his demands on white and black, but the black were in bodily danger. One Negro had been so terribly beaten that he was pointed out as an awful warning. I saw him, bent double, tottering down the road. A woman had been severely beaten because, against orders, she had sent her child to Calhoun School. All the tenants were in great poverty.

Next door to this plantation was a much smaller one, owned by a man of a different caliber, Edward Chesnutt. His father, before the war a prosperous carriage maker, had like many others opposed secession, and like others called it "a rich man's war and a poor man's fight." He continued his trade, and by buying his way, only fought for ten days. He could not afford schooling for his son, but he educated him in his own ideas, for Edward was a Populist and told me much about Weaver's fight. "Some of the Negroes voted with us. I know because I saw them," he said. He had now sold the bulk of his property to Calhoun, and was made its manager. A man of native kindness, sympathetic, ready to learn, he was a great acquisition to the school. The purchase of his land made possible an experiment in a model community. Thus Calhoun was not only a school, it was also a collection of homes, bought on easy terms, where Negroes might live and cultivate their own land, and where they could send their children to as good a school as they could find in the country.

These children constituted only a small number of the scholars. Calhoun was a boarding school, and young people came from all parts of the state. One ambitious boy whom I met had walked a hundred miles to attain the chance for an education. Such students, as at Hampton, worked their way, attending evening school. It was a busy community, striving prayerfully for a free, happy life that had never before been possible.

Miss Thorne had the power of interesting people in her work, and her school flourished. It was a lovely place, the school buildings white, roses growing about the houses, the paths from building to building edged with flowers. A few were in blossom even in December, when I made my visit. Miss Thorne's home with its open fireplace, its hundreds of books, its antique furniture, was a bit of the Connecticut from which she came. With her reddish-gold hair and blue eyes, her quick speech, she was alien to that red soil growing its cotton and corn. She made it her own, however, going about whenever needed, alone at night if a call for help came. We talked far into the night our first evening. Visiting her was Emily Hallowell, a musician, deeply interested in Negro music.

I stayed at the school six weeks, visiting the classes and the pleasant homes of the community, once the Chesnutt plantation, and trying to understand the Negro in this environment. It seemed the most favorable environment in which I had seen the poor of the race. They were deeply religious, not dogmatically, but emotionally—their emotion illuminated by imagination. They visualized what they read, and Biblical figures stood alive. And when they met for their Sunday afternoon services, the singing of the spirituals and the reciting of Bible texts, they were without self-consciousness. It was not church, a place away from the world that a boy or a girl visited occasionally in a busy life, but a part of home.

At Calhoun I felt that I had heard the spirituals for the first time. I had heard words and music beautifully sung at Atlanta, but in classic form. At Calhoun, I heard them as they were originally sung, primitive music, great group singing. It was disappearing even then, but in schools where this music alone was heard, where the hymnbook and the book of popular songs had not penetrated, folk singing still existed. By now it must have disappeared.

They sang at Calhoun as their fathers and mothers must have sung, always in harmony but always unexpected. A cry came from a tenor voice as startling as lightning. I used to hear that on San Juan Hill, but not the extraordinary harmonies that accompanied it. They sang with the sorrow of the slave. Again I heard,

> Bye an' bye, bye an' bye
> I's gwine ter lay down dis heaby load.

A hopeless sorrow that lingered in this generation.

The belief that sorrow is something inevitable, to be accepted, while inimical to progress, has a moral quality. At a mothers' meeting which I attended with Miss Thorne, complaint was brought against a woman for drinking to excess. One after another brought evidence, and the woman agreed to all they said. She was tough-looking and a very shabby, black sailor hat did not add to her attractiveness. When, after the accusation, Miss Thorne asked her if she would give up drink, she nodded and said that she would.

I was skeptical. "She won't keep her word," I said later. But Miss Thorne, who knew her well, did not agree. "She'll take going without drink as one of her troubles that has to be endured."

This quiet acceptance of life without dramatization or self-pity was illustrated at Christmas time. It was the great day of the year when the school had all sorts of good times about their Christmas tree and feasted on turkey and pie. In the morning, baskets were assigned to different boys to carry to old persons in the vicinity. All the boys but one came back shortly and joined in the festivities. When evening had come and one boy had still not returned, Miss Thorne became anxious. We walked along the path to his dormitory and suddenly saw him coming up toward us. He explained that the old woman for whom his basket was intended had moved a way out, and he had used up his day finding her. "She seemed right pleased," he added. When Miss Thorne expressed regret at his having missed the good times, he only said he was glad to have gone, and left us with a good night. He did not dramatize the event or pity himself.

Discipline was simple. The boys were proud of their uniforms which they wore at all times. Hanging around the railroad station until the train came in was about the only entertainment Calhoun had, and the colored boys liked to go there. When it was pointed out to them that this did not become their uniform, they agreed to stay away. Ray Stannard Baker visited Calhoun while I was there, collecting material for his illuminating articles, later to be published in *McClure's*, called "Following the Color Line." He asked Miss Thorne whether they had much theft. "I know," he said apologetically, "it's an inheritance from slavery." She answered that they had had two cases since the school started; one of a dress stolen by a woman from outside "for whom we were not responsible"; and one a hair ribbon taken by a school girl. "This girl," she said, "we felt must leave the school grounds for a time, boarding outside, until she could be trusted again." "That was all?" Baker's face was a study. "Yes, that was all."

January first, Emancipation Day, was celebrated at Calhoun and the old people told their stories and sang their songs. Almost every recital began, "I were sold down in Alabama." I collected a number of these slave tales which were later published in *The Independent*. The awfulness of being treated as chattels was the deepest memory in these lives. "Seem lak I couldn't bear it," one said. "I was sol' away f'om my chillen," said another. "I had four chillen but they only lef me my little baby. Dat near broke my heart." I remembered what Viola Roseborough, who was writing her inimitable short stories at this time, told me of her southern mother. "I couldn't understand why she so hated slavery," Miss Roseborough said. "She saw little of it in her own home. Yet when she was dying of a painful illness and started to complain, she stopped herself. 'I have no right to complain of anything,' she said, 'for I have seen the end of slavery.' Many years later," Miss Roseborough continued, "I learned that she sometimes visited her grandparents who lived by one of the roads down which the slaves marched to the far South. She never forgot that procession, its strong youths, its mothers and babies, driven like cattle to new owners."

During this visit, I went with Miss Thorne to the Farmers' Conference at Tuskegee. The beautiful campus of today with its artistic buildings was in embryo, but its energetic principal made one confident that before he was through Booker Washington would have the finest school in America. Scholars marched triumphantly into the auditorium—organ and band rolling out music—a seemingly endless number of boys and girls. But even more interesting, though less impressive, were the farmers who came from all over the state to the Tuskegee conference.

They were very dark, these farmers, dressed in rough clothes and sometimes speaking a difficult Negro dialect. Some were sharecroppers, but most of them owned their farms, and each year tried to make a little better showing than the last. They did practically all the talking. Some of them liked to tell of the help they had from their women folk, at home and in the fields. One clad in homespun, told us his suit had been woven, dyed, cut out, and sewed by his wife. They told proudly of their industrious children, their crops, their pigs, and their chickens. They seemed to have a number of jokes among themselves.

Washington encouraged and reproved and occasionally did some talking. He spoke on beautifying the home. "How many of you have painted or whitewashed your houses?" he asked.

"I want ter whitewash mine," a man got up to say.

"You want to?" Washington replied. "Why didn't you do it last week?"

The man sat down looking shamefaced.

"Don't mortgage your crops," he said another time. "I hope you aren't any of you mortgaging your crops."

"I's speaking der truf," an old man got up to say. "Plenty of us is doing it."

"Not me," one man called out and others rose to say that they were free of debt.

"That's good," said the presiding officer. "Now use your influence against loafing. Let us take a stand here against the Saturday afternoon loafing and the women who hang about corners or go into the courthouse."

And so on. They were told not to support liquor dispensaries and blind tigers, but their churches. A very great deal, it seemed to me, was expected of them.

Before the conference adjourned, Washington made an appeal that had something wistful about it. "Those Negroes up North are hammering at me," he said. "You'll stand by me?"

"Yes, yes!" they said.

I remember especially one face in the audience, an elderly black man, who looked morally indignant, a look that, had he been a preacher, he would have used when hearing of some cowardly sin.

I took this to heart for while I had tried to report sympathetically the Booker Washington meetings which I attended (I was to report this one) I was with the group that criticized Washington's ignoring of Negro rights. Looking back on it now, I think the northern group would have felt less bitter toward this man of whom they could not but be proud if he had been able to delegate authority; but like most self-made men, he took details upon himself. He was appealed to on any and every subject: how many bathrooms to put in a YMCA, whether or not to start a day nursery in some town, and so on. These things came into his office, but were not scattered over the country to be answered by specialists; they were answered by Washington and his coterie. His emphasis on industrial training hurt the colleges, and nearly all had to put some industrial training into their curriculum, a needless expense. Then politically he was supreme. The friend of presidents could hand out many plums. That he kept his dignity, a dignity combined with a modesty of bearing, is very much to his credit, for in the eyes of the world he was the Negro of the hour. "I almost worship this man," I heard W. H. Baldwin, one of his most ardent supporters, say at a Washington meeting. To be worshiped is dangerous to a man who has known the hardship and degradation of poverty—especially when it comes from the rich and powerful. It encourages him to believe in his own infallibility.

Booker Washington was not to live many years after this meeting. He died in 1915. A great educator, a man who rose above obstacles, who became a power in his day, and was destined to be elected to the Hall of Fame. As a teacher, he was in advance of his time. He used farm demonstration work before most educators had heard of it. He knew enough to take George Washington Carver out of his Iowa environment and give him a laboratory at Tuskegee. Both were passionate lovers of the soil, and Washington gave Carver the opportunity to make his remarkable discoveries. I often heard him talk at Carnegie Hall, but I liked best to remember him among the farmers at Tuskegee, meeting these hardworking men with homely wisdom.

It has been interesting through the years to note that whether the school was academic like Atlanta or industrial like Tuskegee, most of its graduates became teachers. Salaries might be insufficient and buildings inadequate, but the need of public education for the Negro together with a demand for trained teachers, gained recognition in the South. Few went into agriculture or the trades.

As far back as the beginning of the century, educated colored people were taking the place of the white Northerners with missionary zeal. Mary Bethune from the deep South, Charlotte Hawkins Brown from Cambridge, Massachusetts, started schools; one at Daytona Beach, Florida, the other at Sedalia, North Carolina. Both are important in the educational world today. Men like Edwards of Snow Hill, Alabama, and Jones of Piney Woods, Mississippi, with Armstrong's courage and belief in work, carried his ideas into remote sections. White churches continued their interest in their home mission educational work, and colored churches supported a large number of schools under their respective denominations. Persons interested in the progress the Negro has made in the South, can do no better than get a list from the General Education Board and move down the eastern coast, through the large cities, and back by the hill country, stopping at private and state schools and colleges. Of course, he will see the best, but why not? When he visits the white South, he does not specialize on its gambling houses and brothels. Those who visit the best get an incorrect idea of the whole; but the American has been made thoroughly familiar with the Negro's worst. So I recommend this study of the colored school and college where one not only meets teacher and student, but also sees a good Negro quarter of a city. When the school is in the country, it usually is able to affect favorably the life of the farmers about it.

One principal of a school whom I met as I journeyed north in Alabama, William Benson of Kowaliga, was trying to combine education with business founded upon proper treatment of its employees. He wanted a business to support his school, and especially he wanted to have a turpentine camp of his own. He wanted a respectable camp, and would not allow the two requisites for turpentine labor, liquor and women. Consequently he attracted few workers. The sap poured into his new cups, overflowed, and dripped to the ground. What Will Benson needed was capital for his years of experimentation. He could not raise the needed money. He learned that it is much easier to get money for a school than capital for a philanthropic business, philanthropic in the sense that it was interested in the welfare of the worker. It was a good dream, this dream of a decent turpentine camp. Bitter disappointment was one cause of the dreamer's early death.

I did not see the southern part of the state where the

land is better, but I grew to understand a little about the soil, after a drive at Calhoun. We came to a mud puddle in the road. I was amazed when the driver was afraid to go on. "Why, that's nothing!" I exclaimed. Perhaps my ignorance encouraged her, or more likely she thought I ought to learn something about Alabama soil. She ventured on—and we were dragged out later by two mules!

Milholland had asked me to visit a white Southerner named Joseph Manning, a Republican politician who was in charge of the post office at Alexander City in the central part of the state. Manning owned a small paper in which he had printed matter favorable to the Negro. For this he had been severely beaten up. I was to see Manning, Milholland said, and get him to continue printing live stuff in his paper. So I journeyed to Alexander City and visited with the Mannings for ten days.

My host called himself a "hillbilly." He had a pasty, ill-nourished look. I became convinced, as I journeyed through the state, that the English type loses much of its attractiveness in a warm climate. Since then, cosmetics have brightened female complexions, but the blush of beauty over which poets rave comes with the foggy air of old England or, in America, of Nova Scotia. A hillbilly diet of corn and pork does not help. At any rate, Manning looked half ill. He was small and rather jittery. He could not have put up a fight even if the men who attacked him had given him a chance.

He wanted to please Milholland, but I realized, after I left, that Manning risked something in entertaining me. I ought to see conditions among the colored and the white in his city, he said, and to see the white first. When through with that, and not until then, could I go among the colored. So I visited the white schools and spoke to the children and attended the white church the Mannings attended. Having spoken at one time to a geography class, I had evolved a speech good for all children who, poor things, always seemed assembled to listen to visitors. I talked about places I had seen in my travels, especially places in the North with ice and snow. I encouraged questions and was floored once by a little boy at Tuskegee who asked me to describe the water system in Iceland!

The minister of the Methodist Church went with us on our tour among the whites and then, to Manning's gratification, remained with us when we turned to the colored. I noticed that the colored grammar school principal seemed honored and surprised to see a white minister. We three spoke in the colored schools and in one colored church. I remember the minister's cordiality to his fellow preacher.

I did not see much of my hostess who had a large family; but one evening, when Manning was away, we had a long talk. She told me of the attack on her husband. In a sentence or two, she described an unforgettable incident of white brutality. In her quiet home, the children all in bed, a single kerosene lamp lighting the dim room, the story burned into my consciousness. Manning had been brought home to her inert, bleeding. She had thought him dead. "They'll get him next time," she said bitterly. "They mean to kill him." The shades were only partly down, and she got up and pulled them all the way, saying again that he was in danger. She may have thought we were all in danger. And at this time Milholland was writing Manning that he ought to speak out more in his paper.

When I left Alexander City—it would have been a town in New England—I had seen white and colored in their schools and churches. I saw few homes, for the colored people, out of consideration for Mr. Manning's safety, did not entertain me, and the whites looked at me askance. The liberal-minded minister asked me to dinner, but his wife never set a date. I left feeling that I had done no good and might have made life harder for my host. A letter received a month later set my mind at rest.

Mr. Manning wrote that they were all well, that the children wanted to know when I was coming back, and that I might be interested to learn what had happened at the church whose minister went about with us. Shortly after my departure, the congregation held a stormy meeting at which the minister was present. Members of the congregation rose to charge him with going to a colored public school and a colored church, and with associating with Miss Ovington, a northern nigger-lover. A simple punishment was open to them: they proposed reducing his salary.

The minister, Manning wrote, was very red in the face when he rose to give his answer. He did not excuse himself but launched out against his critics. Yes, he had gone to the colored church and had met the minister who was a God-fearing man. He had visited the colored school and had talked to the little children, the children whom Christ loved, and would be glad to do it again. He was proud to have met Miss Ovington. Standing up to his congregation, he swung sentiment in his favor, and in the end was voted a raise in salary of $200. "Men like courage," Manning ended.

I had been home some weeks when I was again reminded of Alexander City. An expressman came to my door bringing in a large box with slats at the sides. Within was a sadly frightened animal having a conspicuous snout. The express-man did not know what it was, but I could guess. Just before I left, the Mannings had been shocked to learn that I had never tasted possum! Here was a live one and if it was to be any good to me it needed the attentions of a butcher. The expressman gone and the animal parked in my kitchen, I called up my friend, always my friend in need, Thomas Bell of the colored YMCA. He soon came, talked affectionately to the possum, and brought a Harlem butcher who took away the animal in his cart. Later, Bell said, a good cook would be secured. The plan was excellent but when the box was opened, the animal escaped and was last reported in the back yard of a tenement. I have not yet tasted possum.

When I was at Montgomery, the state capital, I learned a bit of southern history. During the Civil War northern Ala-bama, with a soil unsuited to slave labor, had been cool in its attitude toward secession. "A rich man's war and a poor man's fight," again expressed the opinion of many. Winston County had even gone so far as never to secede from the Union. At this date, 1907, its voters had sent a Republican to the State Legislature, one of two representatives of that party in the House. Shortly after this representative took his seat, a bill was introduced providing that Winston County officers be appointed by the State Legislature, not elected by the people. As one representative said in a speech before the House, "Winston County was in rebellion in 1860 and it is in rebel-lion now. It needs to be disciplined." Nothing but oratory came of the measure, but the Winston County representa-tive invited me to visit his part of the state and stop at his home. I accepted.

The countryside, with its unpainted houses and untidy yards, was not unlike the region I was leaving. The State Representative and his wife had a fairly large house, but I was a long way from the trim neatness of Calhoun and from the comforts of city life. On the front porch a pitcher and bowl did good service during the day for washing hands and face, and were reluctantly handed over to me when I demanded some way of washing in my parlor bedroom. No wonder Lillian Smith in *Strange Fruit* dwells on the physical habits of a population where a privy is a modern invention and running water unknown!

I met the town's young minister, dressed entirely in black, the priest set apart from his congregation. When I commented on this, declaring that he should have a good time with the other young people and not be apart from them, my host replied, "But think of all he is giving up!" I met the boyish-looking doctor who made his visits on horseback, his medicine and instruments in his saddle bags. He pitied me my life in New York, surrounded as I must be by strangers. For himself, he wanted to work where he knew everybody. Where he lived was his world.

On my return to Birmingham I stopped at Double Springs, the county seat. I attended court and heard a wise, kindly judge give instructions to the grand jury, so lucidly, explaining the law so clearly, that even I, who had never before heard a judge give a charge, or seen a grand jury, could not fail to understand. At one point, he spoke of a place he had visited and of the filthy, disgusting accommodations given the Negroes lodged in the jail. This was received with laughter. These country northern Alabamans, who looked like characters from a scene in the Old Homestead of nineteenth-century fame, like too many people the country over, thought of the Negro as a joke. The judge might express sympathy, but they felt none.

Winston County, however, had a legitimate grievance against the Negro, or rather against the use of the Negro in state politics. He had been disfranchised since Reconstruction days, but he was counted in the population and allotted his share of school money. This meant that in the southern part of the state, where Negroes were in the majority, the whites had more money for schooling than white counties North. In Calhoun, Lowndes County, nine-tenths of the population was colored. That they should have nine-tenths of the state appropriation was unthinkable; instead, they got one-tenth. Winston County had almost no Negroes to count in its population—to count and then to steal from—and its schools suffered. One could understand the presence of that Republican Senator at Montgomery.

I was a nine days' wonder at Double Springs. What was a lady from New York City doing there? My suitcase carried a card with my address, but New York did not come to trade at Double Springs. Still, the suitcase looked business-like, and it was settled that I had something to sell. I did not learn what a reputation I had acquired for wealth until I was leaving. My landlady's daughter haunted my room and showed much interest in my belongings. "You're a millionaire's daughter," she declared positively as I was packing my toilet things. I asked what made her think so. "Because you brought your own comb and brush. These were for you," and she pulled out a well-worn brush and comb safely chained to the bureau drawer. Her last question, and she was full of questions, was, "Why don't you dip snuff?"

At Birmingham I met the man who was to remain vividly in my memory among the people I had seen on this southern trip, the state secretary of the Socialist party in Alabama. I was at that time a member of the party, and had asked the New York Central Committee for this introduction. He came to my hotel on my last evening, and we sat in the balcony overlooking the busy lobby where well-dressed people stood at the desk, or followed smartly uniformed bellboys to the elevator, or smoked in the comfortable chairs. My new acquaintance was a sharp contrast. His clothes were cheap, his collar and cuffs were frayed. His face was sickly, blood-less, and he had lost one eye—he told me later—at his trade. Had I seen him on the street I should have classified him as one more ineffectual poor white. Before his visit was over, I felt profoundly his strength and courage.

He was embarrassed at first, and I did most of the talk-ing, describing a recent meeting in New York where Jack London spoke on internationalism. He had thrilled us with his picture of the workers of the world who would unite and win the world. I tried to bring back the enthusiasm of the meeting and London's confidence.

Then my visitor began to talk—not of world socialism but of socialism in the State of Alabama. The movement was small, of course, centered chiefly in Birmingham where labor was organized. . . . Did I understand that meant all labor, black and white? Some Negroes, coal miners, had joined the Socialist party. When he was traveling, once, he had met one, down at the railroad station. . . . I wouldn't understand

how the whites hated this, "me meeting a 'nigger' and practicing social equality. . . . They got hold of us, threw us
together, made us kiss one another. They . . ."

He stopped and began again, this time talking about himself. "I lost my job, of course. I had a good trade, but I
couldn't work at it, for they blacklisted me. Now I print a
little paper for the party. . . . My wife left me. I don't
blame her; I couldn't support her like I used to. We'd lost
our little girl and grieved for her, but maybe that was right
too. I couldn't have done for her. . . . My wife's with her
own folks now. My brother-in-law and I used to be old
friends, but he takes her side. And that's natural."

He pulled a letter from his pocket. "You'll be interested
to see this for it's from a Negro comrade. Nicely written." I
examined the letter. It had the familiar ending, "Yours for
the revolution." The pen had sputtered but the words were
clear. "They make good comrades once they understand,"
the secretary said with pride as he put the letter into his
pocket; and I understood that despite what had happened
at the railroad station, and would happen again somewhere
else, he would go on explaining socialism to the black man.

He had lost his self-consciousness while talking, but when
he got up it returned. I thought him conscious of his clothes,
but no; in his mind was something fine, delicate. "I hope
you'll excuse me if I've been rude," he said at last. "It's a
long time since I've talked with a good woman, as much ?s
six months. I hope I have not been rude."

I hurriedly said, "Of course not," and tried to make him
understand how much I appreciated what he had done for
the cause in which we both believed. We shook hands in

good-bye, and he disappeared in the milling crowd of the lobby.

I was glad to lock the door when I went into my room that night. The day's journey had been hard and disagreeable, beginning at five in the morning. A fellow traveler, once high in the state's service, now a lewd old man, was with me much of the way. When at last I hurried from the day coach into the Birmingham station, I was thankful to get into a taxi and drive to the hotel. All annoyance had been forgotten while talking to my visitor, but back in my room I found myself shaking a little. This was a strange land to me—my only friends in Birmingham were persecuted Negroes and a despised Socialist. How thankful I would be tomorrow when I had boarded the express that would take me to New York. I lay awake, lonely and depressed.

The next morning, settled in a comfortable Pullman chair, my mood remained. The day was cloudy and I looked out on a dull landscape: cotton, straggling pines, squalid cabins, dark-skinned, ragged men and women and children standing motionless watching the train go by. It was depressing almost to hopelessness. We ran past a forlorn little station with WHITE and COLORED over its two doors. The white people were scattered, but the colored were standing by the door bearing their sign.

"It might have happened here," I thought.

Back in New York I wrote my story. It is based on the few words Mrs. Manning half-whispered to me that night. Max Eastman printed it in *The Masses* when that paper was a power. The black brute, attacking beautiful white girls, was the South's excuse for lynching. Remembering this, I called my story

THE WHITE BRUTE

It was a very hot day, and the Jim Crow car was the hottest spot in the State of Mississippi. At least so Sam and Melinda thought as they got out at the railroad station to change cars to go to their home.

"Come out of the sun into the shade, Linda," he said, when, a heavy bag in each hand, they started to move down the platform.

"I ain't minding the heat," she answered, smiling up at him.

He looked down at her, his dark eyes gleaming from his black face. He was a large, powerfully built man, with big muscles under his newly pressed coat, and strong hands that showed years of heavy work in the fields. He swung the two bags into one hand and with the free one drew the girl to his side.

"You's the sweetest thing," he whispered.

Again she smiled up at him and her eyes were very soft and dark. Her new straw hat, with its blue ribbon, rested for a second on his shoulder. Then with a little laugh she started down the platform.

"We'll come inside," she said.

They entered the small, ill-ventilated room marked "Colored." It was a dingy place, for the stove in the center still held the winter's ashes, and the floors were thick with many weeks' dust. At one end was a window where the ticket seller would come a little before train-time to serve, first, the whites from their window in the adjoining room, and last, the blacks from theirs. But no one was about now, and the two settled themselves upon the dusty bench. The girl, with a little yawn, leaned back against the wall.

"Reckon you is feel sleepy, honey," the man said tenderly. "You was up all night mos'. We sure had the finest weddin' in the country. Your folks ain't spare nothin'. I never see so many good things to eat nur so many pretty dresses befo' in all my bawn life."

His bride slipped her hand in his. "We wanted to give you a good time."

"You sure did. It was the grandes' time I ever knowed. Dancin' and ice cream and the people a-laughin' and the preacher a-hollerin' with the res'. And all the while my li'l gal by me and me knowin' she was mine furever an' ever, ter have an' ter hol'."

He pressed the hand that she had given him. "I can't see why you took me, Linda. Tom Jenkins is a preacher and learned in books, and I ain't nothin' but a black han' from de cotton fields."

She pulled his necktie into place, and then, glancing at the door and seeing that there was no one in sight, she drew his black face close to hers and kissed him.

"Tom wasn't much," she answered. "You're so big and strong. You make me feel safe."

He gazed at her and still wondered that she had chosen him. He knew himself to be uncouth, uneducated, scarcely able to read the sign over the doorway, while she had been to school for two years, had worked for white folks, and knew their dainty ways. She had lived in a town with many streets and could not only read the newspaper, but could sing hymns out of a book. Then she was slender, with a soft brown skin, wavy hair, and small hands and feet. When she smiled and spoke to him, he felt as he did when the mockingbird told him that winter was gone and he caught the first scent of the jasmine bloom. How could he ever show her his great love?

He longed to perform some service and noticing a tank in the corner of the room walked over to get her some water. But as he turned the spigot nothing flowed into the dirty glass. The tank was empty.

"That's mighty mean," he objected. "Looks like they

ain't know a sweet little gal lak you was comin' hyar. Jos' wait a minit an' I'll git you a drink."

Leaving her for a few seconds he returned, an anxious look on his face.

"De train am late," he declared.

"Of course it's late," she answered a little petulantly. "I've lived near a station all my life and I never knew a train to be on time. Sometimes it's an hour late, sometimes twenty-four."

"Dis ain't so bad as all that. Dis train am two hours late. De ticket man tole me so."

"That means nearly three hours here. Well, cheer up, Sam. We'll get home sometime, and then you can show me our house with the roses growing over the po'ch——"

"And de clock——"

"And the work-table that you made——"

"And de turkeys——"

"And the cooking stove——"

"Yes, ma'am, don't you forget de new cook-stove!"

She laughed and rose to her feet. "Let's go outside," she suggested, "perhaps there's a breeze there."

They left the dirty room and walked upon the platform. Up the track was the freight depot where were piled bales of last year's cotton crop, not yet moved. A Negro lay on a truck fast asleep. Across the track was a group of tumble-down shanties, the beginnings of the straggling little town with its unpainted houses and fences in ill repair. Only the church, raising its slender spire back of the houses, gave an impressive touch to the village. To the right the platform belonged to the whites, and two men lounged against the wall. They were young fellows with coarse, somewhat bloated faces that betokened too much eating of fried pork and too much drinking of crude whiskey. Both were chewing tobacco and expectorating freely upon the floor. One of the men carried a gun.

"Suppose we cross the track," Melinda suggested, "and

see if we can't get some sarsaparilla. It would taste good."

"I reckon I wouldn't go 'bout hyar much, Linda. Dis ain't no place fur you and me. De whites is mighty mean and de bes' of the cullud folks is lef' town after de lynchin' hyar twenty years ago."

"A lynching, Sam?"

"Yes, they got him outen one o' dem houses right over yonder and tied him to a pos' down de road a bit. He warn't a *bad* feller, but he done sassed de sheriff—wouldn't let him 'rest him widout a fight—and dey is burn' him alive."

"No, no," the girl cried, and turned a frightened face toward her husband. "Sam, it won't be like that where you live?"

"Don't you be 'fraid, honey. De white folks is fine down my way if you treats 'em right. I know; I worked for 'em for years 'til I bought my lan'. Now I pays my taxes reg'lar, and when I comes along, dey says, 'Howdy, Sam,' jes' as pleasant lak. I neber put on no airs, jes' alys pertend as deir cotton am a heap better'n mine, dough it ain't near so heaby, an' we gets along fine. I can't never fergit dat lynchin' dough," he went on reminiscently. "Pop brung me to see it, hel' me high in his arms. It warn't much of a sight fur a little boy though, de roarin' flames an' de man screaming —how he is scream—and the flesh smelling lak a burn' hog."

"Stop!" the girl cried. "Don't tell me any more, it's too horrible."

"I won't, honey. In co'se it ain't for a li'l gal lak you to hear. So you sees I ain't lak dis hyar town much. But we'll go on over dat-a-way and take a walk. It can't do no harm."

"We won't go far, Sam, and you must talk about something pleasant. About the new cooking-stove, eh? You haven't once told me about the new cooking-stove, have you?"

"Don't you be makin' game of me!"

"Get the bags, dear. We don't want to leave them lying about."

"In course we don'. Somebody mought open 'em an' steal dat white weddin'-dress. But 'twouldn' be much widout you in it. You was shinin' lak a li'l white cloud lyin' close down to de black yearth dat's me."

"Oh, go along," and she gave him a shove.

He was gone a few moments and when he returned he saw that the two white men had walked over to where she stood. She hurried swiftly toward him and he noticed that she was breathing fast.

"That's a right pretty nigger," the taller of the two men said to Sam. "Belongs to you, does she?"

"Yes, sir," Sam answered. "She's my wife. Jes' married las' night," he added in a burst of confidence and pride.

"Don't look like it," the white man answered. "She ain't black enough for you, nigger. What are you doing courting a white girl like that?"

Sam threw back his head and laughed. "You sho' is funny," he said.

"Let us go, Sam," Melinda whispered, tugging at his arm. Her face showed both anger and fear and she tried to walk with him across the tracks.

But the men stood directly in her way. The first one went on, "Don't you all be in a hurry. You don't live here, I know that. Reckon we know every nigger in town, don't we, Jim?"

He turned to his friend who nodded assent.

"Enjoying your trip?" He addressed the bridegroom, but his eyes traveled, as they had traveled before, to Melinda's slender figure and soft, oval face.

"Yas, sah, we's enjoyin' it all right. We's waitin' fur de train now ter take us home."

"What train?"

"De train from the South, sah. Ought to be hyar by two o'clock, but it ain't comin' til fo'. Pretty po' train, to keep a bride waitin'." He showed his white teeth again in a broad smile, but his eyes were fixed anxiously on the white man's face.

"That's a right smart time to wait, ain't it, Jim?" The man with the gun nodded. "Reckon we ought to do something for your amusement. Give your girl a good time now?"

Sam laughed again to show his delight at the man's facetiousness. "You's mighty good, sir, to think about my girl and me. But we don't need no amusement. We ain't been married long enough to be tired of one another, has we, honey?" and he looked down into Melinda's face.

She was terrified, he could see that clearly. Pulling at his arm she drew him back toward the waiting room. "Come in here, I want to sit down," she said.

"Sam led her into the room only to find the white men following him. Standing at her husband's side, the girl turned and for the first time spoke to the men.

"This room is for colored," she said.

The man with the gun spat upon the floor, but did not move. The other, an ugly look coming into his thin, unhealthy face, answered,

"There's plenty of places where a nigger can't go, my girl, but there ain't a place where a nigger can keep a white man out, leastaways in this county of Mississippi, ain't that so, Jim?"

"That's so," was the other's answer.

"So listen to what I'm saying. Your train leaves at four?" turning to Sam.

"Yes, sah," was the answer.

"Don't you worry, then. I'll bring the girl to you all right. Won't let you miss connection. We wouldn't part husband and wife, but I mean to have my time before you go."

Sam felt the girl's hands about his arm in a grip of terror. Her hot breath was upon his cheek. Patting her two hands with his big ones, he whispered, "Don't you worry, honey."

Then he looked at the men and laughed a harsh, scared laugh. "I knows white folks," he explained, speaking to her and to them. "I knows dey don't want to do us no harm. They jes likes to play wid us, dat's all. Niggers kin always understan' a joke, can't dey, boss?"

"This ain't a joke," the white man retorted sharply. "We-all mean what we say. We ain't jawing at you all this time for nothing. Give us the girl right quick or we'll hang you to the nearest pole and shoot at you till you're thicker'n holes than a rotten tree full of woodpeckers."

"A nigger ain't much account here," the man with the gun added, shifting his weapon in his hand. "We shoot 'em when we feel like it. There's a law in this state for shooting game, but there ain't no law for shooting coons. We burned a nigger here twenty years ago. Got a souvenir of him. Want to see it?" And he thrust a hand into his pocket.

"Sam!" the girl cried.

He looked into the face that had smiled upon him a few minutes before to see her sweet mouth drawn with fear and her eyes starting with terror. His fists clenched and his body stiffened ready for the battle. He measured the man with the gun. He would strike him first, and then, the weapon secured, he could easily shoot his companion. Or he would squeeze those lean necks, one in each hand, and see the eyes start out from the bloated, ugly faces. He would kill them before her, his mate, who had chosen him as her protector.

And after that, what?

As he stood there, alert, tense, ready to strike, before his eyes there flashed the picture of a man tied to a post, writhing amid flames, while to his nostrils came the smell of burning flesh.

His hands unclenched. Pushing his wife behind him with

a dramatic gesture he threw out his arms and appealed to the two men.

"I know de white folks is master hyar," he cried. "I ain't never said a word agin it. I's worked for the white boss, I's ploughed and sowed and picked for him. I's been a good nigger. Now I asks you, masters, to play fair. I asks you to leave me alone wid what's mine. Don't touch my wife!"

For answer the man with the gun struck him down while the other seized the woman. Reeling against the wall, he saw them drag her to the platform, and when he had stumbled from the room he watched them disappear among the shanties across the tracks.

"Got your girl, eh?" a jeering voice said.

The question came from the Negro who had been asleep upon the truck, and who now sauntered over to where Sam stood. The outraged husband fell upon him in a blind fury, and beat him with his big fists until the other cried for mercy.

"Get out, then," Sam bellowed, flinging the bleeding man from him. "Get out, if you don't want me to kill you."

The man muttered a curse and slunk away.

"I'm sorry for you," a voice said at Sam's elbow.

The Negro turned again with raised fist, but dropped his arm and stood in sullen silence as he saw a white man at his side. The newcomer had emerged from the waiting room, and was looking at Sam in friendly sympathy. He was an elderly man with white hair and beard and kindly blue eyes.

"I'm right sorry," he went on. "I saw 'em just now and it was a dirty trick. I'd like to have done something for you, but, Lord, you can't stop those boys. They own the town. Everyone's afraid of them. Jim there, he's shot and killed two, white men I mean, not counting colored, and Jeff's his equal. They ought to swing for it, but Jeff, he's the sheriff's son.

"You done just right," the man continued. "If you'd a struck either of 'em you'd be a dead man by now—or worse. They won't stand for nothing from a nigger, those boys. I's right sorry," he said over again, and seeing that he could be of no service he went on his way.

The black man in his strength and his helplessness waited on the platform through the interminable hours. The trainmen looked at him curiously as they went about their work, and occasionally a colored passenger spoke to him, but he seemed unconscious of their scrutiny or their words. His frenzy had left him and he stood, keeping silent watch of the shanties in front of the church spire. Once, when a train stopped and shut the town from his view, his eyes dropped and he stooped and picked up the bags at his feet, but there was no bright presence at his side, and as the cars moved out, he put the bags down again and resumed his patient watchfulness. And while his eyes rested upon the dingy outline of the unkempt town, his vision through all the hot, gasping minutes was of a dark-faced, slender girl in the clutches of a white brute.

The men kept their word. As the train from the South drew up they hurried her onto the platform and pushed her and her husband into the Jim-Crow car, "Good-bye," they called and then with lagging steps walked to the village street.

It was late afternoon when the bride and bridegroom reached their home. The western clouds were turning from glowing gold to crimson and all sweet odors were rising from the earth. Violets grew in the grass and honeysuckle clambered over the cabin side. At the porch was a rosebush covered with innumerable pink blossoms. And as though he had waited there to greet them a red bird chirped a welcome from the window sill.

A moment's glow of happiness shone in the man's face and he turned to his wife. Vaguely he felt that the warm earth and the gentle, sweet-scented breeze might heal the

misery that grieved their hearts. They had been like two
dumb, beaten creatures on the train, bowed and helpless.
But now they had quitted the world of harsh sounds and
brutal faces and were at home. The man drew a deep
breath and stood erect as he opened the door for her, but
the woman crossed the threshold with shrinking step and
bent head.

It was such a homelike place. All winter he had worked
for her, fashioning a table for her use, placing a chair here
and a stool there, saving the brightest pictures from the
papers to pin against the wall. The dresser was filled with
blue and white china bought with money he had taken from
his own needs. Many a time he had gone hungry that they
might have something beautiful on which to serve their
first meal together.

"Sit down, Lindy, lamb," he said. His deep, rich voice
had never been so tender. "Rest yo' hat and coat. I'll git the
supper tonight."

He set about his task, lighting the lamp, kindling the fire
in the new stove, and cooking the evening meal. But she
ate nothing. She would startle violently at the fall of a log
in the stove, at the leaf tapping on the window pane, at the
cry of a bird.

"That ain't nothin' but the tu'keys, honey," once he
said soothingly as he saw her tremble, "they's goin' to roost.
They'll be right glad to see you tomorrer."

Presently she arose and in a hoarse voice told him that
she would go to bed. He led her into the little chamber
that he had built for their bedroom. Setting the lamp that
he had carried on the table, he looked up at her, his eyes
asking wistfully for a caress as a dog might look at its master.
But she turned away and he went out to keep his watch
alone.

Sitting in the room which he loved and had fashioned
for her sake, the clock ticking upon the shelf told him with

every second of the happiness that he had lost. "Looks like I's 'bleeged ter bear it," he whispered to himself, "but it ain't right. It ain't right. No man had oughter treat anudder man lak dat. Seem lak dey think a black skin ain't cover a human heart. O God, it ain't right! It ain't right!"

When he crept into the bed beside her he found her shaking with sobs.

"Honey," he whispered, "I's glad you kin cry. Let the tears come. Dey'll help you ter furget."

He would have laid her head upon his breast, but she drew away.

"Lindy," he cried passionately, "I was nigh crazy to help you, don't you know dat? I could hav' kill dem wid my two han's. But it wouldn't have been no use! It wouldn't have been no use! Can't you see dat? If you jes' thinks you'll understan'. I'd seen dem burn a nigger as had struck a white man. Dat's what dey'd have done to me. Can't you see? You wouldn't have wanted to have seen me lak dat?

"And what good would it have done? It wouldn't have made no difference. You'd have had to suffer jes' de same. Listen, honey, I couldn't help you; it'd been jes' de same, only you'd have been lef' all alone.

"But you ain't alone now, Melindy, honey-lamb; you's got me, and I'll toil for you while I lives. I'll help you to furgit. I'll love you and I'll work for you from morn till night. I'll tend you if you're sick lak's if you was my baby chil'. There ain't nothin' I kin do fur you as I'll leave undid. Oh, Melindy, I'm here *alive;* don't you want me? I'm alive. You wouldn't rather have a dead man than a live one, would you?"

He stopped panting and listened for her answer.

At length it came in whispered gasps, "I don't know, Sam; I'm afraid. Every minute I'm afraid."

"Don't be afraid," he cried impetuously, throwing his arm about her. "I'm hyar."

And then he stopped. She had not turned to him, but snuggled close to the wall as if seeking protection there.

Outside were the soft night sounds, the vines rustling against the window, the insects' drowsy chirps. Far off by some distant cabin, came the howl of a dog.

"A dead man or a live cur," he said to himself; and turned upon his face with a sob.

CHAPTER IV

THE NAACP BEGINS

We shall not be satisfied with less than our full manhood rights. . . . We claim for ourselves every right that belongs to a free-born American—political, civil, and social—and until we get these rights, we shall never cease to protest and assail the ears of America with the story of its shameful deeds toward us.

Either the spirit of Lincoln and Lovejoy must be revived and we must come to treat the Negro on a plane of absolute political and social equality, or Vardaman and Tillman will soon have transferred the race war to the North. . . . Yet who realizes the seriousness of the situation, and what large and powerful body of citizens is ready to come to their aid!

THE FIRST of these statements is part of the resolutions adopted at the second meeting of the Niagara Movement. Written by W. E. Burghardt Du Bois, it was read by W. H. Hershaw at Harpers Ferry in the summer of 1906. The second statement is from an article on "Race War in the North," appearing in *The Independent*, Sept. 3, 1908, and written by William English Walling.

Out of these two statements the militant National Association for the Advancement of Colored People was born.

The Niagara Movement took its name from its first meeting-place, Niagara, where, led by Du Bois, a number of colored men and women joined together to fight growing race discrimination. Some came from New England, a few from the West, a very few from the South, many from Washington. Its second meeting was at Storer College, one of the early missionary schools, at historic Harpers Ferry. I was fortunate to be present as a reporter for the New York *Evening Post*. The president of the college opened the conference declaring it was suitable that we should gather in a hall of learning representing, as it did, the belief that the human mind should be unlimited in its development.

Du Bois saw that we had time for walks and discussion; and early one morning we went on a pilgrimage to John Brown's Fort where, with a handful of supporters, John Brown had dared challenge millions of slaveholders. I saw Dr. Waller reverently walk barefooted over the rough grass and stones.

The meetings were concerned with reports of the work done by various committees, most of it legal and political. There was rejoicing at having helped materially to defeat a Rate Bill that would have nationalized Jim-Crow cars. In Chicago, Dr. Charles E. Bentley had secured Negro representation on the Board of Education. Women had done active work. Lawyers had given their services in test cases. The work was crippled by lack of adequate funds, but it was a beginning and I doubt if a more resolute, intelligent set of men and women were assembling anywhere that summer, filled as summers are with various national conventions. Full membership in the Association was limited to Negroes. White men and women could be associate members, but the direction of the movement belonged to the colored.

English Walling's article came out of the Race Riots at

Springfield, Illinois, during the summer of 1908. He and his wife, Anna Strunsky, had just returned to America from czarist Russia where she had been imprisoned for a short time for her alleged revolutionary activities. They were in Chicago when the Springfield riots broke out, and both at once went to investigate them. The worst was over when they arrived, but they saw enough to fill them with amazement and horror. Here in Lincoln's home city, innocent people had been robbed, wounded, and killed. The Wallings, leaving czarist Russia, had felt deep happiness on entering free America, but in the State of Illinois they saw a disregard for law and a venting of hatred of the Negro which they decided was worse than the Russian's hatred of the Jew. In Russia, the Czar had to stir up the people to make a pogrom—race hatred was cultivated—but in Springfield it had broken out unaided and no one seemed sorry or ashamed. Anna Walling, moving among the people, had found only one to express sympathy for the Negro—a Salvation Army worker. Many boasted of what they had done.

Out of his deep concern and his indignation, Walling wrote a stirring article in which he called on the spirit of Lincoln and Lovejoy. *The Independent*, old-time defender of human rights, published it. I saw the article as soon as it came out. Its description of rioting and brutality was terrible, but I was familiar with that. What made me put down the magazine and write to Walling within the hour was the appeal to citizens to come to the Negro's aid. Du Bois was working with his own race. Here was a white man who called upon both races, in the spirit of the abolitionist to come forward and right the nation's wrongs. My letter reached Walling in Chicago. He replied telling me that he counted it of the utmost importance and that he would come shortly to New York where we must meet.

One month, two months, went by. I had heard nothing more. Then I wrote again and the answer came from New York. Walling had been thinking of what I had written; he and Charles Edward Russell had talked of the Negro question often at the Liberal Club. We three should meet at his home, and he appointed the day.

I kept the appointment! Russell, unfortunately, was unable to come. Henry Moskovitz, who took his place for the meeting, was a Jew, and his knowledge of conditions among New York immigrants was of value. English Walling—the Englishes were from Kentucky—represented the Southerner with a world viewpoint; while my background had led me already to give four years to studying the Negro in America.

Once started, Walling was a dynamo. We must begin with publicity. We must draw up a strong statement, to be signed by prominent Americans, recounting the injustices under which the Negro suffered, and calling for a conference to be held later in New York. When could we publish with the best chance for publicity? Why, Feb. 12, 1909, the centenary of Lincoln's birth. We must choose who should draw up this statement and we must all secure signatures that would carry weight with the press.

Oswald Garrison Villard, we agreed, was the man to write *The Call*. We hastened to get signers, and secured fifty-three names—educators, writers, publicists, social workers—an imposing list. Du Bois was at once consulted. Bishop Alexander Walters and Dr. W. L. Bulkley, Negro principal of a New York white public school, helped us in our own city, where we formed a small committee to work at once on the proposed conference.

The Call that came from Villard's pen was powerful, impressive. It recited the wrongs that Lincoln would find should his spirit at his centenary revisit the United States. He would find the Negro suffering disfranchisement and discrimination in education, in employment, in transportation. He would find him denied justice in the courts and lynched by the mob. It ended in calling upon the believers in democracy to join in a national conference "for the discussion of present evils, the voicing of protests and the renewal of the struggle for civil and political liberty."

That is *How the NAACP Began.* We have a pamphlet at the office with that title. I wrote it at the request of the board five years after the meeting in Walling's home, including in it an account of the Niagara Movement. Probably there was nothing new to the Negro in our organization; he might have been amazed that it was so late in appearing. Since the Association has become of such nation-wide importance, it has seemed to some that the story might better begin with *The Call.* But I like to think that the gathering of us three, so different in background, was symbolic of the help that was at once to come to our aid.

The Call was printed Feb. 12, 1909, and a small committee was formed to arrange for a conference in May and to prepare a slate for election. Securing speakers was not difficult. Men of science—anthropologists, educational experts— were glad to come and testify to the possibilities of Negro advancement. The proceedings of that conference were published in book form, and read well today. Livingston Farrand, later president of Cornell University, and Burt Wilder made memorable contributions. And between sessions white and colored met at luncheon at a Union Square hotel and grew to know one another. "I never was so interested in meeting people before," Charles Edward Russell said after one of these luncheon talks. A new world of men and women was opening up to him. Attendance was by invitation, and the hall of the Charity Organization Society was full.

But if choosing speakers went ahead smoothly, the work of those who were to bring in names of men and women to form a permanent committee was far from simple. Certain names occurred at once—Moorfield Storey and Albert E. Pillsbury of Boston, Bishop Alexander Walters of New York, and Charles E. Bentley of Chicago. We could form a satisfactory working committee, but would we be able to raise money unless it included Booker T. Washington?

I have spoken before of Washington's power. Villard, a newspaper owner, appreciated this more than some of the others. If you wanted to raise money in New York for anything relating to the Negro, you must have Washington's endorsement. This was a bald statement, but we had to have money to put over our program. We would need money for publicity, for an office, for legal work. We were a group primarily of white people who felt that while the Negro would aid in the Committee's work (we were then called the National Negro Committee) the whites, who were largely responsible for conditions and who controlled the bulk of the nation's wealth, ought to finance the movement. But how to get such support without Washington's endorsement?

Well, we anti-Washingtonians won out but not without

compromise. Before our report was presented to the evening meeting that ended the two days' conference, a lengthy discussion of the resolutions brought in by the Committee took place. Charles Edward Russell was in the chair, and he and Walling had decided that the fullest discussion should be permitted. And it was. For three hours those resolutions were threshed out. Some of the colored people evidently were distrustful of us. How sincere were we? It was easy enough to talk brotherhood; was not the Christian Church continually talking brotherhood, and sending the Negro into the gallery? In their experience, the boasted bond of brotherly love had always a loose strand, and a good pull broke the white from the black. They asked questions freely and they made many speeches. I especially remember Monroe Trotter of Boston, and Ida Wells Barnett who, when in Tennessee, had fought in her paper the first virile battle against lynching. They were powerful personalities who had gone their own ways, fitted for courageous work, but perhaps not fitted to accept the restraint of organization. There was also the usual crank who rose again and again to make incoherent speeches.

Russell was the personification of courtesy. He let each talk, and yet guided the debate which went on and on. As midnight drew near, the committee on nominations was at length allowed to make its report. It took a middle course and suited nobody. Washington's name was omitted, but also omitted were the names of Trotter and Mrs. Barnett. Their anger as they went out was perhaps justified. Mrs. Barnett took her complaints to Russell who quite illegally, but wisely, put her on the Committee. Not until the following year, when we again met in New York, did we become the National

Association for the Advancement of Colored People, incorporated under the law by the State of New York.

The average age of the five incorporators, Du Bois, Villard, Walter C. Sachs, for a time treasurer, John Haynes Holmes, and myself, was thirty-five. I like to remember this because it is rarely until old age that men are recognized, that their portraits are painted, or their statues placed in parks. I gazed for years at a picture of the Pilgrim Fathers that made each man look at least fifty, and was delighted to learn later that, except for Miles Standish, not one of those men was over thirty. Garrison started *The Liberator* and became the most hated man in America in 1831 at twenty-six years of age; but you see his statue on the strip of green that runs through Boston's Commonwealth Avenue, as an old man sitting in a large, comfortable chair.

There was no especial courage needed by us as we sat about our council board in New York. Archibald Grimke complained of this once saying we were not revolutionary, but he withdrew this criticism when we pointed out that while it was a small matter to demand that a Negro be served at a public restaurant in New York, it was revolutionary to demand that he vote in Mississippi.

In the spring of 1910, we called Dr. Du Bois from Atlanta University, giving him the title of Director of Publications and Research. We told him we had no assurance of money for his salary, but he took the risk and joined the staff. That fall he started *The Crisis*, a monthly magazine. Its success was immediate. Before the year was out it had a circulation of 12,000. In another year it was mailed into every state but one in the Union. Its features, "Following the Color Line" and "Men of the Month," grew to be well known and eagerly read. Colored newspapers were few in those days and *The Crisis* gave the news. But the most avidly scanned section was the editorial page. Always scholarly in his effort to print the truth, in expressing an opinion Du Bois could vigorously voice approval or blame, sometimes with the passion of the poet who wrote the "Litany of Atlanta." His magazine was so great a success that for a few years it was a rival of the Association. I use that term advisedly. Du Bois was a member of the board, careful in his judgment and scrupulous in never demanding his way in matters that pertained to the NAACP. On the other hand, he wanted complete freedom in editing *The Crisis* magazine. But the magazine was an organ of the Association, and Villard, then chairman, believed it should not express views contrary to the best interests of the Association. It was only after Herbert Seligmann was appointed publicity director, and established a news service which was mailed weekly to the colored press, that *The Crisis* became only one medium, though a powerful one, for Association publicity. Du Bois was ably assisted by his business manager, Augustus Granville Dill, Harvard graduate.

Our first practical job was a case concerned with an arrest at Asbury Park, New Jersey, of a Negro charged with murder. There was no evidence against him, but he was black and had been near the scene of the crime. He was put through the third degree before we learned of the case. Our lawyer went at once to Asbury Park and after some days secured his release. A similar case occurred later at Lakewood, New Jersey. This time we moved more quickly, found that there was no evidence, and freed the man. Imagine our satisfaction when we learned that we had been "rather expected," that there was an organization in New York that was looking into these Negro arrests. Our fame had crossed the North River!

The expense of our work fell upon a few people. Oswald Garrison Villard gave us room-rent in the *Evening Post* building and many hours a week of his time. He won friends for us, and gave us much publicity in his paper. It is impossible to overestimate the value of the New York *Evening Post* when under Villard's management—1897-1918. It printed as radical material on the Negro as one would see in *PM* today. We struggled under the expense of irregularly paid counsel until in 1913 Arthur B. Spingarn and Charles H. Studin took over our legal work, carrying it on in their office. "And do you know," Richetta Randolph, our office secretary said once to me, "no matter how many times I call Mr. Spingarn up, and sometimes I call him three or four times in one day, he is never annoyed, never gives me the feeling that I should not have troubled him." This arrangement continued until 1936 when Charles H. Houston, a Harvard graduate and a man of legal experience, became our Special Counsel. He carried on the work of our office and was able to be of definite help. In 1939, William H. Hastie became chairman of the Legal Committee, and Arthur B. Spingarn became the present president of the National Association for the Advancement of Colored People, succeeding his brother, J. E. Spingarn, who succeeded Moorfield Storey. Without remuneration, these two board members, Spingarn and Studin, handled our legal work for us. Their patience and generosity can never be measured. And this was matched by as eminent counsel as could be found in the profession. Moorfield Storey, our president, argued cases for us. Louis Marshall was another of our lawyers, and so was Felix Frankfurter. All the time we were building up a list of lawyers, white and colored, in various parts of the United States, who could be called upon when needed.

The early days of any association are pleasant to dwell upon and may be given undue importance. But our governing body has changed so greatly since we began and bears so little resemblance to the original group that we need a record of it. Death is responsible for many of these changes.

A board meeting in early 1917 finds J. E. Spingarn in the chair. Frances Blascoer, our first secretary, brought him to us in 1911, her great gift to the Association. He has recently completed a second tour in the United States—Detroit, Chicago, Kansas City, Topeka, St. Louis, Indianapolis, Omaha, St. Paul, Minneapolis, Pittsburgh have each heard him make one of his unforgettable speeches. Villard, once chairman, is now our treasurer, and has also spoken for us in five of these cities. Milholland, Walling, Russell, A. B. Spingarn, Charles Studin, all would have come to this meeting. Lillian Wald of the Henry Street Settlement and the Visiting Nurses' Movement, is on the board but we rarely see her. Florence Kelley of the Consumers' League is probably present, and another social worker, Paul Kenneday. Moorfield Storey, our president, never comes but Joseph Prince Loud, one of the officers in the Boston branch, takes his place. Among our colored members are two New York clergymen, Hutchins Bishop of St. Phillip's and William Brooks of St. Mark's. About this time Bishop John Hurst joins us, an invaluable friend. William Sinclair may come from Philadelphia (soon to be succeeded by Isadore Martin), George W. Crawford of the Niagara Movement from New Haven, perhaps George W. Cook, Secretary of Howard University at Washington, and

Dr. F. N. Cardozo from Baltimore. The only colored woman will be Dr. V. Morton-Jones, able physician and head of Lincoln Settlement, Brooklyn. Members from farther away rarely attend our meetings. Du Bois, editor of *The Crisis*, attends board meetings as an elected member.

We used to pride ourselves on never knowing how many white members we had and how many colored—we do still. It would be correct, however, to say that more board work was done at this time by white than by colored. In the field, the situation was the reverse. But in New York we still had only one executive who was not white, Du Bois. Our secretary in 1917, Roy Nash, who was shortly to leave for the war, was a white man; so was Seligmann, director of publicity. So were Martha Gruening, assistant secretary, and May Childs Nerney, secretary for three years before Nash. Legal work that emanated from New York was in the hands of white men.

As our program was directed primarily against segregation, this almost exclusive employment of whites may sound out of place, but it was the result of circumstance. Few colored people were trained to take such executive positions as we had to offer, and also few had the leisure of our volunteer white workers. I had taken the work of the secretary for a year, between Frances Blascoer's regime and May Nerney's. We were very poor and I could give my services. Others gave many hours of every week.

What were we doing besides legal work in these formative years before World War I had put new demands upon us? What direction did our "Advancement" program take?

It did not enter the field of social service and employ-

ment. Most fortunately, about six months after we began,
the Urban League was formed. George Haynes, sociologist
from Fisk University, came into our office one morning with
plans to form a national organization in the fields of employment and of philanthropy. Elizabeth Walton and Hollings-
worth Wood were back of him. Some of us gasped at having
so large a field of "advancement" taken out of our program,
but nothing could have been more fortunate. We could not
have raised money for "philanthropy" as successfully as an
organization with a less militant program, and securing employment is a business in itself. So the two national organizations divided the field, working together from time to time
as action demanded.

The newspapers usually showed the Negro as a criminal.
It made, they thought, interesting reading. We, then, would
show the criminality of the white; we would publicize lynching, interpret the story which, in 1911, appeared in the papers
on an average of every six days—the story of a colored man
taken out of the custody of the law and lynched.

A map of the United States soon appeared in our office
with a pin stuck into every spot where there had been a
lynching. The lower part of the map was black with pinheads.
Our primer was a post card that had been sent to John
Haynes Holmes after he had spoken against lynching in
Ethical Cultural Hall. We had tried to get ministers of
established position in New York to speak at this meeting
but without success. "We must get young men," Villard then
declared, "newcomers who at once will write themselves
down as opposed to this shame of America." We did get two
such men, the Reverend John Haynes Holmes and Rabbi

Stephen S. Wise. John Lovejoy Elliott (descendant of the martyred Lovejoy) presided. Our two young men have become great figures in New York, and have unswervingly followed the platform they set down for themselves that night. Our publicity must soon have reached the South, for shortly after the meeting Holmes came to us with a post card which he had received from a town where a lynching occurred. It was a picture post card. In the foreground was the dead Negro, and back of him, and on both sides, were the lynchers, clear-cut photographs that could have been used successfully for identification. The men's confidence that no one would dream of prosecuting them was the most striking thing about the card. We wondered that it had been permitted to go through the United States mail.

We used that post card with accounts of other lynchings as publicity. I remember the morning Mary Maclean and I got the dummy ready for the printer. It was Sunday; our office, in the New York *Evening Post* building, was on Vesey Street and through the open window we heard the singing at the Church of St. John, one of New York's oldest places of worship. While we read, "They cut off his fingers for souvenirs," and pasted it at the top of the second page, the voices of the choir sang, "We praise Thee, Oh Lord. We acknowledge Thee to be our God." Were those men who had committed murder in some church singing from the hymnbook?

But this first pamphlet contained nothing as horrible as the lynching that soon occurred not in the South but at Coatesville, Pennsylvania. Albert J. Nock wrote it up in the *American Magazine*. "For shooting and killing a constable in a fight, the details of which were not known, Zach Walker, a Negro of Coatesville, Pennsylvania, was taken from the hospital, where he lay wounded as a result of the fight, dragged through the streets on the cot to which he was chained. The bedstead was broken in half and the man, chained to the lower half, was dragged half a mile along the ground, thrown upon a pile of wood drenched with oil, and burned alive. . . . All attempts to indict members of the mob failed. They were given an ovation by their fellow citizens when they returned from the grand jury."

This was a case, Villard believed, that we must investigate, using all possible means to secure evidence against some of the lynchers. It was peculiarly vicious and had occurred almost at our door. We were poor, but money must be raised for this particular piece of work.

Martha Gruening was in charge of the campaign. Garrison is quoted as saying when Channing chided him for being all on fire, "I have need to be on fire for I have oceans of ice to melt." There were oceans of ice in the homes and the offices of New York that Martha visited and the impatient listeners refused to melt. Occasionally instead of ice she met sympathy and brought us a check that helped pay William Burns's large bill.

For the Association engaged the best detective to be had. Burns appeared in our office, outlined his campaign, and we agreed to put it through. Two men, heavy-jowled and strikingly stupid-looking, opened a restaurant in Coatesville hoping to secure evidence from the talk of their patrons. They heard horrible details but nothing to use as an indictment. Mary Maclean, newspaper-trained, spent two days at Coatesville, learned that politics were back of the trial, and unearthed some nasty details of techniques used to close an honest man's mouth. Burns, in the one talk I had with him, made me nervous by demanding his money at once. His green eyes were a little frightening. We paid him at once, but only because Jacob Schiff came to our rescue. We learned the difficulty in getting an indictment against a lyncher whether he lived in Pennsylvania or Georgia.

Lynching was not the only form of violence that came to our attention. The attempted destruction of homes bought by Negroes in white neighborhoods was becoming frequent, and cities were passing segregation ordinances to prevent such transfer of property. Homes of Negroes who had bought houses in white blocks or nearly white blocks were bombed, dynamited, and occupants were intimidated in many cities. Philadelphia had a case in which a colored woman, buying a home and finding it damaged and her family in danger, demanded and got police protection for six months. Negroes in Baltimore, Kansas City, Louisville, and other cities sent us stories of destruction of property. Druid Hill Avenue, Baltimore, was going the way of hundreds of other fashionable American streets. The Baltimore *Sun* assumed a moral tone, "Most white men have too much self respect to thrust themselves into company where they are not wanted. It would be well if the Negro cultivated the same spirit." The editor must have had his tongue in his cheek when he wrote this since white men, and especially white Americans boast, and act upon the boast, that they can go where their money will take them. But the realtor knew that property depreciated as the well-to-do moved into a new section of a city, more open and attractive than the old. He knew that if the laboring class—which happened to be black—might not acquire the property, it would remain unoccupied and bring disaster to the owner. Old neighborhoods that become unfashionable do best with freedom of sale and get more rent from Negroes than from whites.

When the NAACP brought its test case before the Supreme Court, it was not without some support from real estate operators. The Louisville Segregation Case was a test of the validity of the city's segregation ordinance which the Kentucky Court of Appeals had held valid. When the case came before the Supreme Court of the United States, that court reversed the decision. Justice Day, Nov. 5, 1917, in reversing the Court of Appeals of Kentucky held:

This court has held laws valid which separated the races on the basis of equal accommodations in public conveyances, and courts of high authority have held enactments lawful which provide for separation in the public schools of white and colored pupils where equal privileges are given. But in view of the right secured by the Fourteenth Amendment to the Federal Constitution such legislation must have its limitations, and cannot be sustained where the exercise of authority exceeds the restraints of the Constitution. We think these limitations are exceeded in laws and ordinances of the character now before us. . . . That being the case the ordinance cannot stand.

Moorfield Storey won this, our second case. Our first case, the "Grandfather Clause Case" he also won for us, and his presence before the Supreme Court set the highest standard for our growing organization. The Grandfather Clause of the Oklahoma Constitution was declared unconstitutional in 1915. It was part of an amendment to the Constitution of Oklahoma passed in 1910, and provided that no person should be registered unless he were able to read and write. But should the would-be voter be denied the right because he could not read or write, he still might vote if his lineal ancestor had been eligible prior to Jan. 1, 1866. This ingenious method of disfranchising Negroes while enfranchising illiterate whites with a slaveholding tradition was declared unconstitutional. Chief Justice White found that the amendment made the Fifteenth Amendment wholly inoperative, based as the Oklahoma amendment was "purely on a period of time before the enactment of the Fifteenth Amendment and makes that period the controlling and dominant test of the right of suffrage."

Not all of our work in those first years was concerned with discrimination and crime. Sometimes we had pleasant tasks to carry on, and the award of the Spingarn Medal was one of these. Indignant and weary at seeing the Negro in the press usually synonymous with crime, J. E. Spingarn instituted the Spingarn Medal. This gold medal, not to cost more than $100, was to be awarded each year to the man or woman of Negro descent, citizen of the United States, who should have made the highest achievement during the preceding year in any field of elevated or honorable human endeavor. A committee to be appointed by the NAACP board should each year determine the award.

The first recipient of the medal was Ernest Just, a young professor at Howard University and student at Wood's Hole, Massachusetts, who had done important biological research. The medal was presented by the Governor of the State of New York, escorted by a number of his brilliantly uniformed aides. Just murmured a "thank you" as he received the award. It was a stimulating evening, and the next morning the news-

papers, for once, featured a Negro not in crime but in connection with excellent scientific achievement.*

In the early days, interest in art, or rather in a young artist,
came to the NAACP. George de Forrest Brush, represented
now in the Metropolitan Museum of Art, wrote Villard about

*Winners of the Spingarn Medal

1. Professor E. E. Just, research in biology, 1915
2. Major Charles Young, U. S. Army, 1916
3. Harry T. Burleigh, composer, pianist, singer, 1917
4. William Stanley Braithwaite, poet and critic, 1918
5. Archibald H. Grimke, seventy years of distinguished services to country and race, 1919
6. William E. Burghardt DuBois, author, editor, founder Pan-African
   Congress, 1920
7. Charles S. Gilpin, actor, created role of *Emperor Jones,* 1921
8. Mary B. Talbert, for service to the women of her race, 1922
9. George W. Carver, agricultural chemistry, 1923
10. Roland Hayes, singer, 1924
11. James Weldon Johnson, author, diplomat, and public servant, 1925
12. Carter G. Woodson, publisher, 1926
13. Anthony Overton, business career, 1927
14. Charles W. Chesnutt, novelist, 1928
15. Mordecai Wyatt Johnson, president of Howard University, 1929
16. Henry A. Hunt, Principal of Fort Valley High School, 1930
17. Richard Berry Harrison, actor, *The Green Pastures,* 1931
18. Robert R. Moton, Principal of Tuskegee Institute, 1932
19. Max Yergan, Y.M.C.A. secretary, 1933
20. William Taylor Burwell Williams, dean of Tuskegee Institute, 1934
21. Mary McLeod Bethune, founder of Bethune-Cookman College, 1935
22. John Hope, President of Atlanta University, 1936
23. Walter White, secretary of the National Association for the Advance-
    ment of Colored People, 1937
24. Marian Anderson, singer, 1939
25. Louis T. Wright, surgeon, 1940
26. Richard Wright, author, 1941
27. A. Philip Randolph, labor leader, 1942
28. William H. Hastie, jurist and educator, 1943
29. Charles R. Drew, scientist, 1944
30. Paul Robeson, actor, singer, and humanitarian, 1945
31. Thurgood Marshall, lawyer, 1946

(Winners of the Spingarn Medal through 1969 may be found in the
Appendix on p. 300.)

a young colored boy in whose pictures he was interested. Would Villard come to his studio to see them? I was sent instead and learned to know the pictures and the artist, Richard Lonsdale Brown. Richard was born in West Virginia, and grew up to love the beauty about him. Without instruction, without having seen great pictures even in photographs, he made watercolors of trees and sky and hills that were true and beautiful. They reflected a quiet and deep personality.

The West Virginia State College that he attended gave him an order for a drop-curtain which today they display with pride. For this he was offered a job at house painting! Instead, stopping at Pittsburgh where he visited the Carnegie gallery, he made his way to New York.

It was hard to get any work, however menial. The two dollars in his pocket did not last long. He had his pictures, and with his portfolio under his arm went into the great galleries. No one paid any attention to a colored boy with a portfolio of watercolors. I have often wondered whether if the head of one of those galleries had seen Richard Brown, he might not have received attention. His modesty and the expression of his face would have appealed to a man of fine discernment, but who ever sees the head of any concern!

At the Metropolitan Museum he saw George de Forrest Brush's *Madonna* and felt that this man painted as he tried to paint; and so, looking up the artist's address, he trudged down to Macdougal Street and found Brush at home.

"I liked him at once," Brush said as he prepared to show me the pictures Richard had left. "He was so modest and yet you saw how deeply he felt. After he had shown me his painting he asked, 'Mr. Brush, do you think I can ever be an artist?' I told him, 'My boy, you are an artist.'"

I saw the pictures. They were painted by someone who loved bare trees and a winter sky. I told George de Forrest Brush that I would do what I could.

Mary Maclean, seeing a chance for a Negro news story— not about crime—wrote Richard up for the Sunday *Times Magazine* and found her story on the front page with Richard Brown's photograph. Mrs. Maclean could announce at the end of her article that Brown's pictures would be on display at Ovington's on Fifth Avenue, for a week.

The exhibition was a success. Twelve hundred dollars' worth of pictures were sold. Some of them were painted on the spot, little vignettes of sky, with soft clouds passing over it. Richard would paint them as he sat near the gallery. With his signature they sold for five dollars. He liked especially to sell them to men and women of his own race. Those little sketches must be treasured in many homes. He gave me one of his first paintings, a bare tree against a paling sunset. I gave it later to Howard University since Richard Brown was not represented in their galleries. Sometimes I think I never missed a possession so much, and then I know that it is a part of me and can be recalled at any time, even amid devastating ugliness.

The story ends sadly as so many artist stories do. The boy used the money from the sale of his pictures to try, fruitlessly it turned out, to save the life of his sister, ill from a fatal disease. He made many friends among artists. Hamilton Field gave him a place in his studio and at his country home, and Brush always welcomed him. He studied for a time in Boston, but his world had changed and with it his expression of it in painting.

I saw him for the last time not long before his death. He

came to see me in my Brooklyn office, a room overlooking the East River and New York. It was late afternoon and as we talked we could see the lights come out, like flashing stars, in the office buildings. He told me of what life was growing to mean to him and said something like this, "You see I never noticed people much in the old days. I wanted to get away and look at the hills about my home. I wanted to paint them and I still want to. Sometime I hope to go back and see if I can really paint them as I feel them. . . . But now, you see, now I've become interested in people . . . in my own people, they're so real and so sad. I look out on the street from my window and see the people as they go to work. There are girls out of high school. They're going to get jobs. I've watched them since last fall. They start out interested, walking briskly. Then they begin to lose courage. You see it in their walk. Nothing ahead, only the work they've seen their mothers do. They don't have the opportunities white girls have. Then in the evening, I'll meet one with a gay hat and a gaudy dress and I know what's ahead for her. They're so bright when they start off. . . ."

As he went away he stopped in the doorway and said, "You won't lose faith in me, will you? I can paint before long."

I hope he understood what I tried to say, that nothing could ever make me lose faith in him. I never saw him again.

Brooklyn had a colored settlement at Fleet Place, of which Dr. Morton-Jones was head. She told me that the little mission around the corner on Hudson Avenue had started a class for boys in painting. "In house painting?" I asked. Dr. Jones laughed. "No, in art painting. And why," she went on, "couldn't the artist, Mr. Cody, have knocked at my door? I would have loved to help him." The boys were crazy over the class, she went on to say, and wanted to go every day.

Mr. Cody (he was ill then and died within the year) believed in giving children materials and letting them go ahead, while he stood ready to answer any question that came up. The result of a winter's joyful use of watercolors and oil was an exhibition in one of New York's smaller galleries and a reproduction in color in *The Survey* of "Ham and Eggs." "Ham and Eggs" was an ambitious depiction of a long table, guests on each side and at the ends, enjoying America's favorite dish. It was full of color, and each figure had life and individuality. Another of the pictures exhibited was a sailing-ship on a deep blue-green ocean, ploughing fast through the waves. "That boy used to paint lying on his stomach," Cody said, "his feet kicking in the air, his head bent. He never painted anything but ships, and they always moved through a heavy sea."

The ships sailed, the pictured people moved through the streets, the mission room was filled with color and noise and busy small boys. Then one day word came that Mr. Cody would not come again. No one was found to take his place, and in a little while the boys went back to aimless racing up and down the squalid street, to crap games around the corner, and when occasionally they were bored, to coming to one of the settlement clubs where they would be given some simple handicraft or parlor game. They who had learned to paint the world!

In 1912, the case of Virginia Christian of the State of Virginia was brought to the attention of the NAACP by the

National Association of Colored Women. Virginia Christian, a strong young girl, in a fit of rage at being struck, jammed a towel down her mistress's throat and killed her. There was no question as to her guilt, but as to the extent of her punishment. Her age was determined to be seventeen and she was subject to the full penalty of the law.

The trial was over when we were told of the case, and all we could do was to add our plea to that of the National Association of Colored Women that, as the act was not premeditated, the girl should not be given the extreme penalty. It was decided otherwise by the State, and Virginia Christian was electrocuted.

The National Association of Colored Women felt this execution keenly. It had been raising money for a reformatory and had it moved faster, it might have saved Virginia's life. That such a thing might not happen again, it bought a farm a few miles from Richmond, fixed up the buildings, and installed Janie Porter Barrett as matron. The place was at once a success. Mrs. Barrett was familiar with reformatory methods but her place was unlike a reformatory; it was a home. Her children did well. "One of the best reformatories in the country," Hastings Hart said, "and in spirit the best of all." When I visited it, the girls looked happy and though the buildings were ugly and the furniture crude, beauty was present. Violets were in bloom, and the girls had placed big bunches of them on their dining room tables. "We have a mile and a half of violets at the side of our paths," one of the girls told me, "Come and see." I went and found it true. Each path was edged with fragrant violets.

The colored social worker was just beginning to appear at the Conference of Social Work. At a meeting I attended—

I think in 1907—I met Mrs. Sarah Fernandis, a social worker in Baltimore, the only Negro representative. In 1904, Jessie Sleet of New York was that city's first colored nurse in social service employed by the Charity Organization Society. The National Association of Colored Women had been doing much work of its own especially in the South.

The NACW had a dramatic beginning. In 1892, a white doctor in a public statement had declared that there was not a virgin in the United States among the colored women over sixteen. He based his statement on hospital examinations. His accusation received wide publicity and was bitterly resented. Members of small social clubs among the colored met to decide on what to do. The group represented women who had known a stable home for generations. After sending a strong letter of refutation to the press, they accepted their social responsibility. Recognizing that the mass of their people was only a generation from slavery, they felt that it should be assisted in its struggle for a secure family life. It was then they formed themselves into the National Association of Colored Women and took as their motto, "Lifting as we climb," thus recognizing their common aspiration and their common womanhood. They entered upon needed social work, day nurseries, kindergartens, playgrounds, old people's homes, personal charity. Reports at their conferences showed gallant gains made against a wall of indifference. When some day the story is written of the work the voteless women of America did for this Republic, the National Association of Colored Women should have a chapter all of its own.

Negro women enjoy organization. They are ambitious for power, often jealous, very sensitive. But they get things done. Our Advancement Association would be a mere National

Negro Committee but for the organized work of the women in the branches. The Washington branch, in our very early days, at the crucial moment, met a deficit of $2,000. Archibald Grimke headed the branch, but the women did most of the teamwork. They learned organization in their churches; and it is to the women that the minister turns. "My church has forty clubs, less than half a dozen officered by men," a worker in an imposing New York church, Mount Olivet, tells me. "These clubs can be said to be the backbone of the church, apart from the spiritual side, because they are continually working on their various programs and thus keeping alive interest throughout the church." The Reverend A. Clayton Powell, Jr., minister of the largest church in New York not excepting the Riverside Church, is at the head of a great organization of which the women form the self-sustaining foundation. Contrary to popular belief, the ability to work successfully in organizations has been the Negro's greatest weapon in an unequal battle.

The NAACP's third annual conference was held in Boston where we were received with every consideration from colored and white. The fourth conference met in Chicago, and we were introduced to one of the religious forces in the world today, the Bahaist Movement.

At the World's fair, in 1893, America learned of the Bahaists and their Persian background. The movement gained many followers and, in 1912, the third prophet in its trinity, Abdul Baha, came to America to meet his followers and give them his commands. He had been in New York only a short time when the Sunday *Times* gave Mary Maclean, one of its feature writers, an assignment for an interview. Mary Mac-

lean was helping Du Bois with *The Crisis,* and never lost an
opportunity to discuss the Negro. After noting what the
Persian prophet had to say on the Bahaist Movement, she
began to ply him with questions on the Negro problem. But
he needed no questioning. He was full of interest and spoke
unequivocally against racial lines. Shortly after this, we invited Abdul Baha to our Chicago Conference. He spoke to
us in the courtyard of Hull House. He wore Eastern dress,
his face ennobled by suffering, with deep, burning eyes and
soft white beard. Many years of his life had been spent in
prison from which he had but recently been released. The
long years of contemplation and suffering had not led him
to dwell on the differences among men; rather he saw and
preached their common brotherhood. Differences of skin
meant no more than differences of color among flowers. As
he talked, hurry and nervous tension left us, and we felt
the harmony that he described.

Abdul Baha died not many years later, but he understood
our race problem. In Washington during that city's race riot
of 1919, he was profoundly impressed, not only by the brutality but by the indifference of the whites. Like English
Walling at Springfield, he felt the callousness of the race
in power, and told his followers that the problem of race was
the most serious one America had to face. He commanded his
followers to attack prejudice without equivocation. Physical
differences were nothing; only the spiritual should govern
men in their relation with one another. He told his followers, white and colored, to associate together, and they have.
The Bahaists are scattered throughout the country; they
carry their message north and south, and like all spiritually

courageous people, they gain the respect of their communities.

When the *Birth of a Nation* flashed upon the screen in 1915 it gave employment for some time to the national office and the branches. This celebrated film by David Wark Griffith was an adaptation of Thomas Dixon's *Clansman*, and as a novel had received much publicity. The motion picture, good photography for that time, was likely to be a success. It was in two parts, the first portraying scenes in the Civil War, the second Reconstruction.

It was the second part that aroused antagonism among old-time northern friends of the Negro and among all Negroes. In a series of exciting pictures it said three things: first, that the Negro, if emancipated and treated as a citizen, had one paramount desire, to possess a white woman. (This was portrayed by an educated Negro who made himself obnoxious to a white girl of fine family; also by a brutal, ignorant black man who pursued a lovely white girl, lust portrayed in his face and in his grasping hands. The first girl easily got rid of her unwelcome suitor, but the second escaped the rapist only by throwing herself over a cliff, dying from her fall.) Second, that the legislature of South Carolina, dominated by Negroes and Northerners, was disgusting in its uncouth manners and ignorance. And third, that the Ku Klux Klan, made up of noble, humane youths, rode out to rescue maidens in peril and to restore good rule to the State of South Carolina.

The first gun in a campaign against the picture was fired by Oswald Garrison Villard. The *Birth of a Nation* opened on a Monday. On Tuesday Villard refused to accept a lengthy advertisement offered the *Evening Post*.

On Wednesday, the Association sent me to Boston to a hearing before the Mayor since I had seen the film. I was to explain what it was and why it should not be given in the city of Boston. Curley was then Mayor, beginning his long political career. He seemed anxious to give everyone a chance to talk. Only one person beside myself had seen the picture. Many had read the *Clansman* from which it was taken, and a number spoke against that, including Moorfield Storey. But the *Birth of a Nation* was on trial. At length my turn came to testify.

I had decided to speak only of that part that treated the Negro as a dangerous, half-insane brute. To me the whole picture was false. I had read thousands upon thousands of pages in the *Report of the Congressional Committee on the Ku Klux Klan*. I knew of the aspiring Negroes the Klan had beaten and lynched, of the homes and schoolhouses burned, of women treated with brutality. But the picture, the *Birth of a Nation*, was the South's side of the story and I was not there to ask that sectional history be censored. If I could show, however, that the method of presentation might injure the Negro in the city where it was shown, if it was so bestial as to create antagonism, even violence, then it should not be produced. I made my plea on this line, dwelling especially on the flight of the white girl whose pursuer, his great clutching hands repeatedly pictured, was enough to make a Bostonian on Beacon Hill double-lock the door at night.

"Was it as bad as *Macbeth?*" Mayor Curley asked.

I thought of Lady Macbeth washing her hands of imaginary blood, and said, "Much worse."

"As bad as *Othello?*" the Mayor persisted.

"Yes, worse than *Othello*."

(All but the beginning and the end of that scene was omitted in Boston, and the audience wondered why the girl was found dead.)

Griffith, the producer, spoke pleasantly of freedom of speech as represented by Boston, and of his pleasure at being at the cradle of liberty. The Mayor said he could censor but had no power to stop the production. With this announcement the hearing was over.

Moorfield Storey had spoken for a few moments and as he moved to leave the platform, Griffith turned to him saying, "I am glad to have the opportunity of meeting you, Mr. Storey," and held out his hand.

Storey said quietly, "I do not see why I should shake hands with you, Mr. Griffith."

Griffith dropped his hand and turned away, but Mrs. Butler Wilson, standing near them both, tears on her face, said agitatedly, "That was wonderful, Mr. Storey, that was wonderful!" And it was wonderful. It was the first time, and it might be the last time that she or I would ever see a northern gentleman refuse to shake hands with a southern gentleman because he had given the country a malicious picture of the Negro.

The *Birth of a Nation* was an enormous success. After one production was over and we thought it gone, a revival would be advertised. It must have been a decade before it ceased to educate our children on the southern conception of the Negro. Where the Negro was a voter, it encountered resistance. Political power kept it out of the State of Ohio. The Governor of Pennsylvania, at one time, forbade its being shown, declaring it a gross libel on a great statesman, Thaddeus B. Stevens. NAACP branches developed a technique of resistance, and their hectoring had a considerable nuisance value. But its design to discredit the Negro and bring the South back to its historic role of knightly men defending beautiful women was accomplished. Textbooks of American history changed. Reconstruction was viewed from the standpoint of the man of wealth.

But the story of that South Carolina legislature depicted in the *Birth of a Nation* awakened my curiosity. One of our board members, William Sinclair, a man of education and excellent judgment, once told me his father had been lynched. Now I learned that his father had been in that very legislature. I knew that not ignorance, but intelligence, had led to the lynching. That the legislature had been corrupt and extravagant went without saying. During the Civil War, stealing from the Government had been a business, and during Reconstruction, especially in the cities, stealing had been a pastime. My first bank had been named Bill Tweed, and I dropped pennies in his capacious pocket while hearing about the diamond buttons on his daughter's shoes paid for by the city of New York. But was no decent thing accomplished when the Northerner and the Negro held the balance of power in South Carolina?

The only way to learn was to read the proceedings. They were not in the New York Public Library. They were not in the Library of Congress. I decided I must go to South Carolina to find them. "They won't be at the State Library in Columbia," Sinclair said. "The State made every effort to destroy them. White men went into our houses and took the copies off our shelves." I did not go to Columbia, the capital, but in Washington I found the Acts that had been passed. They showed the beginning of public school education and of care of the aged. Some library, I hope, has records of the debates.

The summer of 1911 found Milholland, Sinclair, Du Bois, and myself at a Races' Congress in London. Milholland with Spiller, leader of the London Ethical Culture Society, had organized the conference which gathered together races from all over the world. Culturally, it was charming. We first met at "Fishmongers' Hall," a name that delighted Americans. I fear I made myself conspicuous at this gathering. The English rarely introduce, and here were men and women gathered from all parts of the earth, yet for the most part sitting silent against the wall. No old-time settlement worker could endure such a situation. I went about talking to strangers, trying to help them to talk to one another. Jean Finot, famous for his book on race prejudice asked, "You seem to know everyone here, will you kindly introduce me to M. Légitime, president of Haiti?" I had not met the president but he was a striking figure, quite dark and with a mass of white hair. He was most courtly, a French gentleman in manner and language, when I made the introduction.

Later the Congress spent a day at Warwick Castle, and there I saw Mlle. Légitime, recently returned from Paris, very beautiful with dark eyes and dark face and strikingly graceful. As she walked across the perfect English lawn, she picked up a peacock feather and held it upright like a scepter. She might have been a young queen honoring England with a visit. I was with Eastman, an American Indian, that day and we sat under the great cedars of Lebanon while he talked of the worship of trees, as Turk and Persian, Chinese and Liberian, European and American representatives of modern races and of antiquity moved over the grass. The Countess of Warwick was our hostess but was not with us.

We Americans had a good time, but the conference was called for a purpose, the establishing of a permanent world organization, and Milholland who was back of it, felt a hostile influence. At first we had excellent written addresses, radical and conservative, but all provocative. Then the papers stopped. They had criticized imperialism. Speeches were limited to seven minutes. The French—graceful with felicitations, and references to their *égalité* and *fraternité*—could say less in seven minutes than any other nationality. We met at London University in a hall with a glass roof and in weather hot even to a New Yorker. One person, however, refused to abide by the seven-minute rule, Annie Besant. Tossing back her shock of gray hair, she paced up and down the platform like a lion in a cage, and shouted her criticism of British rule in India. The presiding officer rose, but she only raised her voice. He rang his bell, but she continued until she had made her points, then she sat down amid wild applause.

After the Congress, which alas adjourned *sine die*, I went with a college friend, Frances G. Davenport, of the historical division of the Carnegie Institution, on a trip to Norway. I was happy in her company and in the contacts I made, not only at the Races' Congress, but in Norway where I introduced myself with my old socialist ticket. One day, after a long visit to the headquarters of the Hanseatic League and the museum, Frances and I sat on a bench in the park at Bergen, and discussed Germany and European politics. This was the time of the *Panther* incident and the trouble in Morocco.

Frances Davenport believed that war was near. Her knowledge of European politics was profound, but while I knew nothing of European treaties, I believed we would not have another great European war. I based my argument on the demand of the working class for peace. I had heard of the ordered march of the workers in Berlin taking hours to pass by a single spot, a silent demonstration for peace. Two weeks later I was to see a workers' demonstration in Paris. Forbidden to march, the French socialists and syndicalists sang the "Internationale" inside their park, while outside old women hissed and spat upon the guarding mounted police. I did not believe these countries, with a republican form of government, would dare disobey the will of the people.

Frances assured me that I was wrong, that war was on the way if not this year, soon. I must remember, she said, that political democracy had no part in foreign relations, that the vote was only powerful in relation to certain functions within a country. She spoke with authority.

Well, she was right and I was wrong. When the German troops marched into Belgium, every third man a socialist and an internationalist, I remembered our talk. But if I had been wrong in my estimate of the strength of the working class, at any rate I understood the significance of war. The workers had grown powerful and their governments were imperialistic. I could quote Catherine of Russia who frankly said, "The only way to save our empires from the encroachment of the people is to engage in war *and thus substitute national passions for social aspirations.*"

The outbreak of the European war in 1914 found the NAACP of many opinions. On the board were two out-and-out pacifists, Oswald Garrison Villard and John Haynes Holmes. I joined with them though I did not believe in nonresistance. The war seemed to me to be fought for purely imperialist motives and there was little to choose between English and German imperialism. Pacifism was the word applied to those who did not believe in the war, so why not take it? It had become a conviction with me never to try to explain away an opprobrious epithet. A new idea, a new method of life, is bound to be hated by those who see in it a change in their thoughts and in their way of living. So they hurl some names at you, as boys when a foreigner appears yell "Dago," or "Chink," or "Sheeny."

J. E. Spingarn, another board member, believing that America would enter the European war, was among the first to enroll at Plattsburg. He went further than that. He wanted young, educated colored men as officers in the Army. To train them with the whites was unthinkable to the Army and President Wilson. Then they must have a Negro camp on the lines of Plattsburg. At Howard University, Washington, Spingarn met hundreds of colored youths anxious and ready to enter such a camp. Many from other sections responded, the Department of War became interested, the camp was secured and training began. When we entered the war in 1917, this camp was abolished with other civilian camps and the Negroes were removed to Des Moines where they trained under Colonel Ballou. On Oct. 14, 1917, there were commissioned 106 captains, 329 first lieutenants, and 204 second lieutenants. They were a fine looking set of men, many of them college graduates. Subsequently additional Negro officers were commissioned.

All of us familiar with the Negro world believed that the man to command a Negro division was Colonel Charles Young. Graduated from West Point in 1889, he had been in active service and was known as a capable soldier and a man of fine character. I met him first in Boston when he was given the Spingarn Medal in 1916. He had recently returned from service in West Africa and made a great speech, endearing himself to all who heard him. Later I was with him at the Henry Street Settlement after we had entered the war, and I saw young East Side boys in their new uniforms gathered about him drinking in every word he said. Could he have been placed at the head of Negro soldiers led by the new Negro officers, the success of his Division would have been assured.

But the Army had no intention of allowing him to hold a position of importance, and he was put off in one way and another. He was reported as having high blood-pressure and thus unfit for duty overseas. When Negroes urged that then he be used at home, he was retired. Later, as a retired officer, he was placed in charge of colored troops at Camp Grant, Illinois. The war over, he was reinstated but sent to Liberia. Some years previously he had had black fever in Africa, so this meant being sent to his death. Thus race prejudice lost the nation a noble soldier and dampened the high enthusiasm of many a Negro recruit.

General C. C. Ballou, West Point and New York State, was made commander of the new Ninety-second Division made up of Negro troops. For a time everything went well. Then a sergeant at Camp Funston, Kansas, bought a ticket for an orchestra seat at a movie and was sent around to the gallery. The matter was taken up with the theater management and segregation of the Negroes stopped, but General Ballou issued an order that at once estranged him from his troops. They had the right to be seated in the orchestra, he said, but they should not exercise this right. They should accept existing discrimination.

Emmett J. Scott, formerly Booker T. Washington's secretary, was made an assistant to Secretary of War Baker, and he tells how his department was flooded with complaints that Negro soldiers were grossly maltreated by white officers, often physically assaulted, called "nigger," "coon," forced to work under unhealthy conditions, and threatened long periods of imprisonment in guard houses and stockades if they dared question this treatment. Many white officers refused to salute colored. The young men whom Spingarn had rallied to the defense of their country were finding that their patriotism came up against something as deep if not deeper than the love of country, the love of caste.

Of course, among some commanders the attitude was the opposite of this. At Camp Upton, New York, where 4,000 Negroes were in training under General Bell, a Texas regiment arrived. Some of these men entering the Y saw two Negroes seated reading. They threw the men out of the window. The matter came to the attention of the general. He is quoted as saying, "Gentlemen, I am the General in this camp. Something happened in this camp last night that has never happened before, nor will it happen again. If there is any trouble here you will be held responsible. Your men started the affair and if there is trouble, every one of you will be disgraced and put in the guard house for the duration of the war. You won't be tried by a Texas jury. I shall be both judge and jury. Secretary Baker and the Chief of Staff, General Meade, have said that every man in uniform is the equal of every other man. They are my superiors and I am yours. I am soldier enough to obey orders and you must do likewise." The Texas colonel answered, "Yes, Sir."

Unfortunately at this time, rioting occurred at Camp Logan, Houston, Texas, where Negro soldiers of the Twenty-fourth Infantry were in training. A Houston police officer, known for his brutality, entered the home of a respectable colored woman, ostensibly to search for someone. The woman, who had a little baby by her, complained of his entrance. He threw the baby under the bed, and dragged the woman, half dressed, into the street. A colored soldier went over to inquire what was the matter, and was beaten up by the police officer. Then Corporal Baltimore, a member of the military police, came to ask what the trouble was, and as the colored military police was unarmed, he fled as the policeman shot at him. He was soon captured and put under arrest.

When this was known at the camp, the men were in an uproar; Baltimore was popular and the soldiers meant to avenge him. Some were drunk and their major had no control over them. They stormed into the city and in the rioting that followed 17 persons were killed. When quiet came, the battalion of 636 members was removed to Columbus, New Mexico. Thirty-four men were charged with murder and 13 executed.

This had a bad effect on the Negro camp, but fortunately the 370th Infantry that followed gained the respect of the community. The NAACP concerned itself with those of the men who were sent to prison and ultimately procured their discharge.

✦

Troops began to be sent overseas, the "Buffaloes" going first, and as regiment after regiment crossed the Atlantic and landed on French soil, they found a sinister influence crossing with them. The officers suffered most. The French hotel would welcome the Negro; the white officer would order him thrown out. Insult would follow him into a restaurant. And there was a constant effort, especially where the troops were efficient, to oust the colored officer and substitute a white officer. Promotions for Negroes, again and again recommended, were held up. Especially the well-educated Negro who acted like a gentleman, was persecuted by white officers whose advantages may have been less. Captain Matthew Boutté was an example of this. Speaking French like a native, Captain Boutté was quite at home in France and received socially. He was sent from Brest to Bourbonne-les-Bains to serve as billeting officer, but when it was found that he with his officer friends were received in French homes, he was relieved of this duty, and returned to his company. Then, although he was commended for his work with his men in machine-gun practice, he was placed under close arrest. That his spirit might be crushed, he was forced to ride in an open wagon between two armed guards. At length he came before the Efficiency Board. The Major charging him said he was "mentally and morally efficient but otherwise he was not." Boutté engaged a colored lawyer in his defense, kept his temper throughout the case, and was returned to his company while the Major went to the stevedores. But not all officers had such self-control, nor could all write letters like this colored official who after saying that his camp was a penal institution, and that complaints were useless, ended, "I am beginning to wonder whether it will ever be possible for me to see an American white man without wishing he were in his Satanic Majesty's private domain. I must pray long and earnestly that hatred of my fellowman be removed from my heart and that I can thankfully lay claim to being a Christian."

Another type of prejudiced treatment was more easily dealt with. As the war progressed, a Negro regiment might occupy a village that the white troops had left. When the black men marched in, the children ran into the houses and the women stared, fearful. They had been told that black devils were coming after them. Some of the talk was only American humor but some was malicious. Dr. H. H. Walker of the medical corps, retired as Major, told me how he met this. "Two of our doctors," he said, "were Catholics and they would go to the village priest and explain the situation. In twenty-four hours the children would be running after us." *Life* at that time had a picture of a colored soldier taking her heavy pail from an old woman who stood by a well. The soldier must have been glad to be of service, homesick as he was for his own folk.

For some reason, the YMCA and the Red Cross were chary of sending Negro women abroad, the YMCA allowing only three among the combat troops. Two of these women, Addie Hunton and Kathryn Johnson, in their book, *Two Colored Women with the American Expeditionary Force*, show how much the troops needed them, and many more like them. Mrs. Hunton told me that when they first showed a film with colored actors, the soldiers ran down the aisles and stroked the figures on the screen, so homesick were they for their own.

✦

Handicapped as he was by race prejudice, how did the Negro fight when he got overseas? In the first place, of the 200,000 who crossed, 150,000 were used as labor battalions. They were stevedores, road builders. Much was written of the stevedores, and they were credited with reducing the time of unloading a transport from 28 days, English record at Liverpool, to 44 hours, American Negro record in France. The general opinion regarding the labor battalions was that they worked fast and efficiently and with a gay and gallant spirit.

Of the 50,000 who did combat service, some arrived too late to be of much use. Others, just as they were reaching distinguished victory, were mercifully stopped by the Armistice. But others, and especially those billeted with the French, and that included the Ninety-third Division and some of the Ninety-second, were at the front and knew the danger, the horror, and the fierce excitement of war.

When it became evident that the Negro troops were a center of controversy, a thorough investigation was started by the Federal Council of Churches in America and the Phelps-Stokes Fund. This was done with the recommendation of the Secretary of War and the Adjutant General of the United States Army. The man chosen for the work was a Hampton teacher of Physical Training, Charles H. Williams. I quote a part of what he has to say of the Negro regiments in his book, *Side Lights on Negro Soldiers.**

The 367th Infantry, Ninety-second Division, nicknamed the Buffaloes, received its colors from the Union League Club when it marched up Fifth Avenue in February 1918. It was the first Negro regiment to go overseas, and it returned with many hon-

* Published by B. J. Brimmer Co., copyright 1923.

ors. The entire First Battalion was cited for bravery and awarded the *Croix de Guerre*. This entitled every man and officer to wear the French decoration. Colonel Moss, from Louisiana and West Point, said of these men: "At no time did they ever falter or hesitate at the order to charge."

The 369th Infantry, Ninety-third Division, the old Fifteenth, New York, when it marched up Fifth Avenue on its return from France, was like a mighty army. I have seen many parades in New York, but never one more magnificent than that, with Lieutenant James Reese Europe as band master. Colonel Hayward said, "They never lost a trench or a foot of ground."

The 367th began with a few colored officers, but Colonel Hayward, before he went into battle, had dismissed every colored officer except the chaplain and Europe. The non-commissioned officers, in many cases were tried men.

The 366th Infantry, however, had a number of colored officers. Major Alfred Sawkins of this division worked unflaggingly for its success. Whatever fare his colored officers had, he shared with them, and the spirit of his men when they went into battle was always high. They suffered many casualties and won nearly half of the distinguished service medals given the Ninety-second Division.

The 317th Engineers worked, according to their Lieutenant Colonel Cassidy, "in accordance with the best traditions of the Engineer Service." The sanitary train, the field hospitals, the work of the physicians, generally were highly praised. Many of these Negro physicians have become distinguished in their profession since those days in France.

There had been doubt as to whether Negroes could use machinery. The 167th Field Artillery under General Sherbourne of Massachusetts, from November 4 to November 11, had the chance to do most effective work. Sherbourne, November 18, said, "You have been zealous soldiers and skillful artillery men. By day and night, often under the hail of shrapnel, often through clouds of deadly gas, you have marched and fought, dragged your guns, sometimes by hand, into line, kept lines of communication and brought up your supplies with a cheerfulness that has won the admiration of all." And Wade H. Carpenter, West Pointer and South Carolinian, spoke of the 351st Artillery with equal praise.

The 325th Signal Corps, new work for Negro soldiers, did well. It had six colored officers. It had the best health record of any corps in France with no case of venereal disease.

In the Ninety-third Division, the 371st Infantry was at the apex of attack. Out of 2,384 men attacking, 1,165 were killed. The regiment was never at rest and showed "unflinching conduct in the face of withering machine-gun fire." They were awarded every citation, 123 *Croix de Guerre* in various grades.

The 370th Infantry, the old Eighth Illinois, is of special interest as it carried a full staff of colored officers. At its head was Colonel Franklin A. Denison who had served as judge of claims at Santiago. Born in Texas, he moved to Chicago where he became an assistant corporation counsel. His regiment went to Camp Logan, Houston, after the rioting, and maintained order throughout its stay there. There was talk of leaving it behind, but its record was so good that it was sent overseas.

The regiment landed in Brest in April 1918. It was at once attached to the French Seventy-third Division and completely integrated with that army. The soldiers ate French food and used French equipment. On June 21, they were in the St. Mihiel sector; on July 25 they were behind the lines at the Argonne; and on September 15 they were at the Meuse. In a five days' attack they showed great bravery, a platoon capturing a large section of the enemy's works. When the Armistice was signed, they were pursuing the Germans through the woods, and were on the eve of further victory.

What most heartened these men and made them thankful they had been able as American soldiers to cross the sea, was the gratitude of the French. When the time to leave came, letters poured in from the mayors of the towns in appreciation of the Negro soldiers. The leave-taking with their French commander was filled with emotion and glowing praise. As the Negro boys marched away, French women kissed their hands, blessing them for all they had done. They blessed the living and prayed for those who had given their lives for France.

Charles H. Williams was not the only person sent to investigate conditions among the Negro troops. After the Armistice, Robert Russa Moton, principal of Tuskegee Institute, went over and among other matters took up the charge of rape made against the Negro. Persistent rumor declared rape common among our black soldiers. General Ballou is reported to have spoken of his "rapist" division. General Martin was specific and said that 26 cases had occurred in the Division up to Dec. 16, 1918. Moton asked to see the record. They demurred and then Moton said, "Gentlemen, the reputation of a race is at stake. I beg of you to show me these records." At his insistence a search was made and only seven cases were found in which rape had been charged.

Of these seven cases there were only two convictions, and of those convictions one had been turned down by general headquarters. One Negro had been executed for rape.

The National Association for the Advancement of Colored People sent its investigator to France, the editor of *The Crisis*, Burghardt Du Bois. Du Bois had been in favor of our entrance into the war and full of enthusiasm over the Negro officers' camp. He went to France after the Armistice and learned a great deal regarding the persistent effort to keep the Negro in the position of an inferior. He sent back to us several important documents which were printed in *The Crisis* of June 1919. The edition of 100,000 was sold in a few days. Here was documentary evidence. I give the most important of these documents in its entirety, for it goes much further than General Ballou's order. It instructs the French, an older and more cultured nation, as to the attitude it must take toward the Negro. It also declares American opinion unanimous on the color question. This document was sent out in August 1918, by a French committee at the request of the American Army.

To the French Military Mission stationed with the American Army—Secret Information concerning the Black American Troops

It is important for French officers who have been called upon to exercise command over black American troops or to live in close contact with them, to have an exact idea of the position occupied by the Negro in the United States.

1. America's attitude upon the Negro question may not seem a matter for discussion to many French minds. But we French are not in our province if we undertake to discuss what some call "prejudice." American opinion is unanimous on the "color" question, and does not admit of any discussion.

The increasing number of Negroes in the United States (about 15,000,000) would create for the white race in the Republic a menace of degeneracy were it not that an impassable gulf has been made between them.

As this menace does not exist for the French race, the French public has become accustomed to treating the Negro with familiarity and indulgence.

This indulgence and this familiarity are matters of grievous concern to the American. They consider them an affront to their national policy. They are afraid that contact with the French will inspire in Black America aspirations which to the whites appear intolerable. It is of the utmost importance that every effort be made to avoid profoundly estranging American opinion.

Although a citizen of the United States, the black man is regarded by the white American as an inferior being with whom relations of business or service only are possible. The black is constantly being censured for his want of intelligence and discretion, his lack of civic and professional conscience, and for his tendency toward undue familiarity.

The vices of the Negro are a constant menace to the American who has to repress them sternly. For instance, the black American troops have, by themselves, given rise to as many complaints for attempted rape as all the rest of the army. And yet the (black American) soldiers sent us have been the choicest with respect to physique and morals, for the number disqualified at the time of mobilization was enormous.

Conclusion

1. We must prevent the rise of any pronounced degree of intimacy between French officers and black officers. We may be courteous and amiable with the last, but we cannot deal with them on the same plane as with the white American officer without deeply wounding the latter. We must not eat with them, must not shake hands or seek to talk or meet with them outside of the requirements of military service.

2. We must not commend too highly the American troops, particularly in the presence of (white) Americans. It is all right to recognize their good qualities and their services, but only in moderate terms strictly in keeping with the truth.

3. Make a point of keeping the native cantonment population from spoiling the Negroes. (White) Americans become greatly incensed at any public expression of intimacy between white women and black men. They have recently uttered violent protests against a picture in the *Vie Parisienne* entitled "The Child of the Desert" which shows a (white) woman in a *cabinet particulier* with a Negro. Familiarity on the part of the white women with black men is furthermore a source of profound regret to our experienced Colonials who see in it an all over menace to the prestige of the white race.

Military authority cannot intervene directly in the question but it can through the civil authorities exercise some influence on the population.

(Signed) Linard

When the French Ministry heard of the distribution of this document, it ordered such copies to be collected and burned.

CHAPTER V

JOHN R. SHILLADY

1918-1920

Who Put Our House in Order

IN 1919, our office was in a mess. We had no secretary.
May Childs Nerney, who succeeded Frances Blascoer,
had left, and Roy Nash, who took her place for a few
months, had gone to the war. Our new field secretary, James
Weldon Johnson, was doing what he could but of necessity
was away much of the time. I was puttering in the office one
morning when Villard came in and earnestly urged that we
secure a man well trained in secretarial work on social service
lines. Thus far we had had a business woman, a librarian, and
a writer. The time had come for a man with experience in
handling organizations as well as a desire to help the Negro.
Our Association should stand high among national social
service bodies in New York.

"But can we pay an adequate salary?" I asked.

We would have to, but we would soon find under trained
guidance that we were on such a financial footing that we
would not only meet the increase in salary but would find
ourselves with money to spend on added work.

Villard brought the matter up to the board and then proceeded to recommend a candidate, John R. Shillady, a man

of largo experience who had just finished a piece of work for the Charities Department of Westchester County. He was an able executive and in deep sympathy with our work.

We met him and liked him at once. Tall, fine-looking, with gray eyes and graying hair, he approached our proposition in a businesslike way and assured us that he was ready to throw all his energy and experience into our work and our problems. So, despite our depleted treasury, we offered him the position and in April of that year, 1918, he became executive secretary of the NAACP.

I had been doing the work of chairman in J. E. Spingarn's absence and later became chairman, but before that I had volunteered to assume the work of the branches. From the first I had been interested in branch work, and while I could not give any amount of money, by taking over this job I could give a salary. So I added branch director to the less arduous position of chairman.

At this time, on Johnson's recommendation, we added a very young man to our force. While organizing in Atlanta, and after the branch had begun to function, Johnson had noticed an energetic youth who, he was told, had been out of Atlanta University for a year, and who was then working for an insurance company. Certainly he was working for the NAACP and with a high enthusiasm that made whatever he touched a success! Johnson recommended our securing him as an assistant secretary. We accepted his judgment, and Walter White began the work that he today heads.

With a competent though small office force, our new secretary went about methodically acquainting himself with our work and our needs. He had known of Moorfield Storey and the decision handed down in the Louisville case, and he went to Boston to meet Storey in person. The lawyer was approaching his seventieth birthday and the branches were discussing holding banquets in his honor. He did not want this, but he wanted above all things to see the Association become a power, and this he told Shillady. Shillady secured his consent to organize a Moorfield Storey Drive. The paid membership was about 10,000. Should we make 50,000 a possible goal? Storey agreed and our campaign began.

The Crisis opened with a statement by Moorfield Storey himself. "Do not hold laudatory meetings," he said. "I shall feel best repaid if every branch will join enthusiastically in the effort to secure 50,000 members." We put a date for the opening of our campaign and sent out carefully prepared literature. Ambitious work had begun.

At once we met with generous response. Memberships came in so fast that we had to employ a clerk to help our bookkeeper, Frank M. Turner. We outgrew our quarters in the Educational Building and secured more space at 69 Fifth Avenue, with ample room for the stenographers, and pleasant private offices. Shillady's correspondence soon required two stenographers for he was meticulous in clearing up his desk before the day was done. He could delegate authority to those under him, and I found the branch work absorbingly interesting. Walter White was frequently on the road at his dangerous task of investigating lynchings, and James Weldon Johnson was South, North, and West visiting branches. The popularity of *The Crisis* helped him since it was known in many places where we had not organized.

After starting the drive, Shillady's next piece of work was a thorough overhauling of our lynching material. We had kept a record of all lynchings, and had investigated a large number. These, the secretary felt should be listed and tabulated in various ways, the most dramatic stories told in some detail, and the whole published as a study of lynchings in the United States.

Fortunately we had been raising money for some time for anti-lynching work and were able to make an appropriation for this book. It was prepared by Franklin Morton and was printed early in 1919 under the title, *Thirty Years of Lynching in the United States, 1889-1918*.

In those 30 years, 3,224 persons were lynched. They were tabulated by geographical divisions, by sex—61 women were lynched—and by offenses charged. Here our figures surprised us. Only 19 per cent had been lynched for the alleged cause of rape, though a second heading, attacks upon women, brought the percentage up to 28.4. The second classification was made because from the press accounts, upon which we usually had to rely, it was not clear whether rape was attempted. The largest percentage was for murder. Miscellaneous crimes were 12 per cent, and absence of crime 5.6 per cent.

The book opened with short chronicles of one hundred lynchings, all of them either special investigations or reports from *The Crisis*, the Chicago *Tribune*, or the New York *Tribune*. I do not intend to retell these stories, but I will outline two as representing the danger to two different classes among the Negroes, the prosperous and the very poor.

Roy Nash investigated the lynching of Anthony Crawford in 1916. He went to the town of Abbeville, South Carolina, where it had occurred and gave us a picture of a pleasant street with princess-feather growing by the attractive houses.

He saw the home of the dead man. Anthony Crawford was middle-aged, a hard working farmer who had accumulated a little fortune, $20,000. His sons had worked with him. He had a large family and a pleasant home. He had no dealings with white people except on business. His life was with his colored friends, in his recreations, in his church, and in his home. But he was a proud man and understood his danger. He had been heard to say, "The day a white man strikes me, that day I die."

So it proved. One day, taking his cotton into town, he got into a dispute with the dealer and cursed him. He was arrested for disorderly conduct but released on $15 bail. Here the matter should have rested and doubtless would have, had not an ignorant, lawless element entered the picture. A mob collected; it drove Anthony Crawford into a cotton gin, someone struck him and he struck back, knocking down an assailant with a hammer, a bad blow but not fatal. The sheriff with difficulty rescued him and locked him in the county jail. This officer of the law did his best but the mob was frantic and broke into the jail, dragged Crawford through the streets to the Fair Grounds, hanged him on a tree, and riddled his body with bullets.

Not one of the lynchers was indicted. We, sitting safely in New York, always say this with scorn, but we fail to consider the danger to the man in a small community who brings a charge against his neighbor when that neighbor has proved himself capable of violence.

Abbeville lost a valuable citizen, a hard worker, a producer of wealth, a man who minded his own business, but lost his temper when trying to drive a bargain. He was killed because the town could not control the ignorant, brutal element of its population. The rate of illiteracy was and is high in South Carolina, and poverty among both races is shocking.

The second lynching concerns a different type of individual. Mary Turner, an ignorant, hard working woman, was the wife of a tenant, really a peon, on a plantation at Valdosta, Georgia. The trouble began when a peon, beaten and abused by his landlord, turned on the man, shot him to death and wounded his wife. After some days, he was found dead in his home but the mob in the meantime had killed three innocent Negroes, one of them Haynes Turner. His wife, Mary, after her husband's death, mourned and loudly proclaimed his innocence. For this she was slowly burned to death, watched by a crowd of men and women. She was pregnant, and as she burned, the infant fell to the ground and was trampled under a white man's heel. White children were held up in their fathers' arms to witness this brutality.

As Garrison, in *The Liberator*, relentlessly held up the horrors of chattel slavery to the world, the National Association for the Advancement of Colored People relentlessly broadcasted this and other stories of the horrors perpetrated against the black man. Our hundred-page study went to libraries, not only in this country but throughout the world. Today, lynchings have nearly disappeared. Many factors have contributed to this: the spread of education, better roads, the church, the courageous workers against it in the South, and the fear of a Federal Anti-Lynching Law. But it was necessary to shake the nation out of its complacency and to superimpose on the picture of the black brute, dealt crude justice for his unpardonable sins, the picture of the white brute, taking his pleasure in a bestiality that we now understand only too well, and that we have learned to fear as we fear nothing else in this passionate world of today.

Besides the publicity of the printed word, we used the public meeting. Here again our secretary worked methodically, planning a conference on lynching that would have names so distinguished as to force the attention of the press. It was months before we were ready. The Conference opened in May 1919 with a meeting at the Law Building on the legal aspect of lynching, and was disappointed at the indifference of the New York lawyers, who were conspicuous by their absence when Moorfield Storey opened the session. But our Carnegie Hall gathering occupied a considerable amount of space in the morning papers. Charles Evans Hughes, then Governor of New York, was our star speaker and with him Anna Howard Shaw and Emmet O'Neal, ex-Governor of Alabama. James Weldon Johnson was eloquent and terrifying. We reached a high water mark.

I can think of no more nauseating work for a kindly set of people than this task of setting forth brutality. We felt it was the only way to end a method of community life in which a dark-skinned group was denied education, economic opportunity, and a full, cultural life, while another group, the poor whites, also ill-educated, penniless, were encouraged to consider themselves inherently superior to the blacks because their own skin was white—or, more accurately, sallow. This second group was never punished for violence against the first, and so it indulged in brutalities partly for the fun of it, as boys torture animals. Their lives were as barren as that. We could not tabulate all the suffering and harm that they caused, we did not have the facts. Maimed black bodies floated down the rivers and if recognized were never identified. After every rioting, the black man fled the community, leaving behind him home, personal property, the bed, the table, that had been an integral part of family life. Through no fault of their own, the Negroes had to leave their friendly associations and start an impoverished life in some new place.

Money for our propaganda came from all types of people, colored and white, though we had not begun to penetrate the labor world. We had dreamed of a full-page advertisement in the New York *Times,* and colored women, under the leadership of Mary B. Talbert, made this dream come true. We opened the morning paper to see THE SHAME OF AMERICA staring at us in great capitals, and below, the story of lynching and America's shame. A full page! It was a proud moment when we could reverse the usual crime story in the press and show the crime of the white against the black.

On Oct. 2, 1919, we learned of a Negro uprising in Phillips County, Arkansas, an eastern county in the rich bottomlands. The Negroes had arisen, were rioting and shooting down their landlords. This was the feature, but the story went on to tell that the Negroes were organized into an association called The Progressive Farmers and Household Union of America. That they were growing strong and powerful. That they held meetings at which they proclaimed their determination to join their forces. They had a song that began "Organize, Oh, Organize." The rioting had started in a Negro church at Hoop Spur and had spread throughout the community.

That this story should center on the riot theme was not strange. Rioting had begun in June at Longview, Texas. In

July it struck Chicago. It moved to Omaha where a Negro was lynched, the courthouse burned, and federal troops sent to maintain order. What more natural than that a riot should occur in Phillips County, Arkansas?

But to those of us who discussed the story at the office, the emphasis was different. Colored, evidently tenant farmers, were organizing. Something was said in the story about a lawyer named Bratton. These men were trying to improve their condition by legal means. If rioting broke out it was not part of their unionizing activities.

We wrote our Arkansas branch and found out the truth of the matter. The Negroes on the cotton plantations, many of them illiterate, had been intelligent enough to see that they would probably get no advantage from the new high price paid for the cotton they were picking. Their landlords would make a lot of money but their status was such that they could be kept in debt or receive much less than their share. The most progressive started the union and in the latter part of September went to a white lawyer, U. S. Bratton, known for having worked against peonage when Theodore Roosevelt was president. They asked him to look into their cases and help them to secure better terms from the men or corporations for whom they worked.

Bratton knew enough to see that, if he accepted these cases, he would be engaged in difficult and perhaps dangerous work. But he was a man of courage and told them, if they were in earnest, to raise $50 for a retaining fee and meet him, at a specified date, with the money. They agreed to raise the money and met at a colored church at Hoop Spur. Here after discussion and securing the needed funds, they sang their song of organization. A few white men passing by stopped,

looked through the window, and became suspicious. Someone fired into the church. A few Negroes were armed. Shots
were returned and rioting began. When it ended, a few
whites and many Negroes had been killed. Bratton's son,
who had gone to the wayside station to get the money for
his father, only escaped with his life by being thrown into
jail.

The Governor of Arkansas was most anxious to avoid any
lynchings. He at once appointed seven white men to investigate the situation while the lawless element was assured that
justice would be done and speedily. At this time, at his urgent
request, the NAACP board sent Walter White to Little Rock
to investigate for us. We feared the danger, but his fearless-
ness broke down our caution. White went to Little Rock, of
course, as a white man, and talked with the Governor who
gave him an excellent autographed photograph. From Little
Rock, White went to Helena where twelve Negroes sentenced to death were held in jail. Here conditions were very
different. Little Rock was a progressive southern city but
Helena was a small, bitterly prejudiced town where any
stranger was looked upon with suspicion. Moreover, someone
had recognized him and word had gone out that a "nigger"
masquerading as a white man, had gone to Helena.

When White left the train he started, bag in hand, to
walk down the street toward the jail. He had gone about one
block, parallel with the railroad track, when he heard a
voice from a heavily built black man say in a whisper as he
passed, "Turn to the right at the next corner." Obeying instructions, White turned. Two men of the town passed. Then
the black man overtook him and said softly, "I don't know

who you are but I think you're friendly. These folk here are fixing to do you harm. Get away!"

They were near the station. White jumped on a train pulling out for Memphis. When the conductor came for his ticket, White explained that he had been suddenly called away from Helena and had not had time to buy one. While the conductor took his bill and made change, he condoned with his passenger. "There's a damned yellow nigger down here parading for white," he said, "and meddling in our affairs. He won't pass for white any more when the boys get through with him." It seemed a very long way to Memphis.

White did no more investigating of the Phillips County riots. The trial came. It was rushed through. The men had a counsel appointed but he did nothing for them. The jury was out five minutes. Twelve men were condemned to death and seventeen to imprisonment for from one to twenty-one years. Outside a threatening mob awaited the hostile verdict. The date of execution for the twelve Negroes was December 27. English Walling used to call this "lynching by law."

At this point we definitely entered the case. Shillady had seen expenditures mounting to many thousands of dollars and held back a little, but we assured him that we could make a dramatic and popular appeal. I was especially confident. I knew that while it is very difficult to raise money for a cause, it is easy to raise it for an individual case. Here we had a case that concerned men who were not of the criminal class—hard-working men who had been fired upon because they had unionized—men with no other crime than that they had opposed their landlords. They had not killed white men but they had been active in trying to kill their own status as peons which held them in wage slavery. What more popular appeal could anyone make!

Agnes Leach, wife of Henry Goddard Leach, opened her home for our first meeting. We found great enthusiasm among the picked group that came to talk things over. Our publicity went out: "Twelve men will be executed on December 27 for attempting to employ a lawyer to secure money from their landlords." Checks came pouring in. Our continued emphasis on lynching was losing its first vivid impression; here was a story of innocent men, hard-working men who were to be killed for the crime of attempting to improve their economic condition. The labor slant made the case at once a success. Sharecroppers, peonage, these conditions were beginning to be known. A revolt against them was not to be disposed of too easily.

The trial brought us in touch with two courageous white Southerners, Bratton who, however, soon left Arkansas and came North to live, and Colonel Murphy, an old man, who took up the case and stayed in it until his death. But it was the colored lawyer associated with the Colonel who was the heroic defender of justice in the story, a Little Rock man, Scipio Africanus Jones.

Jones was middle-aged and well known in the Little Rock Courthouse. His practice was entirely among Negroes, some of whom could pay his fees, others, friendless, for whom the court appointed him counsel. He understood the South's code of manners between black and white. While always respectful, he made his points and even read the law to the judge. He picked up his knowledge of the law in white men's offices and by extensive reading, for he never went to a law school. His legal knowledge was considerable. This man was to assist

Colonel Murphy, which meant that he was to do most
work, in the courtroom and outside.

The story of the defense of the Elaine, Phillips County,
Negroes is a story of acumen, courage, and patience. An appeal was at once made after the conviction and granted. This
postponed the execution. When the case came up in March
1910, six of the men were given a new trial but the case of
the other six was to be reviewed at Helena. This made two
distinct cases, one at Little Rock and one at Helena.

Little Rock was a progressive southern city, and Jones was
at home there but Helena, from which Walter White had
escaped, was a different community. Still vindictive, it
wanted vengeance, and one night shot and killed four
Negroes, well-to-do, respected professional men who happened to be visiting in Phillips County and had gone out
squirrel hunting. No one was indicted for these murders. It
seemed safe to kill any colored man in Phillips County.
Scipio Jones knew this, and had no illusions about the seeth-
ing race bitterness that treated even a man of Colonel
Murphy's caliber with disrespect that verged on insult.

The case lasted a week. Murphy became ill, and Scipio
Jones handled it alone. He had little time for preparation but
his cross-examination was masterly. When the court adjourned, he would slip into a colored drugstore to watch
the people as they dropped in, occasionally speaking, often
silent. When night came, he stole out and walked the streets
until he had chosen a home to enter. Though he was never
expected, the door always opened when he knocked. He
knew his danger as did those who sheltered him. To make
this danger less, each night was sp   in a different home. So
he went through the week in safe

...e case was lost. The men were convicted and sentenced ...death. Counsel appealed to the Supreme Court.

Back in Little Rock, Jones turned to defend the other six men. Their case had been held in abeyance pending the outcome of the Helena trial. An effort was made to carry it directly to the Supreme Court on a writ of certiorari but without success. On the day this writ was denied, Colonel Murphy died. His firm continued, but the work and responsibility were on the shoulders of a small dark-skinned lawyer of Little Rock, Arkansas.

The Supreme Court reversed the decision of the Circuit Court in the Helena cases on the ground that no Negroes had been on the jury. A change of venue was granted to the Lee County court. But Jones had no respite. The Little Rock cases were desperate. Leading white citizens believed that there must be some executions, if not at Helena, then at the Capital. The Governor set the date of execution for June 20, 1921. The city's Rotary Club, the American Legion Post, and the press demanded that nothing should stop the death of these Negroes, and back of them were the planters who wanted their tenants to have an object lesson.

The days went on and the six men were assured by their jailers that there was no hope. June 18 came and went. June 19, the Negroes were brought into the jail yard and shown six coffins for their burial. "You'll die there tomorrow," the jailer said. "No," was the answer. "Scipio Jones won't let us die!"

And they did not die. On June 19 their counsel petitioned for a writ of habeas corpus in the chancery court of Chancellor John E. Martine... ...dge Martineau, after grave consideration, issued... ...d the execution was postponed.

But the Supreme Court of the State decided that the Court of Chancery did not have criminal jurisdiction, and Governor McRae again fixed a date for execution. On the presentation of new evidence, September 26, an appeal was granted by the Supreme Court of the United States.

We in New York watched the case with eager interest, signed many checks for this lengthy litigation; and, like the men in prison, put unbounded faith in Scipio Jones.

Moorfield Storey, white haired, clear-cut featured, the New England patrician at his finest, argued the case before the Supreme Court. New evidence told of the torturing of some of the men before the trial to terrify them into testifying against their fellows. The Supreme Court heard the argument. The case rested.

The six Helena Negroes were discharged before the Supreme Court had rendered its decision. Their counsel, knowing that ugly feeling was still abroad, was at hand to meet them. He carried them in automobiles to Little Rock where homes had been found in the Negro population. They were free men.

On Feb. 19, 1923, the Supreme Court of the United States handed down its decision, Justices McReynolds and Sutherland dissenting. Justice Holmes spoke for the majority and held:

. . . If in fact a trial is dominated by a mob so that there is an actual interference with the course of justice, there is a departure from due process of law; and that if the State, supplying no corrective process, carries into execution a judgment of death or imprisonment based upon a verdict thus produced by mob domination, the State deprives the accused of his life without "due process of law" . . . If the case is that the whole proceeding is a mask—that counsel, jury and judge were swept to the fatal end by an irresistable wave of public passion, and that the state courts failed to correct the wrong, neither perfection in the machinery for correction nor the possibility that the trial court and counsel saw no other' way of avoiding an immediate outbreak of the mob can prevent this Court from securing to the petitioners their constitutional rights.

The cases were remanded for a new trial. But they were not retried. On Jan. 14, 1925, the men were granted conditional pardon and released from imprisonment, four years and two months from the time they were first condemned to die.

Scipio Jones came to our office when it was all over, tired but quietly triumphant. He brought with him a picture of the twelve men. Not one had the least look of the criminal. They were hard-working farmers who tried to better their conditions, came up against a powerful, vicious economic system, and escaped with their lives. Their long case had wearied the Negro haters, and the element in the state that stood for order was doubtless glad that the men had not been killed. At any rate, the state elected John E. Martineau as its Governor—the judge who granted the writ that stayed execution.

A few days after the Supreme Court decision, the NAACP received a substantial check from one of New York's great constitutional lawyers, Louis Marshall. In the letter that accompanied it, he congratulated us on obtaining a decision that he had failed to obtain in the Leo Frank Case. Later, he joined our Legal Committee of Lawyers who gave their services to the Negro cause. Of the many favorable decisions that we have obtained from the Supreme Court, this is the most far-reaching, affecting as it does colored and white alike, forbidding that "legal lynching" that Walling feared.

So we won a great case and we had a right to rejoice over it. But how about the sharecroppers who had formed the Progressive Farmers and Household Union of America? Were they getting more money for the cotton that they planted and cultivated and picked? Hardly. Their union was destroyed and they were back in the position from which they had tried to rise. The landlords had triumphed and the abortive attempt would soon be forgotten. Perhaps; and yet when the Southern Tenant Farmers' Union had its beginning in July 1934, in a dingy little Arkansas schoolhouse, the Elaine trials were not forgotten. Peonage was to be attacked but the men faced the race problem. Should they or should they not have two unions, one for whites and one for colored? One white farmer believed that since the churches were divided, the union should be. Another said the planters wouldn't stand for a mixed union. And then, as Howard Kester tells the story in his pamphlet on the sharecropper, "an old man with cotton-white hair overhanging an ebony face rose to his feet." He had been in unions before, he said. In his seventy years of struggle the Negroes had built up many unions only to have them broken up by the planters and the law. *He had been a member of a black man's union at Elaine, Arkansas.* He had seen the union and its membership wiped out in the bloody Elaine massacre in 1919. "We colored people can't organize without you," he said, "and you white folks can't organize without us." And he added, "Aren't we all brothers and ain't God the Father of us all? We live under the same sun, eat the same food, wear the same kind of clothes, work on the same land, raise the same crop for the same landlord who oppresses and cheats us both. For a long time now the white folks and the colored folks have been fighting each other and both of us has been getting whipped all the time. We don't have nothing against one another but we got plenty against the landlord. The same chain that holds my people holds your people too. If we're chained together on the outside, we ought to stay chained together in the union. It won't do no good for us to divide because there's where the trouble has been all the time. The landlord is always betwixt us, beatin' us and starvin' us and makin' us fight each other. There ain't but one way for us to get him where he can't help himself and that's fer us to get together and stay together." The old man sat down. The men decided that the union would welcome Negro and white sharecroppers, tenant farmers, and day laborers alike into one fold.

So the spirit of the Elaine farmers and their suffering were of use. It went on in the heart of one old man who, by his wisdom, made the Southern Tenant Farmers' Union, still bi-racial in Arkansas, the most persecuted and the most courageous of the many unions in the United States.

The Elaine cases started when Shillady was secretary. He learned quickly of conditions among colored and among white, and he worked to remedy them as he had worked to remedy conditions near New York. He believed that if our problem were put clearly and dispassionately before the people of intelligence and property in the centers of unrest, that conditions would be on the road to recovery. He used this appeal when he spoke in Memphis, Tennessee, before the Chamber of Commerce. Handsome, friendly, he presented his case without emotion, appealing as he believed to the best interests of the community.

"Tell us all about it," we demanded when he came back. "What did they think of your speech?"

"They received it," he answered, "with varying degrees of disfavor." But he added that one man had written to him at his New York office assuring him of his interest and that "they needed more talks of that sort." He believed the net results to have been good. What he had done had been to speak to them as citizens of the same country, under the same Constitution and governed by the same legal system. Did they not all desire education, intelligent labor, cessation of rioting? He thought that they agreed with him in principle.

Something of this sort was in the back of his mind when he made his report at the annual meeting in January. After telling of the year's accomplishments, he envisaged our Association as a great, peace-loving power working everywhere for justice to the Negro. "We aim to weld the supporters of the Association into a compact, unified, thoroughly organized and intelligently directed whole," he said. "Striving to be strong in numbers," he continued, "and so effective in method that no president, no governor, North or South, no member of Congress of any party, no mayor of any city, will dare commit an indignity against colored people without realizing that their legitimate and constitutional rights will be defended in the press, on the platform, at the ballot box and in the courts." With this goal in view he did his work.

It was a time of great unrest. Race riots had occurred and were occurring over the country. Longview, Texas; Chicago,

Illinois; Omaha, Nebraska, all had civil war that ended in many deaths. At Omaha the courthouse was burned, and federal troops were needed to restore order. Washington, the capital of the nation, witnessed a horrible riot. Carey McWilliams tells us that twenty-six race riots were recorded in the year 1919. These were undoubtedly wars, for both sides fought. The Negro was defending himself, fighting for his life, his family, his property. I remember a Washington woman writing with fierce joy when at last she saw the men of her race fighting against their enemies. She flung herself onto her bed, beat her pillow with her two hands, crying out, "They're fighting, they're fighting, they're defending us."

Such stories as came to our office! One from the Southwest told of the escape during a riot of six educated Negroes whose homes had been burned; who had fought back and were now fugitives. They spent two hours at a railroad station acting the fool, talking the broadest dialect, playing craps and guffawing, while word of the escape of six dangerous Negroes was coming over the telephones and the telegraph from town to town. They told of quick glances down the track where the train, as always, was late; of its arrival at last, the six men boarding it, to the last playing the fool to conductor and trainmen; of the blessed sight of Negro soldiers in the Jim Crow coach to whom they could whisper the name of their town. The soldiers were quick to act, treating them like the ignorant field hands they pretended to be, clapping gas masks over their heads, joshing with them, keeping them disguised, and in the end saving them to set foot on northern soil.

That was our most dramatic story, told us by one of the six men, but half a dozen other escapes were filled with wild excitement. Of the many who died we had no record, nor did we know about the women and the children left after the fighting was over. In time they might meet their men folk in the North, but their treasured homes were gone.

The conference of 1919 was to be held in Cleveland, Ohio. The Cleveland office asked my help with the program, the work fitting into my growing knowledge of the branches as director. Many were the letters that passed between the two cities. While the star speakers for the evening meetings would be decided upon by a joint committee, my interest was in the day sessions when the various branches were to participate both in prepared papers and in the discussion. To direct the Association wisely, we wanted a thorough expression of opinion and we wanted it from all over the country. That conference set the pattern that we have followed ever since.

A conference is a difficult thing to tell about. Doubtless this one was most interesting to Shillady and to me, of the white race. We were trying to direct and yet continually learning how little direction was needed, meeting people with whom we had had correspondence and finding the contacts different from those of other great national gatherings we had known, especially the one with which we were both familiar, the National Conference for Social Work. The latter discussed what should be done for the poor, the sick, the disinherited. It was the wisdom of the well-to-do, the philanthropically-minded. But at the Cleveland conference, we white delegates were working *with* the people we were trying to help, were discussing not their economic problems but their status as citizens, and were constantly learning from them. Time has shown that white direction was short-lived.

Few white people came to our meetings though what they heard would have been interesting to any thoughtful person. If a social service worker dropped in, it was noticeable. This was partly because the social cleavage between the races was considerable, North or South, but it was also because few are interested in others' problems. White people were interested in a story of distress, like that of the Arkansas peons, interested to the extent of giving money as they were giving me money for a colored day nursery or a boys' club, but philanthropy and justice often stand apart. The very recognition of the need of philanthropy denies justice. So the National Association for the Advancement of Colored People, started by whites, was being organized all over the United States by Negroes.

The Cleveland conference was the longest we ever had. It lasted for a week—morning, afternoon, and night. Meals were served at the church where we met, and over luncheon and dinner we went on discussing the colored tenant, the colored landowner, the city schools, housing, the right to vote, and, discussion over, told stories of injustice, of imprisonment and death.

Archibald Grimke was awarded the Spingarn Medal and he and Shillady almost fell into one another's arms. We had had much help that year from many cities, but the District of Columbia branch, by its unquestioning, continuing loyalty, its magnificent leadership under a man of Grimke's high reputation—a leadership to be followed by Neval Thomas whose name will always be associated with courage—made the capital of the nation a place to which we looked with glowing pride, and the award warmed our hearts.

Major J. E. Spingarn, recently returned from France,

spoke and told the story of the persecution of the colored soldier, putting much of the blame on the South's lack of education. He had on one occasion commanded a displacement battalion in France in which were many poor whites from the rural South. "Where do you come from?" he asked one man. "Toombs County, Sir." "Where is that?" "Toombs County, Sir." "In what state?" "I never heard tell, Sir." "And it is in the hands of such ignorance as this that the destiny of the American Negro rests," he said.

He spoke of those white officers who deliberately failed to give to the colored division the training that was its right, and who thus deliberately attempted to weaken the military efficiency of their country. They were traitors in that they preferred to lose a battle to seeing the colored officer return home distinguished, honored. The speech, as I reread it today, came from a man on fire at race prejudice, who hated as he never hated the enemy, those Americans who worked to destroy the Negro as a soldier and to asperse his character. It is an issue that has not yet disappeared.

At our conference we had often had representation from the South. At Cleveland we were especially fortunate. Leo M. Favrot, Louisiana State Agent for Rural Schools for Negroes, read us a carefully prepared paper and stayed through many of our meetings. He created the impression of being unusually kindly, an impression that one so often gets when meeting and discussing the race question with residents of that half-French state. Louisiana had only begun seriously to consider educating all her whites, and her progress had been slow. It would be still slower in providing educational facilities for her Negroes. Favrot believed that it was on the way, and seeing his earnestness, and hearing his

figures of the increase in appropriations and the improve-
ment in the quality of the Negro teacher, brought us hope.
He gave high praise to the Association and especially to
Moorfield Storey and the National Conference on Lynching.
His speech was far from the excited battle cry of the other
speakers, but his tribute to the Negro was sincere and lacked
the condescension usual with the "old school" Negro's friend.
He said:

Let me pay a tribute to the race for whose advancement I have
the privilege of working. (He is speaking of the rural colored
workers of Louisiana.) It is not possible to work for these people
and not feel for them sympathy, admiration, and respect. The
sacrifices they are making for the education and the enlighten-
ment of their people, their kindly disposition and the sincere appreciation they show for the smallest service rendered them, their
patience, the philosophical way they generally take discourtesy and
brusque treatment, their cheerfulness even in adversity—all of
these things make it a source of never-ceasing wonder to me that
for so many years I have lived among these people and knew them
not, that for so many years I saw in them only the faults that
are bred of ignorance, depravity, and neglect, and not the inher-
ent good qualities with which our Almighty Creator has endowed
them. I am grateful that my eyes have been opened, and that it is
my privilege to help open the eyes of others in my state.

At the end he pleaded that our Association "recognize the
serious aspects and innate difficulties of the problems that
beset us, to help us with constructive suggestions, and to give
the colored people of the South some encouragement by bearing witness to our efforts in their behalf."

But those who listened were in a different mood. We were
not in the cotton fields of Louisiana but in the City of Cleveland of the State of Ohio, that had bred abolitionists, and

started Oberlin. We felt our wrongs and we meant to voice them. Only James Weldon Johnson spoke in the quiet mood of Favrot, warning us against hoping we had a panacea, that our organization was the next step, but only a step. We liked better Bishop Hurst when he cried, "We have been lulled to sleep under the delusion that justice would come if we quit crying out so loudly for our rights and go to work. . . . Anthony Crawford was not a shiftless, lazy, undesirable neighbor, and what did they do with him? Every step of progress realized by the black man seems to be an occasion for the South to renew its assaults upon him. . . . We will die if need be for what belongs to us. No matter how long the delay, we will continue the agitation and will push forward with steady tread and uplifted faces until America becomes equally the inheritance of our children as it is for the rest of its citizens."

There were thirty-four states represented at the Cleveland conference. As we ended our week's gathering singing "God be with you till we meet again," representatives from every branch, from Los Angeles to Bangor, were resolved to carry on the work and to win more men and women to the cause.

It was a disquieting summer. Negro soldiers were coming home and some were in no mood for a return to their former position. There were many clashes. The exodus to the North that had been going on now since our entrance into World War I absorbed a number of the men, but the tension was still there.

Early in August we received a disquieting letter from our branch at Austin, Texas. Texas had become a banner state with 29 branches—those in Dallas and San Antonio had paid-up memberships of 1,000 and 1,500. The Austin news might affect all these branches.

What had happened was that white politicians in Austin had seen *The Crisis* on some newsstand, had bought and read it, and had then examined a few colored newspapers where they found the resolutions adopted at the Cleveland conference condemning segregation on public carriers. There had been a riot not so long ago at Longview, Texas, where colored soldiers had killed whites, and the politicians felt that if white Texas was to maintain its sovereignty, this talk must stop and this Austin branch cease its activity. The Attorney General, the Austin branch wrote us, had demanded their books. Would he try to prove that the board was operating illegally?

What should we do about it? Shillady and I talked it over in the security of our New York office. This trouble was occurring at the capital of the State of Texas. We were a membership corporation of the State of New York with branches all over the United States. If our position was explained to the Attorney General, and if necessary, to the Governor, surely they would withdraw their opposition. I looked up at Shillady and asked him if he would go.

"Do you think there is any danger?" he asked. I thought of our secretary's wife and recalled that she had been highly nervous ever since they had lost both their children, but I answered with complete assurance that of course he would be safe. Were he colored, I thought, there might be reason for the question but that anything more could happen to this quiet, pleasant gentleman than had happened in Memphis, was unthinkable. There the businessmen of the Chamber of Commerce had merely viewed him with disfavor. Was he not now to meet the officials of the State of Texas, the Attorney General and the Governor?

But August is not a month when a Governor or an Attorney General is likely to be lingering about a state capital. After an interminably long railway journey, Shillady reached Austin to find both these gentlemen away. He was received by the Acting Attorney General to whom he explained the legal character of the Association's work. The Acting Attorney General answered that while the Association might be thinking of the future, the "niggers" would be expecting to break down segregation "right now." The talk turned to lynching and Shillady produced the list of signatures for which he had worked so long and which he had appended to the address to the Nation issued at the Anti-Lynching Conference held at Carnegie Hall three months before. He assured the Acting Attorney General that no Association that had secured signatures of such eminent men as the Attorney General of the United States and the Governors of several states could have any connection with organizing Negroes to attack whites. He was dismissed in a courteous manner, and left the building.

Before he had walked any distance he was touched on the arm by a constable, served with a subpoena, and hailed before a secret session of what was called a Court of Inquiry. Here the tone was hostile. He was in the hands of tough politicians. They quoted the resolutions of the Cleveland conference and accused the Association of attempting to violate the laws of Texas by abolishing the Jim Crow car. Shillady answered that any proposed action would be by the Federal Congress. He was asked the stock questions, "Would you want your daughter to marry a nigger?" "Why don't you stop at a nigger hotel?" And while answering this heckling, Shillady managed to write into the record the names he had mentioned to the Acting Attorney General, including those of two prominent Texans.

He was allowed to go at last, and returned to his hotel. He should have left at once, but he had promised to call in the morning at the office of the branch president and he went out to make this call. On his return, when just opposite his hotel, he was again tapped on the arm. He did not turn, thinking it was another summons, and was struck in the face and beaten almost into unconsciousness. Among his assailants was a county judge who had been at the evening hearing.

He got into the hotel, secured a doctor who took needed stitches, called up the mayor and demanded protection to the railroad station and into his train. The mayor was not enthusiastic but he gave the protection. There were many ugly faces at the station, but Shillady got his reservation and started on his way northward. The train would not be out of Texas for twenty-four hours.

He had a porter make up his berth at once, and lay high-pillowed watching the monotonous landscape until someone drew aside his curtains. He grabbed his typewriter, the only weapon he had, and was greeted by a pleasant-faced reporter. If he wanted to say a word, it would go at once to the Associated Press. We read this story in the afternoon papers at the office, "Shillady beaten up at Austin, Texas."

Those of us who went to meet the returning secretary at the Pennsylvania Station, heard the cry of "Shillady," as the train came in and saw Red Caps, dozens upon dozens, tearing down the platform, crowding to meet the man who had suffered in their cause. It was a great demonstration.

Later, back in the office he told the story and then Mrs. Shillady carried her husband away with her. His face was not seriously scarred.

He sent in his resignation with the new year, but stayed on to have everything in perfect order for the incoming secretary.* The demonstration for which we had hoped, a dramatic trial down in Austin, was not to be. We could not have it without the victim and the victim was like a shell-shocked soldier. He had believed in the way of order and law and he learned that this way did not exist when the right of the Negro or of his friend was in question. He wrote in his resignation, "I am less confident than heretofore of the speedy success of the Association's full program and of the probability of overcoming, within a reasonable period, the forces opposed to Negro equality by the means and methods which are within the Association's power to employ."

* Incorrect. Shillady actually resigned in August of 1920 (*Ed.*).

CHAPTER VI

JAMES WELDON JOHNSON
1920-1931
We Meet the Nation

IN 1920, James Weldon Johnson became the executive secretary of the Association. Thoroughly familiar with the field work, he knew the details of the office. His coming marked a change. The president, the chairman of the board (I had been appointed to that position), and the head of the Legal Committee were white but now the executive officers, those who did the day by day work, were colored. Robert W. Bagnall had taken over the department of branches; Daisy Lampkin and William Pickens now did the field work. Walter White was assistant secretary, and Dr. Du Bois edited *The Crisis*. Herbert Seligman was the only white employee. All the members of the office force were colored. The board was small and thoughtfully debated questions brought before it, but decisions must sometimes be swift. The responsibility was now squarely with the secretary and his executive associates.

James Weldon Johnson was well fitted to take his new position. Brought up in Jacksonville and for a time principal of the colored high school, he had moved to New York and made a remarkable success as a writer of lyrics for musical comedies. After seven years of this work, he entered the consular service. During a revolution in Nicaragua, he guarded the lives of many men and women at the consulate. Capable of deep indignation, he yet had the quality that Matthew Arnold desired for us all, "sweet reasonableness." Given authority, he knew when, and when not, to use it. His years of service as secretary were of incalculable value to the Association.

The Cleveland conference had chosen Atlanta as its place of meeting for the following year; but before the summer was over, Shillady had been attacked in Austin, and letters came to the office suggesting that we change our meeting place. A few of the board were hesitant. Antagonism was developing against the organization. Not only Austin but other southern branches were affected. In one way, the Association could feel this a compliment, we were being noticed; but it was also a menace. Was it wiser to defy this danger or to lie low for a while until persecution had spent itself? James Weldon Johnson had organized in every southern state, and Mary B. Talbert, then president of the National Association of Colored Women, had given months to spreading our doctrine and forming southern branches, especially in Texas. She, with her army of anti-lynching crusaders who raised the money for the full-page advertisement in the New York *Times* against lynching had proclaimed for one day the SHAME OF AMERICA to everyone who turned over the pages of that sheet. How could this work best be served; how could we best represent the thousands of new members whose brave stand made them marks for the Ku Klux enemy?

The matter was decided by the members of the Atlanta branch. They told us that we need not hesitate to come to their city, that we should be welcome and that the conference would help our common cause in the South. Atlanta had and has an unusually large population of successful colored men and women in business and the professions. After the Civil War, its surrounding hills became landmarks for Negro education—Atlanta and Clark Universities, Morris Brown and Moorhouse Colleges, and Gammon Theological School. Atlanta was not a small town like Austin. The president of the branch, Captain Walden, a tireless worker, urged our coming, and our hesitancy over, the board voted to accept Atlanta's invitation. It made, however, two changes—a session of only four days, and a date in April, not June.

The city did all and more than it promised. The mayor spoke at our first meeting held in the largest colored church of the city. Our day sessions were in another church. The hospitality of the Negro churches and the helpfulness of their ministers, their readiness to be of service, is so usual that we are in danger of merely taking it for granted. We should not today number a dozen branches without this help. We were entertained pleasantly and fed bountifully at our midday luncheons together. Edward Bernays handled our publicity in Seligman's absence and the press did well for us. I cannot forget how fully and correctly the Atlanta *Constitution* reported our meetings. Bernays's technique was to make friends of the reporters and do all their work. City officials were courteous and overlooked the occasional breaking of Jim Crow rules. I hope the branch was jubilant; I know we were.

A few white men attending some of the meetings were most courteous. After her terrible riots, Atlanta had formed an Interracial Committee and two of its members were on our program: Plato Durham, dean of Emory University, and the Reverend C. B. Wilmer, a well-known minister. I also remember a businessman, John J. Eagan, who took a serious interest in our program. North and South talked earnestly to one another, and listened impatiently or resignedly according to his or her temperament. The minister, Dr. Wilmer, came down to the train with Arthur Spingarn and myself and argued with us until we reluctantly mounted the steps. Last words were shouted as the train moved out of the station. Of course, no one changed an opinion. Who ever does?

One amusing thing had happened. The Interracial Committee had called a meeting for us, inviting a selected group of white and colored members. The room was not large and the chairs were scattered. I dropped into one near the door and, a minute later, Florence Kelley, secretary of the Consumers' League, entered and walked directly across the room to take her seat by William Pickens. No one said anything, but later committee members, whites and blacks, looked perplexed, not knowing where to sit. The segregation pattern had been broken when the meeting began. It was some minutes before Mrs. Kelley realized what she had done, but when she did, her enjoyment endured all the way to New York.

Had we helped the Negroes of Atlanta? Would our insistence on the horrors of lynching and the wrongs of discrimination only anger people who had been influenced by the Interracial Committee and were beginning to think of the Negro with sympathy? Is it well to demand everything of people who interpret our demands for equality as revolution? There is no blanket answer to these questions, but history seems to show that loud agitation must precede any change that affects a redistribution of social and economic power. To get something worth while you must ask for every-thing. Anyway, Will Alexander, for years the dynamic sec-retary of the Atlanta Interracial Committee, used to tell Walter White, when he dropped into Alexander's office, to go ahead with all his demands and all his anathema! It is good for men to be aroused.

Speech was not our only medium of protest. Besides con-ferences and meetings held in Carnegie Hall or the parlor of a private home, besides the written word in pamphlet and newspaper and magazine, New York saw a silent protest parade. Down Fifth Avenue to the sound of muffled drums marched thousands of Negroes. It was shortly after the riots of East St. Louis about which Congressman Rodenberg of Illinois said in the House, "The plain unvarnished truth of the matter is that civil government completely collapsed at the time of the riots." He told a pathetic story of the shoot-ing of an innocent child.

That child and others called out the Negroes of New York in the strangest parade the city has known. It was led by little children dressed in white, not more than five or six years of age, all trying soberly to keep in step. It looked like the Sunday School parade we have in Brooklyn on Anni-versary Day. But instead of Bible texts these children asked, "GIVE ME A CHANCE TO LIVE" and "MOTHER, DO LYNCHERS GO TO HEAVEN?" After them, also dressed in white, marched the women—mothers, sisters. Then, dressed in black, came the men. "TREAT US THAT WE MAY LOVE OUR COUNTRY." The march went on, black and white, the colors of mourning in the East and the West, to the roll of muffled drums.

The parade was short. The crowds on the sidewalk moved quietly away. From their faces one could see that a few were deeply moved.

A few weeks before the Atlanta conference, the Association had voted that James Weldon Johnson be sent to Haiti to obtain information regarding the American occupation. Since 1916, when the United States, Woodrow Wilson as President, took over the island and its finances, we had received complaints against the occupation. Although for over a hundred years the Haitians had scrupulously paid interest on their bonds, their debt was now repudiated. Americans were insolent, and their soldiers were brutal. The Haitians had won their freedom in their fight with the great Napoleon. Were they to lose it now?

"The trouble with Haiti is that these niggers down here with a little money and education think they are as good as us," one of the Marines told our secretary while accepting a glass of excellent Haitian rum. They were at a café in Port-au-Prince, a beautiful city like a town on the Riviera, the blue tropic sea in front, and back from the sea high cliffs dotted with villas. Johnson was familiar with the Spanish tropics but this was French, more cultured and more beautiful. Parisian French was spoken all about him. The American, sitting opposite him, used rough, incorrect English.

"You should'a seen what I seen the other day," he went on. "A man black as your shoes in a Prince Albert coat and a high silk hat. Know what I done? I give him a kick that landed him in the gutter. He went one way and his damned hat another. You gotta let these niggers know their place."

Johnson, whose French was excellent, was entertained in many homes. He was captivated with the place and found

its old world courtesy charming. Here was a French civilization as cultured as France. Children went to Paris to be educated. It had its poets and musicians. There was little use
opposing the administration, but an election was soon coming, and our secretary meant to make good use of it. He returned to the United States, wrote four articles for the
Nation, and then called on Warren G. Harding, candidate
for the presidency. Harding found his story excellent ammunition for his campaign. After his election, conditions improved, but it was some time before the Marines were with-
drawn. The Haitians are still dissatisfied, especially regarding
the control of their finances.

The airplane is bringing us closer to this island which soon
will be known to the tourist. It must be very beautiful with
its superb bay, its purple mountains and, last but not least, its
cleanliness. Johnson found that, per capita, Haiti imported
more soap than any other country in the world. Its peasantry,
while very poor, own the earth that they cultivate, for Toussaint L'Ouverture did more than Abraham Lincoln did when
he freed the slaves. Toussaint also abolished the landlord.

In the hills are the little villages attractive with their
thatch-roofed huts, their walls whitewashed or tinted blue
or green or yellow, and with tropical flowers blooming gaily
in their yards. The huts are usually two-roomed. The peasants speak a patois but, when the tourist comes, gesture will
serve in selling their handicraft. Moreover, Haiti has a
citadel, built by its Liberator, that is one of the stupendous
ruins of the New World. And if the peasants will only stage
a voodoo play, the success of the tourist route will be assured! Prehistoric man tamed the wild cock not only for food
but for use in ritual. That this remote rite lives side by side

with cultivated French civilization, adds piquancy to the enchanted isle.

The Association, through its distinguished editor, Burghardt Du Bois, engaged in one other enterprise outside the United States. With a leave of absence, small financial aid but indomitable energy, Du Bois succeeded four times in gathering Negroes from the United States, the West Indies, Europe, and Africa at a Pan-African Congress to discuss the wrongs of Africa and their possible remedy. In 1919, the Congress met in London, Brussels, and Paris. Blaise Diagne, high official in French Colonial Africa, was made president, Du Bois acting as secretary. In 1921, the Congress met in Paris, in 1923 in London and in Lisbon. It interested such important men as Senator La Fontaine and Professor Otlet of Belgium, Sidney Olivier, the Webbs, and H. G. Wells of England. It visited the League of Nations with a petition. The European press took wide notice of its proceedings. In 1927, with the assistance of Addie W. Hunton and the Circle of Peace and Foreign Relations, the Congress met in New York. Visitors came from Liberia, Portuguese West Africa as well as from the West Indies. Speakers of authority could be secured in New York and many thousands of visitors learned of the Pan-African movement.

Du Bois left New York to accept the chair of Sociology, a graduate department of Atlanta University. He returned to the NAACP in September 1944, and turned again to Africa. In conjunction with George Padmore who has written many illuminating articles for *The Crisis,* a world Pan-African Congress was called in October 1944. This time it was not in London but in Manchester, England, and the moving spirits were the trade union delegates. Du Bois was present at the

San Francisco United Nations' Conference as one of its associate consultants representing the NAACP for the United States delegation, and at this fifth Pan-African Congress held in Manchester he was elected its president.

What was the object of these gatherings? To me, they meant keeping alive in the hearts of American Negroes their African origin and their obligation to the land of their race's birth. Africa has suffered as no other continent, not even Asia, has suffered. Africa is still suffering. Ruled by alien peoples, it is so stripped of its wealth that its very life is at stake. Hunger brings lack of resistance, and lack of resistance brings disease. "There is hardly a healthy Negro in Africa," I have heard say. "They are impoverished beyond belief." American Negroes must know this though the knowledge may only arouse a gesture of understanding. Ultimately it will bring more.

While the decade of the twenties began in unrest, the country settled into a period of prosperity of which the Negro had a modest share.

The exodus to the North, employment with fair pay, brought courage and the chance to better conditions. The professional class, the doctor, the lawyer, the minister, dependent on their race for support, found a more stable demand for their services. Negro banks and Negro insurance companies increased their capital and were able to operate more efficiently. Real estate men helped in the passage of property from white to colored hands. The Negro Business League, under Albon W. Holsey, discovered wholesale firms ready to trade favorably with small business. Harlem became a place of much interest, and its cabarets rang with the latest jazz and the bell of the cash register. With Andrew Mellon, Secretary of the Treasury, telling us that unemployment had gone never to return, we spent our money and some of it went into the black man's pocket.

It is when a nation enjoys prosperity that the arts thrive. Expression is irresistible, for the artist has found his audience. Two unforgotten sonnets of protest appeared at this time. One was written by a young Jamaican, black, not one of the privileged "colored" class, who came to the United States seeking knowledge and economic opportunity. Claude McKay found something of both, but what astounded him was America's record of lawlessness, her race riots and lynchings. He cried to his fellow black men,

> If we must die —let it not be like hogs
> Hunted and penned in an inglorious spot,
> While round us bark the mad and hungry dogs,
> Making their mock at our accursed lot.
> If we must die —oh, let us nobly die,
> So that our precious blood may not be shed
> In vain; then even the monsters we defy
> Shall be constrained to honor us though dead! *

The second sonnet is in a quieter mood. Leslie Pinckney Hill (now principal of Cheyney), after leaving Harvard, taught for a time at Tuskegee. Stung by the pain of long-looking at youth's discouragement, he wrote,

> ". . . Build we our best.
> By hand and thought," they cry, "although unblessed."
> So the great engines throb, and anvils ring,
> And so the thought is wedded to the thing;

* From *Harlem Shadows* by Claude McKay, copyright 1922, by Harcourt, Brace and Co., Inc.

"But what shall be the end, and what the test?
Dear God, we dare not answer, we can see
Not many steps ahead, but this we know—
If all our toilsome building is in vain,
Availing not to set our manhood free,
If envious hate roots out the seed we sow,
The South will wear eternally a stain." *

In fiction dealing with lynchings no novel, I believe, equals in power and authenticity Walter White's *The Fire in the Flint*. The story was in his mind, clear in its detail, when, on vacation, he sat down to write it. In the quiet of the Berkshires, with no greater atrocity to stir his emotions than a robin eating a worm, he pounded on his little portable typewriter and in twelve days finished his book. I know, because he wrote it in my cottage where he and his wife spent their two weeks' vacation. He said in my diary,

"At 4:28 P.M. today began my novel, *The Fire in the Flint*, one hour after reaching Riverbank on Sept. 5, 1922. Is 63,350 words long. Wrote eight hours a day—sometimes longer. Finished it in twelve days of actual writing. The most thrilling, enjoyable experience yet in my life! *Ora pro nobis!*"

His prayer was answered by Alfred A. Knopf, who not only published the book but did not try to make the author change his tragic ending as Irvin Cobb would have had him do. At once a success, *The Fire in the Flint* went through three large printings. It has been translated into several European languages and into Japanese.

Walter White, a "voluntary" Negro, since he is so light

* Reprinted from *Wings of Oppression* by Leslie Pinckney Hill, copyright 1921, by permission of The Stratford Company, Boston.

in color as to be mistaken for white, traveled Pullman and spent much time in the smoking car. Certainly he had first-hand information on the South's opinion of the Negro. This information, his intimate knowledge of the ambitious, college-trained Negro, coupled with his many lynching investigations, gave his word authority.

But neither sorrow nor anger against injustice characterized the writing of this time, rather grandiloquently called "The Negro Renaissance." Like the literary movement in Ireland a generation or two before, it was an attempt to substitute reality for the stereotyped figure drawn by an alien race. This figure was a caricature and, surely, the person to portray the truth was the Negro himself. To do this he must not turn his back on the past. Paul Laurence Dunbar, who wrote fiction as well as poetry, had once said, "We must write like the white man. I do not mean imitate him; but our life is now the same."

"The New Negro"—I use Alain Locke's term, for he has a delightful book of that name—must get away from this attitude. He must not be a black shadow of the white, drawing from old patterns. If he must use an old pattern let it be an African one. Moreover, to get away from the stereotyped figure created by whites he must know more about his own race—its poor and ignorant members as well as its intelligentsia. With infinite effort his grandparents, and now his parents, have educated him and built up a society that rivals the whites' in snobbishness. He must turn from this pattern lest his culture be neither white nor black, only a dull gray.

New York, where this movement centered, had no lack of material. Museums, public and private, contained African collections; the libraries abounded in African folklore and history; and when it came to the study of primitive culture, of turns of speech, of the black man's dancing, singing— there was always Harlem.

Arna Bontemps, known to many as a writer of poetry and adult fiction as well as juveniles, has a thoughtful and amusing article on the "Two Harlems" in *The American Scholar*, Spring 1945. He describes what he saw and felt when, just of age and leaving home for the first time, he opened the window of his small bedroom at 129th Street and Fifth Avenue and looked over "the rooftops of Negrodom." How his heart beat fast, and how excited he was when he went outdoors! "Up and down the streets of Harlem untamed youngsters were doing a wild dance called the Charleston. They were flitting over the sidewalks like mad, while their companions, squatting near by, beat out tom-tom rhythms on kitchenware. The unsuspecting stranger who paused to observe the performance was in danger of being surrounded, shoved into their circle, and compelled to attempt the camel walk."

Bontemps was only one among these young strangers, newcomers to Harlem, who "had been regarded as anything but remarkable in Topeka and Cleveland and Eatonville and Salt Lake City—young people who more often than otherwise had seemed a trifle whacky to the home folk. In Harlem we were seen in a beautiful light. We were heralds of a dawning day." And Bontemps goes on to tell of how they were taken up by the whites.

There was much genuine talent. One finds it in back numbers of *The Crisis, Opportunity*, the *Messenger*, three well-printed, carefully edited Negro magazines. Some gained a larger audience. Books by Negroes, especially of poetry, were published in numbers—a few by old firms, more by comparatively new ones: Harcourt Brace, Boni and Liveright, Alfred A. Knopf, and Viking. Reviewers wrote appreciative notices. Poetry and fiction about Negroes and by Negroes, were for sale in numbers at the bookshops. The New Negro had arrived.

The poet who was to remain the best known of this group was not a New Negro, but a man whose reputation was already established—our new NAACP secretary, James Weldon Johnson. With his brother Rosamond and his friend Bob Cole, he has written the words and music of many of the most popular songs of the time, songs that still linger, such as "The Old Flag Never Touched the Ground," "Mandy," and "Under the Bamboo Tree." He had also written verse; "Oh Black and Unknown Bards" is one of his best known. But freer forms were in his mind and while he was campaigning against lynching, he was mulling over his contribution to the Negro Renaissance.

We two were lunching at the Civic Club with William Stanley Braithwaite, on the staff of the Boston *Transcript*, and began talking of the possibilities of folk material, and of freer verse. Braithwaite was entertained, but, I thought, had no idea of applying this talk to himself. His own verse was as lyrical as any Elizabethan's. He afterwards brought out an anthology of Elizabethan verse, the best of which I know. So he only smiled on us, but James Weldon Johnson was in earnest and told us of a sermon he had heard when traveling for the NAACP. He had spoken at four Sunday meetings and found himself at night in a fifth church, tired and sleepy and not knowing at what time he would mount the platform to give his speech. At the conclusion of a hymn he thought his turn had come, but instead, a country preacher, an exhorter, mounted the pulpit stairs. It seemed just too much to the weary secretary—but the poet in him woke up when he found that he was listening to an old-time folk sermon.

"The Creation," a Negro sermon, by James Weldon Johnson, was first published in *The Freeman*, Albert J. Nock, editor. Later it opened the volume, *God's Trombones*, published by The Viking Press. Johnson's verse at once became known. His book had a remarkable sale, for pulp and predigested facts had not yet begun to dig the grave in which the poet now rests. *God's Trombones*, especially the sermons "The Creation" and "Go Down Death" was soon well known over the radio.

> And God stepped out on space,
> And He looked around and said:
>   "I'm lonely—
> I'll make me a world." *

The New Negro movement was justified when it gave us this verse.

A second poet was Countee Cullen, not a visitor to Harlem but a boy born at its busy center. Cullen was the son of a minister, and was educated in the city schools and at New York University, also taking an M.A. at Harvard. Before this he won the Witter Bynner prize for undergraduates in American colleges. Reserved, studious, he felt this new call for Negro self-expression and voiced it in his poem, "Heritage." His tom-toms were not on Seventh Avenue but in far away Africa.

"What is Africa to me?" he asks.

* Reprinted from *God's Trombones* by James Weldon Johnson, copyright 1927, by permission of The Viking Press Inc.

One three centuries removed
From the scene his fathers loved,
Spicy grove, cinnamon tree,
What is Africa to me? *

The answer is a description of the jungle and its creepy
fear that Kipling might have envied. It is a cry against
civilization and a longing for the savage life which, alas,
when we study it, we learn has more rigid conventions than
our own. Countee Cullen wrote other delightful verses, but
"Heritage," as far as we can look ahead, will make a well-
thumbed page in many of the anthologies.

When hard luck overtakes you,
Nothin' for you to do.
When hard luck overtakes you,
Nothin' for you to do.
Gather up your fine clothes
An' sell 'em to de Jew.†

So said Langston Hughes, the writer, who to many seems
best to reproduce the black man's singing, aloud and in his
heart. He comes from Kansas where his mother made sure
that he was educated in the public schools and that he read
The Crisis. Later he spent some time with his father in
Mexico. Returning to go to college, he chose a Negro one,
Lincoln. He has wandered in many lands; his autobiography,
The Big Sea, sees him on three continents, but he is all
American. Among the many Negro writers of this period, I
think he is the only one who has continued to make litera-

* Reprinted from *Color* by Countee Cullen, by permission of Harper
& Brothers. Copyright 1925, by Harper & Brothers.

† Reprinted from *Fine Clothes to the Jew* by Langston Hughes, by permission of Alfred A. Knopf, Inc. Copyright 1927, by Alfred A. Knopf,
Inc.

ture his career. He has tried his hand at drama, and his play, *Mulatto*, had a season's run in New York. He is a gleeman, traveling about and reciting his songs, if not in a castle, in a school or college, where he is received with enthusiastic applause. He holds his head high as he swings down the road.

Aaron Douglas, best known for his murals at Fisk University, has illustrated both Hughes's and James Weldon Johnson's poems. His striking work shows the influence of African art.

Some worth-while books of fiction came out at this time, but on the whole they were disappointing. I suspect that the writers, forced to support themselves and their families by other means than their art, did not have enough physical strength left for prolonged writing. They began well, the settings were excellent. Whether in Philadelphia with Jessie Fauset, in Harlem with Rudolph Fisher, or with Henderson in the deep South, to name a few, we saw characters clearly, and were ready for what might happen. But little did happen and sometimes we saw the strings that pulled the puppets.

To those watching Negro talent these were good days. We did not have to read books to know this. On the stage, Bill Robinson, one of the great dancers of our time, began tapping down the staircase; while Rose McClendon, in her beauty and dignity, in the opera, *Deep River*, was showing a reluctant heroine the way up the stairway. Who, of the many that saw her, can forget her gesture as she stood at the bottom of the steps? No theatrical producer thought any longer of putting a black-faced white man in a Negro's part. The race had demonstrated for all time its histrionic ability. Charles Gilpin, as the Negro in Drinkwater's *Abraham Lin-*

coln, was the best actor in that play, and was promoted later at the Provincetown Playhouse to the creation of Eugene O'Neill's *Emperor Jones.* Paul Robeson, who later succeeded to that part, was enthralling his audience by his singing of the spirituals and of Negro work songs. Jules Bledsoe brought to life the tragic figure of a defeated idealist in Paul Green's tragedy, *In Abraham's Bosom.*

The cinema was still in its infancy and showed only the stereotyped Negro, the only type it knew or was to know for two decades; but it found able artists to fill its threadbare parts.

In 1917, the Civic Club, of which I have spoken, was incorporated in New York. By 1920, it had a membership of 900. Qualification for membership was "an active and sustained interest in civic affairs." It drew no race or color line and Du Bois and James Weldon Johnson were charter members. Its East Indian members, among others Lajput Rai, author and patriot, educated us in the working of British imperialism: a knowledge of value today. The Club attracted conservative as well as radical, and continued its free discussions during World War I—a really liberal forum resembling Percy Grant's at the Church of the Ascension, two blocks below.

The Club rented a house at Twelfth Street near Fifth Avenue formerly occupied by the Salmagundi Club. Its spacious rooms were used for spirited forums, art exhibitions, musical programs, plays, and poetry contests where Babette Deutsch, Pierre Loving, and Countee Cullen were among the contestants. Its dining hall was on two levels, a large, cool, beautiful room, usually well-filled, for its Belgian chef, a concessionaire, never cost the Club a penny and served as good meals as any club in New York. Dr. Ira S. Wile and Dean George W. Kirchwey were its best known presidents. It ought to be alive today, but its landlord, the Presbyterian Church at the corner, wanted the house for its own purposes; while Achilles, our priceless chef, decided to return to Belgium with his capable Scotch wife. All this slowly brought the Club to an end, which came at the time of depression.

It meant more to us of the NAACP, working in our offices near by, than to other members. We could go there for luncheon or dinner, could take in a guest or two, and be sure of a good meal and a hearty welcome. Few white New Yorkers, unless they have colored friends, know the unpleasantness, to put it mildly, of finding a place where the two races can eat together comfortably and well. The State of New York has a stiff Civil Rights Law, but its enforcement is difficult and justice only obtained after a lawsuit. What hungry guest wants a lawsuit for a meal? The Civic Club welcomed us and gave us of its best. We ate together, smoked together, and perhaps planned our program for the coming week. I doubt if the colored membership was ever over twenty-five, but it did more than its share for our entertainment.

One evening Taylor Gordon and Rosamond Johnson delighted us with their rendition of some of the spirituals. Big, dark, and boyish-looking, Gordon sang the songs with gusto and with almost primitive abandon. The smile on his broad face was contagious.

> When I get to Heben gwine ter try on my shoes,
> Gwine ter shout all ober God's Heben.

At the piano Rosamond Johnson not only played the accompaniment but struck in occasionally with his deep, powerful bass, the two giving the effect of a half dozen voices. It was an extraordinary rendering of folk music. "As exciting as grand opera," one of the members said.

Another evening James Weldon Johnson, Du Bois, Dill, and Walter White told us how near they came to being lynched. It was my program, and I shiver now at the thought of how ready I was to make use of my friends. They must have been reluctant to show how close they had been and still were, to others' savagery.

Of the stories told, Johnson's was the most fraught with danger, though White in Arkansas came a close second. Perhaps an air of detachment made the older man's incident the more poignant. It happened when he was a young man, and in Jacksonville, his native city, where he was well known and had many friends. Among his acquaintances was a colored woman from New York, who had come to the city on a newspaper assignment. Jacksonville had just been through a great fire and she was writing an account of its effect on the Negro population. Though classified as colored she showed no sign of it except, perhaps, in the blackness of her hair. Her skin was dead-white and, altogether, she was a striking-looking woman. She went to Johnson one morning at the place where he was working and asked him to go over her manuscript before she sent it to New York. He told her he would not be free until late afternoon, so they planned to go out to the new Riverside Park. The day was hot and it ended with the woman deciding to start early and to be near the entrance when Johnson arrived.

His work done, Johnson took the street car, went to the

end of the line, got off, and seeing no sign of the woman, returned to the car, believing that she must have gone home. But just as the car was about to start back he saw the woman at a distance, walking toward him. Of course, he again left the car, lifted up the barbed wire that separated the park from the road—at this time the place was unfinished—and walked up the path toward his new friend. The two spent a profitable hour together going over the manuscript and enjoying the view of the river, miles wide at this point. The sun was low and the scene tropical in its beauty.

This was what really occurred. But what the conductor and the motorman saw in their imaginations was a "nigger" running after a white woman! They sent the empty car bouncing and screeching back to the city and reported to the authorities.

In his autobiography, *Along This Way*, Johnson tells this story more fully than we heard it at the Club. He describes a subconscious uneasiness while discussing the manuscript with the woman. Something was happening back of them, dogs were barking, men were calling to one another as though on a hunt. When, their work over, the two decided to walk back to the street car, the subconscious became conscious. The barking grew louder, and as the two reached the fence they saw the militia and civilians with their dogs.

"I lose self-control," Johnson writes. "But a deeper self springs up and takes command; I follow orders. I take my companion's parasol from her hand; I raise the loose strand of fence wire and gently pass her through; I follow and step into the group. The spell is instantly broken. They surge round me. They seize me. They tear my clothes and bruise my body; all the while calling to their comrades, 'Come on, we've got 'im! Come on, we've got 'im!' And from all directions these comrades rush, shouting, 'Kill the damned nigger! Kill the black son of a bitch!' I catch a glimpse of my companion; it seems that the blood, the life is gone out of her. There is the truth; but there is no chance to state it; nor would it be believed. As the rushing crowd comes yelling and cursing, I feel that death is bearing in upon me. Not death of the empty sockets, but death with the blazing eyes of a frenzied brute. And still, I am not terror-stricken, I am carrying out the chief command that has been given me, 'Show no sign of fear; if you do you are lost.' Among those rushing to reach me is a slender young man clad in a white uniform. He breaks through the men who have hold of me. We look at each other; and I feel that a quivering message of intelligence to intelligence has been interchanged. He claps his hand on my shoulder and says, 'You are my prisoner.' I ask him, 'What is the charge?' He answers, 'Being out here with a white woman.' I question once more, 'Before whom do I answer this charge?' 'Before Major B——, the provost marshal.' At that, I answer nothing beyond, 'I am your prisoner.' " *

From that moment Johnson was safe. The lieutenant arranged that his prisoner and the woman walk quietly on ahead of him to the provost marshal's tent. No one saw an arrest.

"I told the provost marshal that the lady, according to the laws of Florida, was colored and he dismissed the case with many apologies. And here I am," James Weldon Johnson

---

* Reprinted from *Along This Way* by James Weldon Johnson, copyright 1933, by permission of The Viking Press, Inc.

ended, looking down on us from the platform with his kindly smile.

"But what about the woman?" one of the Club members asked. "Why didn't she say at once that she was colored?"

"She said it again and again," the speaker answered, "but a crowd of angry white men would never listen to her much less believe her. However, she had her chance at last. After the case was dismissed she turned on the provost marshal and spoke slowly and deliberately at first; then with words that came like torrents. She laid on the Major's head the sins of his fathers and his fathers' fathers, and she charged them and him responsible for what had happened. We left the Major flushed and flustered."

I cannot express how much I, for one, miss the Civic Club. I wait for the day when the colored people will form a club along its broad lines, a club that will promote civic and social work, and represent a variety of cultural interests. The founders can do plenty of picking and choosing while deciding who is eligible for its white membership.

On a late Saturday afternoon, Sept. 12, 1925, our secretary was on a New Jersey golf links. He had reached the seventh hole when a boy from the clubhouse ran up to him saying he was wanted on a long distance phone call from Detroit. When he picked up the receiver, he found an officer from the Detroit branch eager to tell his story. The conversation lasted half an hour. Johnson learned that a certain Dr. Ossian Sweet, a prominent colored surgeon of Detroit, his wife and his two brothers with seven friends, had all been arrested and charged with murder in the first degree. A shot had been fired from Dr. Sweet's newly occupied home in a white neighborhood and a man in the mob surrounding his house had been killed. Many details followed concerning the mob and the desperate position of the Sweets. The Detroit branch of the NAACP had at once become interested in the case, but it wanted New York's help immediately.

Johnson never finished his game. Back in New York he conferred with Arthur Spingarn and Walter White, and the latter, who always welcomed difficult assignments, was asked to go immediately to Detroit to investigate conditions and report as soon as possible. In a very few days, he gave us a detailed story.

Dr. Ossian Sweet had built up a good practice in Detroit and wanted to move from his small flat to a house in a less crowded neighborhood. He could not find a house that he and his wife liked in a Negro neighborhood. Negro sections where anything suitable was for sale were frightfully over-crowded, so they ended up by getting a house in a white neighborhood at the corner of Garland and Charlevoix Streets. The block was not exclusively residential. It had a grocery and a public school, but the corner house which was for sale was attractive, and after much searching this was the best thing the Sweets could get.

Hardly had the doctor made his first payment in May and acquired title than he began to receive threatening letters. No "niggers" were to be allowed on that street, "he had better not show his damned black face there," and sometimes definite threats were made. Mrs. Sweet, who had lived on a white street with her mother before her marriage, and who had had a pleasant time while at public school, discounted much of this. There were always a few nasty people, but she did not believe anyone would bother much about them—one

rarely knew one's city neighbors. But the doctor was southern born and had serious doubts. In his boyhood, spent in a
small Florida town, he had passed one morning by a tree
under which the charred body of a Negro lay still smolder-
ing, and that sight was burned into his spirit. He decided to
wait a little before moving until the excitement had had time
to die down.

But excitement against the Negro and the Negro's entrance into a white neighborhood grew. After Dr. Sweet had
purchased his property, three Negroes, good workers and
good citizens, were dispossessed with their families from their
newly purchased homes. Their property was completely
ruined. In one case, that of Dr. Turner and his wife, the
couple barely escaped with their lives. The Detroit that
Gladys, Dr. Sweet's wife, had known as a little girl, no
longer existed. The city had become a great factory center,
securing labor from every part of the country—the Negro
population had increased from 8,000 to 80,000, and the population of white Southerners had increased proportionately,
bringing in its train active prejudice and the Ku Klux Klan.

Wherever situated, the Ku Klux Klan was active in politics, and some of its members held appointive positions in the
Detroit city government. Candidates for elective offices, while
sympathetic to the Klan, found it wiser not to be identified
with the movement. Such a sympathizer was prosecuting attorney, Robert M. Toms, who entered the Sweet case from the
start. Since his election in 1923, he had shown indifference to
police brutality when directed towards Negroes, and 55
Negroes had been killed while being arrested. Not one of
the policemen was prosecuted. Neither were those whites
who were advocating and practicing violence against Negro

residents. The Klan was holding meetings throughout Detroit, meetings designed to keep Negroes out of white neighborhoods. In early July, the Detroit *Free Press* gave a detailed, first page account of one of these meetings where fiery crosses decorated the platform. So called "improvement" associations sprang up with the object of "improving" their neighborhoods by ejecting colored residents. In late July the schoolhouse in the Sweet block was used for a meeting where violence was advocated, and an improvement association was formed. The meeting was addressed by a man who had taken a prominent part in the Turner eviction. Small riots occurred.

Dr. Sweet's office was downtown. Through the hot summer months he continued his practice, but remained in his little flat. With the beginning of September he decided that he would take the risk and move. The mayor had called upon the city to stop rioting, the summer was over though the heat continued, and he might as well go now as any time. He had bought the house and meant to occupy it. His wife had been impatient to move and on September 8, under police protection but carrying firearms if that failed them, Dr. Sweet and his family took up residence on Garland and Charlevoix Streets.

There was little sleep the first night, for the street was crowded and noisy, but nothing happened. The second night the doctor came back from work to his new home and waited while his wife prepared a dinner they were never to eat. With the doctor was a younger brother, Henry, a student at Wilberforce University. Henry was expecting the following year to enter the law school at Howard University, Washington. His brother was helping him with his education. Henry had with him a classmate from Wilberforce, and Gladys Sweet, the doctor's wife, set them to making ice cream.

Friends of the doctor joined them until there were eight persons in the new house waiting for dinner.

In the street was a constant noise of footsteps and voices. The shades were down but Henry went to one of the windows, and, pushing the curtain aside, looked out.

"My God," he cried, "look at the people!"

The schoolhouse yard was full of people, men were everywhere, on the roofs of the houses, seated on their porches with their women folk, milling up and down. The police, twelve of them, kept the people in the street moving, but did nothing to disperse them. Suddenly Dr. Sweet's brother, Dr. Otis Sweet, a dentist, with a friend, drove up in a taxi, and jumping out, rushed to the doctor's door. They were at once admitted.

The sight of two Negroes running into the house, the shutting of the door, turned the crowd into an active mob. The "damned niggers" were to be treated as Dr. Turner had been treated, and despite the presence of the police, stones were thrown, bricks—anything that could be found. Then firing began. No one ever knew how many shots were fired. One policeman in his testimony said he had shot into the house.

After this, two things happened. A man named Breiner, a resident from a neighboring street, fell dead from a bullet and Henry Sweet, on his own admission, fired from the house. There was no question of his having killed Breiner. The bullet when found did not fit Henry's gun, but one shot at least was fired from Dr. Sweet's window.

This brought police into action. Entering the house—there

were fifteen of them now—they pulled up the shades, turned on the lights, and arrested all the household. The men and Mrs. Sweet were hustled into a patrol wagon and taken to prison where they learned of Breiner's death, and that they were all charged with the murder. Demanding legal counsel, they were refused, questioned separately, and kept under a fierce grilling until three in the morning. Lawyers, furnished by Mrs. Sweet's mother, reached them the next day; and the day after, Saturday, they were arraigned before the court and all declared guilty of murder in the first degree. Later Mrs. Sweet was released on bail.

These facts, and many others, were given us by Walter White when he returned to the office. It was not difficult to understand what had happened. Again and again the Association had had cases brought to its attention of the use of violence in keeping colored men out of their newly purchased homes. In Baltimore, the once famous Druid Hill Avenue, finding itself deserted by fashion, tried to restore the value of its real estate by dynamiting houses when black people started to move in. In Kansas City, Missouri, the same thing happened. Was this violence to be upheld by law or was the legal right of a man to defend his home to be recognized whatever the color of his face?

The Association, without question, must make this case its own, and it must get the best lawyer in the country to defend it. This best person, all agreed, was Clarence Darrow.

Darrow was then in New York, having just returned from the heat and the fatigue of the Tennessee Scope Case, where he upheld the right of a public school employee to teach evolution. The heat and the strenuous arguing had killed William Jennings Bryan, Darrow's opponent, and Darrow himself wanted nothing so much as quiet and rest. He said so when approached by the head of our legal committee, Arthur Spingarn, by James Johnson, and by Walter White. He continued in his refusal after he went to Spingarn's home to spend the night. But in the course of the evening, Walter White, blue-eyed, light of complexion, was spoken of as a Negro. Darrow was incredulous. When forced to believe that the young man had colored blood, he said he would take the case.

All the prisoners were tried together in the late autumn. The jury disagreed. A second trial was ordered, this time of Henry Sweet who had admitted that he had fired from the house. Frank Murphy, now a Supreme Court Justice, was to be the judge at this as at the preceding trial. Judge Murphy was in his early thirties, learned, just and courageous. He showed his courage when, after the first trial, he released all the prisoners on bail. He was very popular and had been elected by the largest majority Detroit ever gave his office. The Association would have fewer lawyers (three), Darrow, Clarke, and a colored lawyer, Julian Perry. The lawyers would have more time for preparation and the Association would have time to raise the needed money.

We had raised money for legal cases and had received generous support, but the response to appeals in the Sweet Case was beyond all expectations. Our publicity was clear, appealing; the press had already given publicity and would give more. Darrow's name was of incalculable value. But while to the white press the case revolved around Darrow, to the colored the great issue was the right of a Negro to defend the home he had bought. He might buy, no city could contract to prevent him, but might he protect his home? The

Sweet Case was based directly on this point and its decision would create a precedent.

Neatly written checks came in, illiterately addressed envelopes held smudged money orders, and dirty dollar bills dropped down from Yazoo, Mississippi, or Bangor, Maine. It looked as if the Negroes would send the bulk of the money until the Garland Fund, Roger Baldwin, president, voted to match the Association's every two dollars with one of its own. The branches, as always, responded and contributions came from all over the country.

Even after the trial was over, money came in, and, with the consent of the donors, this excess was used for the nucleus of a legal defense fund.

The second trial began on April 19, in Judge Murphy's beautiful but small courtroom. "No one is to be hurried," the judge said, and a week passed and 169 men were summoned before 12 jurymen were secured. Their occupations vouched for good caliber: three engineers, three high-skilled workmen, two business managers, a retired steamship steward, a pharmacist, a water-board employee, and a night watchman at the Sacred Heart Seminary. This finished, the case opened for the State.

Though Henry Sweet was charged with murder in the first degree, his gun, as I have noted, could not have fired the bullet that killed Breiner. The case against him was conspiracy to murder, that Henry Sweet was one of a group of men who had gone to Dr. Sweet's house with intent to kill. If he had aided or abetted some one of the persons in the house who caused the death of Breiner, his act would be their act, and their act his. The prosecution did not question Dr. Sweet's right to buy the house, but contended that he had gone there with a supply of ammunition that was used on slight provocation and with intent to kill.

The prosecution produced its witnesses, all but one of them upholding its allegations that the neighborhood was orderly on the night the Sweets shot, that it was indeed "neighborly"; that there was no crowd, no danger to the Sweets, and no violence. To prove this they called their witnesses: policemen, including an inspector, neighbors from Garland and Charlevoix Streets and adjoining streets, men and women and boys—seventy-one persons in all.

The second night of the Sweet's occupancy was hot and these witnesses were out to get a breath of air, or just happened to pass by. Under oath, the police, including the inspector, testified that there was no crowd, only "a few people." Boys on the witness stand, and men and women saw only a "few" people. They also remembered nothing that was said at the meeting they had attended in the public schoolyard in July. One person, looking across the street, might admit that she saw a dozen persons on the night of the Sweet's arrest, but the next witness, looking in the same direction, saw no one. It seemed as though the boys had been coached as to what they saw and what they didn't see, when to talk and when to keep silent. One made a slip but after recognizing it, knew nothing. A high school teacher took great pains to spell her name that the jury might be sure who she was—Miss S-t-o-w-e-l-l. Whether the jury remembered or not, Darrow did not forget it. "Just a few" was used by the witnesses so often that Darrow said he heard it in his sleep. "I don't know" was equally popular. Decidedly an unobservant group of people, these witnesses, who saw little and knew less.

The last day of the week, however, a man of different caliber took the stand. Reluctant, unsympathetic, he yet respected his oath and under persistent questioning, gave a detailed account of the July meeting when the "improvement" association was formed. He told of its size, so large that it was adjourned to the schoolyard, and of what the speaker had said. "He was a radical. . . . I am not a radical," and at last, "He advocated violence." On cross examination, Toms tried to get him to modify this, but the witness reiterated, "He advocated violence."

On this admission of the hostile character of the whites, the friends of Henry Sweet and his cause took heart and listened hopefully as Darrow, on the following Monday, began to present his witnesses. They were few in number but they all counted. To prove that there had been a crowd he presented a big-hearted, comfortable-looking woman who lived in an alley back of the Sweet's house. She had started that evening to go to the grocery on Garland Street, but seeing a great crowd, had turned back. Then, after hanging a few clothes in the yard, "I stepped me by the alley door," where she saw policemen run through the alley into the Sweet yard and heard three shots. This corroborated Henry's story that he heard shots before he fired. A second witness was a reporter and special writer on the Detroit *News*. He had been in the Sweet neighborhood, and testified that hundreds of people were moving about and that this crowd became riotous, so riotous that though he wanted to find out what it was all about, he turned homeward, as he feared for his little girl, who was with him.

Among the colored witnesses were Mr. and Mrs. Spalding, both educators, who had been out motoring and had found themselves caught in a crowd of several hundred, and had had difficulty in getting away and home. John C. Dancy, secretary of the Urban League, testified regarding housing conditions and the overcrowding of Negroes in Detroit. The Negro population had doubled from 1920 to 1926. "Of this group, the largest number," he said, "came from the South." "I suppose by 'group' you mean 'a few,'" Darrow interpolated. Dancy's testimony was so interesting that the prosecution as well as the defense hated to be obliged to end it.

The courtroom was always crowded, a few seated, many standing. Ann Harding was there often; had she not played the part of a prisoner at the dock accused of murder? And Jeanne Eagels, beautiful, intelligent, who had stirred us all by her acting in that deeply significant play, *Rain*. Among our Association people were Arthur Spingarn, Charles Edward Russell, James Weldon Johnson, Walter White. Our work went on at the office, letters were read, typewriters clicked, publicity was sent out, but every mind and heart was with Henry Sweet in the courtroom at Detroit.

The receiving of testimony ended and the arguments began. Toms dramatically summed up for the prosecution, but the trial was Darrow's and his argument became history. He spoke for nearly seven hours, beginning as he ended with the assertion that the case was one of race prejudice, not of murder. "Every one of you is prejudiced," he said to the jury. "You are twelve white men trying a colored man. I want you to be on your guard, I want you to do all you can to be fair in this case—and I believe you will." Darrow was famous for his attitude toward a jury, his genuine sincerity, his belief that they wanted to do what was humane and right. The prosecution lawyers had said this wasn't a race question, it was a murder case. "I insist," Darrow went on, "that there is nothing but prejudice in this case; that if it was reversed and eleven white men had shot and killed a black while protecting their home and their lives against a mob of blacks, no one would have dreamed of having them indicted. I know what I am talking about and so do you. They would have been given medals instead."

This was the theme of his argument; where a white man would be applauded for protecting his home against a mob, a black man was prosecuted for murder. The fundamental law of the land, which Henry Sweet was upholding, was denied him because of his race. Darrow never let the jury forget the injustice that custom meted to the Negro. "How would you like, gentlemen, to wake in the morning to find yourself colored?" He never let them forget the difference between their daily life—they who might go into a hotel or theater or restaurant without rebuff, who might live where their money could take them—and the life of the black man who was always self-conscious, always in danger of insult. Never since the first slaveship, had the Negro been given a fair chance. The jury must know this, must feel it.

But Darrow did much more than show the Negro's wrongs —he showed the culture and the character of his colored witnesses and of the Sweets and set them up against the witnesses for the State. The president of Wilberforce, a scholar and gentleman, came to Detroit to vouch for Henry's scholarship and his good name. Mrs. Spalding was a charming woman, her husband a pleasant, cultured man. Dancy's interesting facts were made doubly interesting by his pleasing manner of presentation. And over against these dark people were the white residents of Charlevoix and Garland Streets.

Darrow recalled them to the jury, one by one. "Miss Stowell, gentlemen, you remember her? You ought to for she spelled her name for us. Miss S-t-o-w-e-l-l. She could spell her name but she could not pronounce Goethe. You remember? She was telling us about Goethe Street. She called it Go-the. The Sweets could teach her how to pronounce Goethe. Another witness, a man named Draper, "that long, hungry-looking duck," had said he didn't want Negroes living on his street. Questioned further, he had added that he did not want "Eyetalians." "Christopher Columbus who, Draper might remember, discovered America, was an Italian but he wouldn't have been good enough to associate with Draper." With merciless satire, Darrow showed up the people of Garland and Charlevoix Streets for what they were, not too literate, prejudiced, ready to perjure themselves to keep a quiet, cultured Negro family out of their block. The contrast was sharp, bold, and in favor of the colored. "If the Negro ever wins his place in our civilization," Darrow said, "it will be by his courage and his culture."

As he drew toward the end of his plea for justice, Darrow turned directly to Henry Sweet. "What has he done?" he asked the jury. "I want to put it up to each of you individually. Dr. Sweet was his elder brother. He had helped Henry through school. He loved him. He had taken him into his home. Henry had lived with him and with his wife and baby. The doctor had promised Henry money to go through school. Henry was getting his education to take his place in the world, and, gentlemen, this is a hard job. With his brother's help he had worked himself through college up to the last year. The doctor bought a home. He feared danger. He moved with his wife, and he asked this boy to go with him. And this boy went to help to defend his brother, and his brother's wife and his child and his home. Do you think the less of him for that?"

Darrow stopped a few moments to gather strength for his last words. He had said to the jury, "I never saw twelve men in my life that, if you could get them to understand a human case, were not true or right." Did these twelve men understand this human case? He went on, "Now, gentlemen, just one more word and I am through. I do not live in Detroit, but I have no feelings against this city. In fact I shall always have the kindest remembrance of it, especially if this case results as I think and feel it will. I do not believe in the law of hate. I may not be true always to my ideals, but I believe in the law of love and I believe you can do nothing with hatred. I would like to see the time when man loves his fellow man and forgets his color or his creed. We will never be civilized until that time comes. I know the Negro race has a long way to go. I believe the life of the Negro race has been a life of tragedy, of injustice, of oppression. The law has made him equal but man has not. And after all the last analysis is what a man has done.

"Gentlemen, what do you think is your duty in this case? I ask you on behalf of the defendant, on behalf of this great state, and this great city which must face this problem and face it squarely, I ask you in the name of progress and of the human race to return a verdict of not guilty in this case."

Darrow took his seat. In the courtroom and standing out in the corridor, men and women were profoundly moved. You saw this, still more you felt it. Our secretary, James Weldon Johnson, rose from his seat and went over to the lawyer to express his appreciation, to try to thank him. Darrow placed his hands on the Negro's shoulders. "I tried to stammer out a few words," Johnson said afterwards, "and then I broke down and wept."

The prosecution presented its argument the next day. Judge Murphy explained the law, covering he believed each point.

The courtroom gradually emptied. The first jury had taken thirty-odd hours before bringing in a divided verdict. It was useless to try to guess how long these men might be. Gladys Sweet was among those who remained in the courtroom. With her were a few friends. Men and women were chatting in the corridors and out in the street.

The afternoon dragged. Once loud voices were heard from the jury room, once the jury asked for further elucidation of the law, but the judge sent word that he had covered everything in his charge. A minute before five, there came a loud knocking at the jury-room door. The clerk of the court had gone out and was not there to answer it. Judge Murphy put his head into the courtroom and said sternly, "Don't bring that jury in until we are ready for them." People came crowding back into the courtroom. Another clerk had to be found. At length all was in order, and the jury was permitted to enter. For a moment, Henry Sweet, his hands clenched, turned his face to the wall. Only for a moment. Then composed, he turned back to face the twelve men.

"Gentlemen of the jury, have you in the course of your deliberations reached a verdict in the case of Henry Sweet and if so who will answer for you?"

The dignified foreman, retired steward of the Cunard Line, answered, "We have and I will." Then, clearing his throat, he said, "Not guilty."

"What!" Toms, the prosecuting attorney, was so amazed that he cried out, not believing he had heard correctly.

The verdict came again, unmistakably, "Not guilty."

The Sweet trial was over.

To make the story complete, Dr. Sweet and his wife and little daughter went back to his house on Garland and Charlevoix Streets where he still lives, at the time of this writing. Henry Sweet returned to college, entered law school the following year, graduated and practiced law until his early death in 1940. The case of Henry Sweet, the precedent it established, became part of the law of the land.

I lost my father in 1909 and in 1927 my mother died. She was ninety and had been failing in mental power though little in physical energy. We traveled a good deal with my father and, after his death, by ourselves. We grew to know certain parts of Europe fairly well but we knew the sea better. My father would have been as horrified at flying across the ocean as Ruskin was at traveling in Europe on a train. The slower the steamer, the better he liked it. We would spend a month on the water and a month or six weeks on land. Kipling wrote,

> I'd sell my tired soul, for the bucking beam-sea roll
>   On a black, Bilbao tramp.*

I was the only weakling when it came to the "beam-sea roll." The other two were stalwarts; they dressed carefully for breakfast, and alone in the long saloon, were invited to eat with the captain.

After my father's death my mother and I took shorter

* Published by Doubleday & Co.

trips, chiefly to the West Indies, though in the spring of 1914 we ventured to North Africa. We saw no Negroes but we saw the Mohammedan women in their long, thick veils, with only a peephole for one eye. Having no souls, they might not enter the Mosque, and their only outing was their visit once a week to the churchyard to mourn their dead. They were slaves, these women, the slaves of the Mohammedan world.

We grew to love islands and spent four weeks in Sicily, so beautiful along the coast, so sad in the interior. Sicily was once called the granary of Europe. Now the interior boasts a few spears of wheat as poor as an escape on a New England hillside. Except perhaps for Madeira we counted Jamaica the most beautiful of islands. Their peasant women, baskets on their heads and striding along like godesses, were wonderful to watch, but we soon learned of their poverty. Indeed, this world is most exhausting for those who alone maintain human life. Few pennies and little but contempt are given those who raise food, yet despite the advertiser's praises, we may not live on automobiles nor drink gasoline with impunity.

After my mother's death I put my things in storage and for nearly a year wandered over this country, sometimes doing a little work, more often at play. I attended the conference at Los Angeles when Charles W. Chesnutt, whose novels still rank high in our literature, received the Spingarn Medal. I stopped at a new hotel, built for Negro trade by Dr. Somerville, and the headquarters of our conference. I met Delia Beaseley who wrote a book on California's colored pioneers; and returning via Seattle and the Canadian Rockies,

I saw one of the younger generation who was to be very close to me in affection, Lorenza Jordan Cole.

I came to know Lorenza in Seattle where I was busy fulfilling engagements for the NAACP. My last day, Sunday, I was to speak at three colored churches in the morning, have dinner with friends, to be followed by a reception, and in the evening take the service at a white church. I had saved the late afternoon for sleep, but I was entreated by the secretary of the branch to hear a young pianist who was recommended for a scholarship at the Juilliard School. She was a pupil of Mme. Leiszniewska of the Cincinnati Conservatory, and would have been a conservatory graduate had not the school denied her access to some of its classes. Of course I went. I stretched out on a sofa to hear the music but soon was sitting up listening to a true musician. The music over, we talked about the scholarship and it ended in my promising to raise money to carry Lorenza through a school year if she could get to New York and support herself for the first weeks. Lorenza fell upon my neck and I became a patron of the arts—the first and the only time I have had the means to occupy this position. Of course, it was a continuous task, one year became three; but my friends, white and colored, were very generous and Lorenza worked with all her strength of hand and brain.

These were golden years in the United States when there was work for anyone capable of it, and when the Secretary of the Treasury assured us that unemployment was gone, never to return. Negroes were pouring into Newark (mistaken for New York), into New York, Chicago, Cleveland, Detroit, Indianapolis, and the far West. In the South they moved from the farm to the city. A few were professional men, a few skilled laborers, the majority unskilled and un-educated. But they had an ambition for learning. They put their children at once into school, and kept them there. De-sirous of improving their position, they were yet not so self-confident, not so wedded to the past, as the European im-migrant. The majority went into domestic service, but a domestic service that paid a good wage and had bearable hours. They were getting a taste, a very small taste, watered, but a taste of the wealth of America.

Returning to New York, I took my goods out of storage and moved to the top floor of a four-story house in Green-wich Village. I was my own mistress and controlled an aug-mented income. No one needed me, and for two years I enjoyed my four sunny rooms, my maid, and my chance to have visitors of any race or any class whenever I pleased. This meant neither worry nor difficulty over their entrance or their exit. The doorman and the service elevator in an apart-ment can mar hospitality. In Greenwich Village, at the buzz of a bell, I had only to push a button and my door opened on a stairway to be used by all visitors, icemen or million-aires.

Number 4 Van Ness Place, then my address, is, I believe, the most difficult address in New York. Van Ness Place is the north side of one block of Charles Street, between West Fourth and Bleecker. Added to that, West Fourth Street has just crossed West Tenth Street. I had a card printed with explicit directions, but few invited guests arrived on time and some never arrived at all. Reading my card, they felt as I do about directions in knitting—the thing printed can't be done.

I stayed two years at Van Ness Place, working a little for

the NAACP, resting from anxiety, and rejoicing in the democracy of the Village. Martha Gruening, who was living there for a time, assured me that I could carry my laundry bag through the street and never be noticed. I knew a few of my neighbors, among them Roy Baldridge whose paintings of African subjects are at Fisk University. Through him, I heard a group of Liberians play unforgettable music on their drums.

Carl Diton and his wife came to dinner one evening and Mrs. Diton told inimitably of the importance of an NAACP in a small town. Not even Carl Diton could hope to secure an audience if he struck a branch meeting. One afternoon Taylor Gordon called, and a friendly mouse entertained us by running back and forth across the floor. One has mice in old houses. Two or three afternoons a week, Lorenza came to practice on my rented Steinway, and I never tired of listening.

By chance I at once became friends with the couple living below me. I had hardly moved in when they gave a party that lasted until dawn. I like "Old Man River," but when the record has been played twenty times, its "rolling" has ceased to attract. However, I made no complaint and virtue was at once rewarded. The party had proved too much for its hostess, and the next night a frightened husband came to my door and begged me to sit with his wife while he went for the doctor. I thus became acquainted with my neighbor who slept directly below the piano and yet declared she enjoyed Lorenza's practicing. Occasionally she came up to hear a complete piece. I felt grateful to the Village, and yet, before I left, race hatred appeared there like a dark cloud.

I planned to spend two months of my summer in my

sister's apartment on East 86th Street, and invited Lorenza
Cole and her friend Grace Postles of Philadelphia to live in
my rooms. Lorenza was to give a concert in the fall to raise
money to go abroad and study in London under Matthay
(which she did) and my place would furnish a piano. Grace,
an Emerson School graduate, was studying that summer at
Columbia. Both girls joyfully accepted my invitation, and I
was glad to have them there caring for my possessions.

Had I been wise I would have left the young people to
make their own adjustments, but hearing that the tenants
below had sublet for the summer, I went down to speak to
the new tenant about my piano. I always felt guilty about
that piano. I would move it to the front room if desired.

The new tenant I met was a young wife who didn't mind
practice in the least. We talked of music and I mentioned
The Green Pastures. She wanted to see it, but her husband
wouldn't go to a colored show. I left feeling slightly disturbed.

The next day I was at the NAACP annual conference
held that year in Springfield, Massachusetts. All who wished
were housed at the Charles Hotel. The city welcomed us as
it would have welcomed any conference of earnest people.
No wonder "the Springfield plan" in education is known
all over the United States.

When I returned to New York with my sister, a letter lay
on the hall table, forwarded from Van Ness Place. My
landlord requested me to eject the young colored women
occupying my apartment. The people living below me were
refusing to pay their rent to the original tenant, who, in turn,
was refusing to pay the landlord. The Negroes must go.

The next morning I went to Van Ness Place. I found

Lorenza in the living room practicing. "Yes," she said, the landlord had told them what he was writing me. They must leave.

"How does Grace feel?" I asked.

"Grace keeps asking me whether you will send us away or not."

"What have you told her?"

Lorenza was still on the music bench. She dropped her eyes and looked at her small, pretty hands, almost too small for a pianist. Then looking up she faced me squarely. "I said I didn't know."

I was silent.

"You see," she went on, "I have experienced things like this before, and every time the white person has gone with her race. She didn't want to, I know she didn't want to, but the pull was too strong. Too much was involved, position, money, convenience."

I looked about the room, at the carefully measured window curtains, at the bookcases made to fit the wall spaces on either side of the fireplace. "Of course you'll stay," I said a little fiercely. "The law is on my side. But be very careful. Don't give parties; don't do anything to make yourself a nuisance." They stayed on. The tenants below, the man at least, would occasionally yell up, "You niggers be quiet." If he met one of the girls on the stairs, he would flatten against the wall as though she were diseased. Grace, her great eyes on the light ahead, would go by dreamily unconscious, but Lorenza, passing the man, felt the hatred ooze out of him. "How terrible," she said to me once, "for anyone to hate like that." The girls were quiet and very busy and after a time, manifestations against them almost ceased.

This was the summer of 1930. The financial crash came and millions of lives were affected by it, my own among the number. The "augmented income" dropped out of sight like the mercury in a thermometer on a cold winter night. The bookcases would have had to come down anyway, I thought. In September, I wrote my landlord that I did not intend to renew my lease. The next morning I received a letter from him saying that I could not come back. As our letters crossed, my pride was saved.

Lorenza went to London, studied for something over a year, and returned to America to find the launching of an unknown pianist impossible. Even the best known could barely draw an audience. She is now teaching music in the public school system of Los Angeles. She recently sent me a picture of the high schoool orchestra she conducts. I count those young people of many nationalities very fortunate to be under her baton.

Conditions are better today in New York since our Anti-Bias Bill, but that summer I was hit in both wings. In my sister-in-law's apartment I entertained some friends from Tuskegee. I was writing my juvenile *Zeke*, and I wanted to ask their advice. It happened they all went out together, and the next morning I was told by the superintendent that, thereafter, my colored guests would have to use the freight elevator. Brenda Moryck was coming to dinner that evening and I had to call it off. "I guessed what had happened," Brenda said when I went to see her, and she told of a recent rebuff downtown. On her return, my sister-in-law took the matter up with the management and did so well that we were again able to entertain whom we pleased. When she had finished her talk, the agent admitted that he had learned a good deal. However, before we moved into smaller quarters the following year, we did not sign our lease until we had a definite promise regarding elevator service.

As the work at the office grew more technical and was carried on by salaried executives, I found that I could be of best service as a field worker. From the beginning, I had often visited branches and was familiar with Boston, Chicago, Philadelphia, Washington, Atlanta, and other cities not too far from New York. But as our work grew, I went further afield. I learned to know not only the South, the Middle West, but the Rocky Mountains, and the Pacific Coast. I did not travel enough to weary of it, and was always glad, when it was possible, to start out with suitcase and typewriter, and to go to new cities or re-visit old ones.

My trips were usually in the spring before our membership drive, which took place in May. Our field work was headed by Mrs. Daisy E. Lampkin whose power of organization is astonishing and always brings results. At times she comes up against internal dissensions, difficulties that seem to make united effort impossible. They do not exist for her, and soon they cease to exist for anyone else. Her work demonstrates the certainty of success if one insists upon considering the constructive, not the destructive side of a question.

With her was our field secretary, William Pickens, Phi Beta Kappa from Yale, now a worker in the Treasury Department at Washington. His oratory is famous. Like Henry Ward Beecher, whom I often heard as a child, he is deeply sincere, with an almost Shakespearian vocabulary and a keen sense of humor. Beecher, a minister, had to hold back some of his humor, but Pickens could evoke laughter as much as he pleased. I made no attempt to emulate either of our officers nor to fill one of the great halls that was needed when the secretaries, or J. E. Spingarn, or Charles Edward Russell spoke. I was just a quiet, feminine emissary who liked the smaller cities, the intimate talks with local organizations, with small liberal clubs and, of course, with the executives of the branch. When the evening came for my talk, I was told to take all the time I wanted. I usually spoke for at least an hour.

My speech was a theme with variations. The theme was the beginning of the Association and its objectives; the variations were immediate accomplishments showing that our dream had become a reality. I liked speaking and, small wonder, for I always had an attentive audience. There were no microphones then, and no photographers creeping and crouching along the edge of the platform to snap pictures.

One compliment I treasured. At a branch meeting in a church at Columbus, Ohio, I noticed a clergyman who listened intently and yet, I thought, glanced too often at the clock. He rose when I was through, and said something like this, "I wondered how long Miss Ovington could hold her audience, using a conversational tone. She did it for an hour and ten minutes. Now if Brother Moore," nodding to the clergyman on the platform, "or I had wanted to hold your attention for that long, we would have had to go in for some skyrockets!"

I visited California branches twice in the twenties, and grew to love the state, especially its women who seemed very democratic. Perhaps the impossibility of securing domestic labor had something to do with this. We in the East are now faced with a similar shortage, but California has always known it. When I was a little girl, our Irish cook left us for San Francisco where she would earn $30 a month! However, she did not help the situation as she promptly married a carpenter and had a house of her own. I met a number of distinguished women teaching at the University of California and found them all doing the bulk of their housework. There seemed, too, many competent and willing husbands. Especially in southern California, a meal took on the quality of a happy picnic. Life like this tends to break down caste.

For a quarter of a century, the Association has been a power in California. When I went there in the early twenties, I did not find a town with fifty colored voters that did not have a branch. I spoke before many different audiences: to classes at the University of California, to women's clubs, to chambers of commerce, and at branch meetings. "It was roses, roses, all the way," or if not roses, geraniums. I was entertained twice by the late Frank Miller, proprietor of the Mission Inn at Riverside and found numbers of white people of prominence in sympathy with our work.

When in California, I stayed some time at Carmel and saw Lincoln Steffens. We talked of old times and of the new. Both he and his wife were enthusiastic over the progress of the Soviet Union about which his wife, Ella Winter, has since written a number of books. That country's amazing strides in education, its children's theaters, its extra curricula for youth (the boys build miniature railroads and then jump into the engine cabs and run the trains), the entrance of women into a full life—even Mohammedan women—all this talk about Russian achievements, instead of Russian politics, was refreshing. Sometimes it seems as though our men thought they were born, first, Republicans or Democrats, and only secondly babies needing to be sheltered and nourished. The ideology of a worker's government is that food and shelter, not politics, come first. Lincoln Steffens knew too much about politics. I wish I could quote him, but it is far back in my mind. He looked very happy in his attractive home within sight of the Pacific, with his wife and their young son. The last time I had seen him was in my settlement days, and then he had heckled me relentlessly.

In Los Angeles I encountered the torrential rains of spring. The water rose high in the streets, stalling the cars. My largest audience on this journey was due to such a torrent. I arrived at Long Beach, a small town, in the afternoon, and as my hostess drove me from the station to her home, she pointed out a huge municipal auditorium. "We have two halls," she explained, "and of course we secured the largest for the chairman of our board." The branch was small, my name carried no publicity value, and I didn't look forward to the evening.

When we were safely home, it began to rain—rain that came down like water thrown out of a pail. At eight o'clock, our car forded streets that had become mountain streams and I ended by paddling through a foot of water to the auditorium door. I mounted the platform. Ten people had come to the meeting! Of course, I left the rostrum, went down the steps to the floor, gathered the ten in front of me, and made my speech. When the meeting was over, an old gentleman came up to tell me how much he appreciated my talking to so small a group. "Some speakers would have left," he said. I told him that I had always resented the preacher who scolded those who came out in the rain because others had stayed away. "If you will come back, I'll fill this hall for you," the man said. The vast auditorium receded into darkness. "I'll come back," I answered.

I was there three weeks later on a bright, sunny afternoon. The old gentleman had kept his promise. Gallery and floor were filled and, not only that, were filled with men. Then a light broke in on me. A "Soldiers' Home," as we used to call it, was not far away. These were Veterans of the Civil and Spanish Wars!

Fashion has entered few Negroes upon its society list, and not many white people have been entertained in colored homes. I have often been asked by the curious what the homes were like. Some represented wealth, but the majority were occupied by people of moderate means—with a northern and western background—or by families recently from the South. They were well kept and, most important, always with an inviting and comfortable bed! Sometimes one of the family vacated her room for me, and I would be bewildered as to where to put my own things. Were I to make any generalization, I would say that my colored friends never liked to throw anything away. Once I amused myself in a young girl's room by counting the number of things that a careful housewife would dust every day. There were a hundred and twenty: photographs stuck in mirrors, magazines, small ornaments, old Christmas cards. A person who loves to keep her possessions should live in an old rambling house with a large attic.

Of course I was bountifully fed. If the good things to eat were a trifle rich, I didn't object. Oliver Wendell Holmes described youth as a time when one can eat anything at any time. By that definition I am forever young. I especially remember a dinner at Avery Institute, Charleston, South

Carolina, when a magnificent planked shad was set down at the head of the table, next to me. And if the food was good it was accompanied by excellent table talk. One evening, at Fort Valley School when Henry Hunt was principal, we did not leave the table until midnight, so engrossed were we in one another's ideas. And it was always conversation, never monologue.

After a round of such visits, I felt sure of one thing— there are no race traits. There are individual differences, so many that they cannot be tabulated, and there is environment. The West Indian Negro, though living in New York, will differ from his Charlestonian neighbor across the hall. The color of their skin is the same, and their forbears may have come from the same African province, yet they differ as whites differ. Climate and social environment influence individual inheritance. Especially environment determines what shall come to blossom.

I used to think, when I was in Greenpoint, that each club boy was a little grab-bag out of which I could pull what I wanted. I could take the children out to a daisy field, not so far from the city then, and let them wander about and pick all the flowers they wanted. The boys changed, their eyes softened, they moved less spasmodically, they still screamed but with a note of delight in the excitement. "Daisyland," they called the place, and they loved it. But the mood died with the daisies held in hot, small hands. Grating trolleys— the company gave us the worst cars in the city—nauseous smells, narrow streets meant nervousness, tough speech, perhaps a raid on an empty flat, and stolen plumbing. Fagin is not needed to teach restless boys to steal. They do it for the fun of it.

While I was unable to find race traits in my travels, I was deeply impressed with the earnestness of the officers of the different branches. No one was paid; presidents and secretaries gave hours of their time day after day. I cannot name a half or a quarter of them, but a few figures immediately stand out: In California it is Beatrice Thomson; in Denver, George Gross and a crowded church that gave me a hearty western welcome. In Kansas City it is Mrs. Myrtle Foster Cook whose Sunday program included short addresses at eight churches, ending with a ninth where I spoke for an hour. In Toledo it is Harrison Fisher. In New Orleans, Dr. Lucas. These two were tall, large, dark, Dr. Lucas coming originally from Texas. He was a member of our board, and often investigated alleged crimes where there might be reason for our undertaking defense. We must have looked very comfortable and safe there in New York, for once he said to us, "Gentlemen, when you ask me to investigate a criminal case for you in New Orleans, I am as safe as I would be in New York. When you ask me to go into the country, that is another matter. But," he added, "I go."

I saw the branches in their relation to our national office. They paid the traveling expenses of our speakers, furnished entertainment, and gave the Association half the dues of all memberships. I am told by other treasurers of national organizations that we receive more help from outside New York than they do. We are indeed national. But this generosity does not preclude local work. The sum of activities in the various towns and cities was and is great. The exact figures have never been published, save in a few cases, and will be forgotten, but the results in better municipal conditions and in an enlarged freedom of action will persist, for the advancement of the race.

I was discouraged at the small effect the Northerner seemed to exert in the South. I stopped at Winter Park, Florida, where Rollins College is situated, and went, of course, to Daytona to see Mrs. Mary McLeod Bethune and the school that she founded. Mrs. Bethune is now a national figure. Hundreds of thousands of tourists must have gone to her Sunday afternoon meetings where the audience listened to a good talk, heard the singing of the spirituals, and were regaled with an excellent tea. Mrs. Bethune is an influential institution in Daytona. But the white Northerner seemed impotent when faced with the injustice of race lines. Rollins College is known for its progressive ideas in education, and for its democracy. The two professors then in the department of economics asked me to speak to their classes, or rather to lead the discussion, and a large majority of the students were liberal-minded. So were the professors, one from the Northwest, one from Virginia. Outside of the college were many visitors, quiet elderly people who, for the most part, were charitably inclined. Yet Winter Park in its way was as prejudiced and unjust in its treatment of Negro citizens as any town in the South. The only place where it showed no discrimination was in the levying of taxes. When it came to the enjoyment of the city's attractions, the whites had everything.

The Negroes lived across the railroad track. Their street was muddy, unpaved. They had only a grammar school. To earn their livelihood, they crossed the tracks and entered the well-kept, attractive white neighborhood where they performed household tasks for others.

Everything that I enjoyed was closed to them. They could not enter the library or the motion picture theater. They could not go to the plays given at the college theater, or to the lectures. They must not bathe in any one of the city's twenty-eight lakes, not even in the summer. Unless they were working for the whites, they must be on the other side of the railroad track by half-past-eight at night. Their section was not properly lighted, and no recreation was provided. I heard disparaging talk about their immorality, but the white people, returning from movies or concerts or drives over the lovely roads (for whites only) were in no position to cast any stones.

One man, a colored chauffeur from St. Louis, tried to arouse the city to some action, and I believe that he obtained preliminary approval for a boys' playground. But I learned of nothing else that broke through the indifference of the tourist who was satisfied that, if he left money for his living expenses in Florida—and prices were then reasonable—he had done all that was expected of him. Too much was already required, he felt, in his own home state.

On my way north, I saw Charlotte Hawkins Brown's colored school at Sedalia near Durham. This institute for girls only, is housed in an imposing building surrounded by beautiful grounds. Mrs. Brown was brought up in Cambridge, and came under the influence of Alice Freeman Palmer, wife of Harvard's famous teacher of ethics. Her school is named Palmer Institute. The old Massachusetts town has reason to be proud of its offshoot at Sedalia.

This trip gave me the opportunity to stop off at Chapel Hill and visit the University of North Carolina. Here I saw Dr. Howard Odum whom I had known when he was a student at Clark University. I met Dr. Guy Johnson and Professor Woofter, and was able to talk frankly about race problems. I missed seeing Mr. Newbold, State Superintendent of Negro Education, who was responsible for a decrease in the inequality between white and colored teachers' salaries from 100 to 25 per cent.

The University of North Carolina had shown its liberality in 1927 when it invited James Weldon Johnson to hold seminars for a week on the sociological and artistic phases of Negro life. In *Along This Way*, Johnson says, "I believe this invitation was unprecedented. . . . As I faced those groups of southern white young men, I felt a greater desire to win them over than I had felt with any other group I had ever talked to; and to win them over by the honest truth. I was not sure that I could do it but I think, to a good extent, I did." He was remembered in the college.

One other trip, in 1933, is of interest. While at Tougaloo, Mississippi, one of the teachers invited me to drive with her to the Women's College Club at Jackson. That a white teacher at Tougaloo should be a member of such a Club was certainly an advance over the treatment that I had seen awarded Atlanta teachers. The president of the College Club was very gracious, and invited me to speak to them on the Negro. All but one of my small audience was attentive, and more than one was sympathetic. Women's organizations on the whole are more democratic on the race question than men's. For one thing, they are not so politically minded and, once convinced of the evil in discrimination, they are more courageous.

From Tougaloo, I went to Alabama where I stopped in Athens at Miss Allyn's excellent school, now taken over by the state. I wanted to meet Miss Allyn, and also to see my young friend, Beth Torrey, a teacher at the school. Born in northern Georgia, Beth had taught at Mrs. Hayford's school in Sierra Leone, and later was to go to the Missao di Dondi, Portuguese West Africa. Like many Southerners, she had an affection for the Negroes, but she was unusual in that this did not decrease when they ceased to be domestic servants. We were wholly in sympathy and we talked and talked and talked. We spoke the same language and we never got tired.

"But you're going to the Scottsboro trial," Beth said.

Athens was only a few miles from Decatur, where the Scottsboro boys were being tried for the second time on a charge of rape. The International Labor Defense Committee of the Communist party was handling the case for the defendants and securing world-wide publicity. The mother of one of the defendants had even been taken to Europe, where she told of the injustice perpetrated on her son. Of course, Beth assumed, I intended to go.

But I was strangely reluctant. Convinced that the charge was a frame-up, I did not want to hear the trial. I said nothing of the sort to Beth, however, and assured her that I would attend court the next morning if she could get me a driver. She secured the local colored undertaker, a man much respected, and the next day I drove with him to Decatur.

The Scottsboro Case was already two years old. The theme of the story was familiar though the setting might be new. It concerned the white's recourse to his prejudice against the Negro to conceal his own crimes. Eight colored boys, poor, without influential friends, were on trial charged with raping two white prostitutes, one of them with a criminal record.

The boys had been stealing a ride on a freight train out of Chattanooga, and their first and real offense was getting into a fight with four white boys who were doing the same thing. The Negroes won and threw three of the four whites off the train. The fourth, who remained, testified later in favor of the women. When the train drew into Paint Rock station, a crowd had gathered to revenge the whites who had telegraphed their story of the fight down the line.

On the same train, dressed in rough overalls, were two white women, also hoboing their way. When Paint Rock was reached they tried to get off unnoticed, for they feared the police. The crowd made this impossible and for their own protection they declared that the Negroes had raped them, thus changing their status from prostitutes to that of somewhat dubious heroines. They were examined soon after they brought these charges by two competent physicians whose reports contradicted their statements. The alleged rape was supposed to have happened in the middle of the day though no one, watching the train go by, had seen anything unusual.

The trial I attended was the second for the Scottsboro boys. The first, sentencing them to death, had been declared unconstitutional by the Supreme Court of the United States on the ground of lack of counsel. This second trial was drawing to a close. There had been much evidence regarding the women's physical condition, and I wondered what to expect when I drew up to the courthouse. I was completely pessimistic. No criminal lawyer, however brilliant his former record, could persuade a southern jury to render a verdict that practically said a white woman was lying and colored boys were telling the truth. Why, these were "damned niggers!" Hadn't they thrown white boys off the train?

My driver drew up to the courthouse entrance and we both went inside. People were rushing back and forth, and I soon saw that my chance of getting into the court was small. The officials I saw were courteous but they did not help me. I wanted a seat at a reporter's table as representing *The Crisis*. Nobody knew what I was talking about, and nobody bothered.

After some minutes I returned to the entrance hall much discouraged, and looked for my driver. I saw him talking to a white man who almost immediately came up to me and said, "Isn't this Miss Mary White Ovington? I am Eleazer of the Atlanta Race Commission. We met at Atlanta." He drew me into the hall and up to a reporter's table.

When I went back to speak with my driver about the return trip, I asked him if he knew Mr. Eleazer. "No, ma'am," he answered. "But I thought you wasn't getting anywhere, and I looked about till I found the right gentleman. I could tell you was getting nowhere," he said a little apologetically.

The courtroom was small, and every visitor's seat was taken and had been since early morning. It was a silent audience. There was no need to call for order, so anxious was everyone to keep his or her seat.

One thing struck me as unusual. The twelve men of the jury sat in front of these listeners on the front two benches. I could study their faces but saw nothing unusual about them. They were from the far South and perhaps showed less intermixture of race than would a northern jury. They were attentive, sober citizens.

In front of the jurors were the lawyers for the prosecution and the defense. The most striking-looking was Samuel Liebowitz, lawyer for the boys, whose New York office overflowed with pictures of young boys accused of murder, whom he had saved from the electric chair. Opposite him were two lawyers for the prosecution, one with a keen look that might well be disturbing to the defendant, Patterson.

Heywood Patterson, whose trial determined not only his fate but that of his companions, certainly needed his able lawyer. There was little in his appearance to plead for him. Two years of imprisonment had taken all expression from his face. His eyes were bleared as if from lack of sleep. Occasionally I thought I saw a look of defiance and I knew that he was said to have struck his guard. He was handcuffed to a guard now.

Then Judge Horton entered and the trial began. Judge Horton lived in Athens. I had already heard much about him, and had met his wife. His conduct of the trial had made him hated by many, and Mrs. Horton knew that his life was in danger. "I am afraid for him whether he is away or at home," she had said. But his quiet manner showed no nervousness. He made me think of the judge I had seen at Double Springs. The word democracy has become hackneyed but these two lawyers gave it new life. When Judge Horton opened the court, it might have been Lincoln rising from his great chair at Washington.

I had been listening only a few minutes when I realized that, had I been able to choose my day, I could hardly have selected one more dramatic, for the defense was putting two important witnesses on the stand.

The first of these was Lester Carter, one of the boys whom the Negroes had thrown off the train. Dressed in a new, well-fitting suit, he made a favorable impression, and seemed sincere in what he said. He had continued hoboing after his fight on the train, and wherever he found listeners, and they were not difficult to find, he talked about the Scottsboro boys. They were not guilty, he felt sure of that. His conscience troubled him and at length, at the urgent entreaty of one of his traveling companions, he decided to go to New York and tell his story to the Defense Committee.

Carter was a long time getting to New York. Hoboes have to work intermittently. But finally he reached the city and talked with the Defense Committee who saw the value of his testimony. And now, two years after his famous train ride, he was on the witness chair giving testimony that the press would send over the world. It was a big moment but he talked as naturally, with as little nervousness, as though in overalls on the freight train, hoboing again.

His testimony concerned the character of the two women, Victoria Price and Ruby Bates, and their conduct the night before the train ride. Ruby Bates was his girl and Victoria Price belonged to Gilley, the boy left on the train when it reached Paint Rock. The night before they boarded the freight train, he with Ruby, Gilley with Victoria, practiced sexual intercourse, wandered about for a time, and then lay down together again.

At one point in the evidence Gilley's wife was mentioned. She worked every day in the mill and was tired. She was always tired, Carter said, and never went out at all.

For a moment Judge Horton, the lawyers, Heywood Patterson, Lester, all disappeared and I was at Greenpoint, talking to a factory girl who was getting a bad name. "Why aren't you at the gymnasium class tonight?" I asked.

"Stuffy old hole," she sneered. "I bin sweatin' in the jute mill all day—me for the Avenue." And she ran down the

236 The Walls Came Tumbling Down

street to a boy friend who also scorned the mild activities of the settlement.

The noon recess came and went. Few of the audience left their seats, certainly few of the Negroes, fearful that they might lose them. One felt the tension. The first trial had been mob-ridden; this was as orderly as a High Church service.

Once the silence was broken, the second witness for the defense quietly walked down the aisle. "It's Ruby Bates!" Ruby Bates, too, had come back and that afternoon was to deny her former testimony. She was a pretty girl, and her new dress and new spring hat gave her quite an air. Her life had not yet coarsened her. Victoria Price who later appeared to contradict Ruby's new story, seemed hardened, but Ruby looked attractive. She was self-possessed, enjoying her notoriety.

The story she told contradicted her former testimony. The boys had not attacked her, as she had said when in court before. That was the feature of the afternoon's testimony, and it did not carry conviction as had Lester Carter's story. It did not help Heywood Patterson who sat chained to his guard. But Ruby Bates looked triumphant as later she stood in the aisle with Lester Carter and posed for the press. The case was lost.

The court adjourned. I said good-bye to Mr. Eleazer whom I was to meet again in 1944 in Nashville, and to find as deeply concerned as ever in the Negro problem. My driver, to whom I owed my day, took me back to Athens.

The most laborious and long drawn out work of Johnson's secretaryship was the campaign to pass the Dyer Anti-Lynching Bill. For two years, when Congress was in session, our secretary spent his time in Washington. He laid the ground-work for the Costigan-Wagner Bill to be described later. He carried on this first battle quietly but with unwearying determination. Our Bill had been drawn by Moorfield Storey in consultation with other eminent counsel. It made lynching a federal offense and provided certain penalties. Introduced into the House by Congressman Dyer, it was passed in 1922 by a vote of 230 to 119.

A wave of thanksgiving, religious in its intensity, swept the colored people of the country. "I was exceedingly happy," wrote Johnson, "but I realized that the fight in the Senate would be harder; and without pausing I started on this second part of my task." In this second fight he failed. The Republicans had a clear majority, but they put a man unskilled in parliamentary tactics in charge of the bill and leaned back to see it maneuvered out of place and finally out of existence. A few senators tried to get the bill passed, but the many did not mean to make themselves unpopular with their southern colleagues. Why create antagonism? Would they not later need some favor for themselves?

During those years of lobbying in Washington, Johnson was in touch with every member of the Senate whom he felt he could possibly interest. Whether they wished to or not, senators were forced to learn the facts about lynching. Johnson made good friends for the Association and he educated the Senate. He understood the intricacies of Senate rules and the ways in which they were evaded. Most senators are lawyers and, advised by Borah, they refused to back our bill declaring it unconstitutional, although the Supreme Court was created to interpret the law. Johnson found that many good bills were lost for lack of a quorum. Men looked after their own interests and in the interim went junketing or stayed at home. The business of lawmaking was seriously handicapped by the absence of the legislators duly elected.

Last, he saw the end of undisputed Negro loyalty to the Republican party. Gratitude for the past was secure, but Republican legislators, henceforth, were to be judged by their actions in the present. No gesture of friendship would suffice. The bill had been introduced, but the ablest men of the party had not intended to bestir themselves to see it pass. Very well! Henceforth the Negro would reward his friends and turn his back on those who had nothing to offer but soft words.

My life was enriched at this time by the acquisition of a house and four acres of land in the Berkshires. I would never have thought of having a country home near New York had it not been for the Cleveland conference. That strenuous week of morning, afternoon, and evening sessions left me breathless and very tired. It was the end of June, and the second week in July, I had an engagement to speak at Zanesville, Ohio. To return to New York would have been foolishly tiring and expensive, so I planned to go to some hotel in the country for the time between the two meetings. But when I began to write to recommended hotels, everything was booked for over the Fourth. I was beginning to wonder whether I would have to stay in the city when Helen Chesnutt, daughter of Charles W. Chesnutt, the Negro novelist, heard of my plight. She invited me out motoring one afternoon, and I left the conference to go twenty miles to a little cottage of hers. With three other Smith College girls, she had bought a bit of woodland at the very end of the formation that runs on through New York State, Watkins Glen being its most famous feature. The cottage consisted of a central room surrounded by porch. I could almost sleep out-of-doors. The place was completely furnished with even an excellent little library. I could eat what I wanted and when I wanted, and with new books and bird-glasses, I should be blissfully occupied. So, the conference over, I moved in. Two or three times Helen Chesnutt came out to see that I was supplied with necessities and to take me on a drive through the quiet country. Otherwise I was alone. Each morning I used to say with Richard Jeffries in *The Story of My Heart,* "Now is eternity." I tried to hold my thoughts within the week's boundary of time and space. Eternity ended, I felt rested and serene and ought to have made a good speech at Zanesville though I don't know that serenity is a quality usually called for in an NAACP speech.

It was the recollection of this lovely week that made me listen the next winter when a Civic Club member told of her little home at Alford in the Berkshires. She wanted to sell and, though she admitted that her house was only a barn, she had four beautiful acres of land with a terrace that dropped to the Green River of which William Cullen Bryant had written. It could all be bought for $650.

I went to see it in May. The apple trees were in blossom and the long meadow was edged with willow and black alder through which you could see the stream. A soft haze was over everything. The river had a fine swimming hole and rippled over the stones, singing in praise of the place. I bought it, though the barn would need a great deal of work done to make it into my needed three rooms, and the land abounded in burdocks. I named it "Riverbank" after Ratty's home in Kenneth Graham's *Wind in the Willows*. The place was mine for twenty years.

It was sparsely settled country. Formerly the stream had been dammed in half a dozen places, but only the swimming holes marked where the dams and small mills had been. Men had settled first on the ridges but soon had come into the valleys, leaving the hill slopes to weeds and sparse timber. Dairy farming was now the chief pursuit. My neighbors went to the town meeting in Alford, but I never mentioned that village in giving directions since I was three miles west of it on the Chatham road. Our most spacious house was owned by Laura Williams Millard, a descendant of one of the original settlers, the cousin of William Williams who signed the Declaration of Independence. In her front bedroom seven generations had been born. The other near neighbors were Swiss-Italian, from the lake country, Delleas, who were invited to come to America to revive the obsolete industry of charcoal-burning.

Great Barrington was our nearest town, seven miles away. Here Burghardt Du Bois was born. Laura Millard had been to school with him and remembered him well. "And if you ask me," she said one day, "Will Du Bois is the most distinguished citizen Great Barrington has ever produced."

Helen Chesnutt's hospitality had entered into my buying Riverbank and I meant to emulate her if I could. I had two young persons in mind who greatly needed a vacation in the country, and I planned that they should spend it in my new home while I went with my mother to Maine. They were Eunice Hunton who had just taken her M.A. degree at Smith in four years, and Augusta Bird, one of the stenographers at the NAACP. (They are now Mrs. Lisle Carter and

Mrs. Roger Courtney.) Would they be happy here alone? Would my neighbors accept them?

To the honor of New England I can say that no one was unkind. Mrs. Millard's daughter, Josephine, went out of her way to be a good companion, and took the girls on their errands and for many pleasant drives. My neighbors were busy people who kept much to themselves. If at any time there was antagonism it came not from country but from city-bred persons.

Some of our office force saw the Berkshires first at Riverbank. I have spoken of Walter White and his wife. Robert Bagnall and his wife spent two weeks there, and Herbert Seligmann, our only white salaried worker, came with his bride. Seligmann painted the first of seven panels that were to make my walls gay and decorative. Much later another panel was painted by Laura Wheeler Waring, a clump of "phlox from a garden in Tyringham." Richetta Randolph also visited me.

Max Yergan, of the African Council, now president of the Negro Congress, used to stop at Riverbank on his way to Vermont. Du Bois came with the Spingarns, two hours late for tea. They had an all-time record of two punctures coming over, and a third on their return. I rented the place for short periods to Brenda Moryck. Before electricity came to our street, you had to be a good sport and accept cold baths, no plumbing but a pump, and candle and lamp light—much more beautiful than the later utilitarian electric bulb. Only in the last years did I have as comfortable a home as Helen Chesnutt's.

The second year I rented Riverbank to James Weldon Johnson, and he and his wife liked it so much that later they bought a neglected barn by the Alford River and created "Five Acres," one of the prettiest places for miles around. When the rambler rose bloomed on the low white picket fence, drivers slowed their automobiles and some stopped to get a better view of the flowers and the low, white cottage that housed hundreds of books, and of a dark poet who wrote some of them, and who could sometimes be seen on the lawn with his beautiful and gracious wife. A stone's throw away, John B. Nail remodeled an old cottage into an attractive place with an orchard the robins claimed as their own. I rejoice that the southern Berkshires hold a few such men and women and that I had a little to do with their presence there.

If the Ku Klux should come and burn its fiery cross on one of the surrounding hills, would tolerance disappear and persecution take its place? Hate is a form of egotism and easy to produce, but I am sure the Ku Klux would have a run for their money. Some of the colored residents have a firm place in the affections of their neighbors, a place that cannot be destroyed by the preaching of prejudice.

I had to sell Riverbank in 1940.

In the summer of 1939, at about noon, I had a telephone call. I took up the phone, said "hello" casually, and learned that James Weldon Johnson had been killed instantly, and his wife badly hurt while crossing the railroad track at Wiscasset, Maine.

After supper was the time they used to visit me. Grace parked in a special place, and she would send Jim ahead. He would walk down the little path by my home, turn the corner, and stand smiling in the doorway. I often see him there. He is my picture of what a man should be, of what men might be if the world wanted such men. Courteous, never boastful, he studied the right and wrong of a human situation and was ready to listen to others. Our country needs his kind, both in our councils at home and abroad. He could do what our scientists say men must do or perish—look with clarity and reason at the problem of human relationship. And this man was the product of the blending of two dissimilar strains among the races of men.

CHAPTER VII

WALTER WHITE
1931–
We Meet the World

DEPRESSION follows a period of prosperity in America as surely as winter follows summer, but we always look upon it with surprise. "And the awful thing is," my father once said to me in a rare burst of emotion, "that when hard times come you have to economize on labor. You must pay your taxes and your insurance; you have to meet the bills for your stock, but you can get along with fewer employees. And you discharge men." I don't remember how he ended, but I saw this in one of his old letters to his wife: "I wasn't meant for business, I worry too much."

Worry over money was the first of the many things that our new secretary encountered in his new office. He attacked it valiantly, urging on the branches and securing large individual contributions. After 1933 our budget expanded again.

I have said that in the beginning we divided the field of advancement with the Urban League, they taking the work of securing employment. But when employment became a national problem, when the Government became an employer, we entered the picture. Increasingly, the National Government was undertaking extensive public works. The

Negro should have the same opportunity as the white man; should be employed at any work he was able to do, skilled or unskilled; should be given equal accommodations and an equal wage. We started our campaign on the Mississippi.

In 1927, the Mississippi had the most terrible flood in its history, and it had had terrible floods. Disaster visited many sections, but the loss was at its greatest over the flat bottom lands in Arkansas, Mississippi, and Louisiana. This was where the sharecropper lived, poverty-stricken, without schooling, held to the land for debt. The Elaine Riots had taught us a good deal. We turned at once to see how, the flood receding, the Negro world fared under Flood Control. For the National Government had decided that it must take over the control of the Mississippi from Minnesota to New Orleans. It appropriated $325,000 and began work before the Red Cross had completed its appropriation for relief.

From the first, the Association received word of discrimination against the Negro worker. The work, although under the Government, was handled by contractors from different parts of the country and by overseers who were Southerners, many from the near-by neighborhood, men who had always looked upon Negro labor as cheaper and deserving of less consideration than white. These men engaged the workers, assigned living quarters, set up commissaries, and in general ran the camps. Had this been private work, the Association could have done little or nothing, but it was Government work, under the Government War Department, paid for with the people's money. It was then possible to challenge conditions.

Before we investigated, facts had been collected by the American Federation of Labor. Two organizers had been sent to the bottom lands and had brought back a story of discrimination in wages, in living quarters, and of cruelty against black men and women. This report was suppressed, and one of the two investigators was dismissed from his organization job. Their report being unavailable, Walter White went first to look over the field, and on his return, the board voted to send a young white college woman, Helen Boardman, to investigate the camps, learn what she could, and report to us. She returned with a sorry story. She found, first: that colored American citizens employed by funds of the United States Government received an average wage of ten cents an hour; that they were worked, with a very few exceptions, twelve hours a day, seven days a week, with no holidays, no pay for overtime despite the fact that the projects were from six weeks to six months ahead of schedule; that a commissary system was in effect in most of the camps and that Negroes were forced to pay out from 50 to 70 per cent of their wages in commissary charges—they had even been charged for water. She also reported that the attitude of the overseers toward their labor was reminiscent of slavery days, with beatings and other cruelty, and that the sanitary conditions were very bad, the colored workers being crowded into floorless tents, without the decencies of life. Disease was rampant.

This report was at once sent to the President who sent it to the Secretary of War. A second investigation was next made in the winter by two men, Roy Wilkins, our able associate secretary and *Crisis* editor, and George Schuyler of the Pittsburgh *Courier,* who for some time did research work for us.

The report of these men confirmed that of Helen Boardman. They went prepared to act as day laborers, getting jobs where they could, and learning the facts of work from their own experiences. They made their headquarters in Memphis with Robert Church. Church looked his visitors over when they appeared in their working clothes, overalls, heavy jackets and rough caps. "You don't look much like the NAACP folk from New York who come down to ask us for money," he said. Duly impressed with the success of their disguise, the two men went out to search for labor so that they might learn the truth of the reports that had come to them. They learned a good deal but they never found work. It was the coldest winter on record and the camps were closing down. "Can't use you," "Close next week," became familiar to them as they went, one south, one west, down the great river, which was still swollen, a rolling, swirling stream that had inundated, it was estimated, 12,000,000 acres and killed thousands of people. Signs of the flood were everywhere, especially in the mud that was now covered with six inches of snow. This might seem of small account to Roy Wilkins who came from Minneapolis, not so remote from the Mississippi's source, but to the shivering black men and women, without warm clothing, who had been sweltering in the summer heat, it was unbelievable, terrible. Along the river our men walked, or got a lift, or took a train. They investigated in and near cities and in places too small to have a name. Wherever they could, they talked with the men. What Helen Boardman had reported was reaffirmed many times. But the sharecropper did not want to quit. He was accustomed to brutality, and though ten cents an hour might be a miserable wage, it amounted to real money when the week was over, and real money was something he had very rarely handled. He could get drunk with it, or spend it visiting, or save it. He had something he had never had before.

Roy Wilkins told of the payment he made for a night's lodging and breakfast in a little cabin on the levee. One room housed the family. The mother with two daughters slept in one bed, the father and their lodger in the other. For breakfast they had coffee, biscuit, drippings. When he started to leave, Wilkins handed the woman a dollar. She smoothed it out in her hand. "This am the first whole dollar I seen in a year," she said.

The contractors varied in attitude toward their labor. One camp was known everywhere for its fair treatment. But the policy of the contractor, no matter from what part of the country he came, was to leave the management of the men to the local Southerner thus perpetuating discriminatory treatment. Neither Mississippi, Louisiana, nor Arkansas furnished much education to its black workers. They knew little of what they were doing and were interested in nothing but their immediate wants. Around Memphis and Vicksburg there was sometimes fighting, shooting. A rough lot who would shoot at the drop of a hat, Schuyler said.

George Schuyler met with an adventure. One early evening, having gone to his room in a boarding house in Vicksburg, he heard tramping on the stairs and his door was flung open by a white man. Without a word of explanation, he was handcuffed and ordered into the street where he was put into a wagon and taken to jail. When he asked on what charge he was being held, he was thoroughly damned and told to shut his mouth. At the jail, he learned the cause of his arrest. A dangerous black bandit was at large, and the police, looking for him everywhere, thought that this strangcr, who went snooping about, might be their man. "I was kept awake all night," Schuyler says, "answering questions, giving information. I told them why I was in the South, and assured them that my investigation, my effort to get more money for the Negro workers was to their advantage. 'See how your stores are closing up,' I explained. 'When the Negro gets money, he's a good spender. It's to your interest to have him receive better wages. I'm doing you a good turn if I can get the Government to put more money in his pocket.' " By morning the chief-of-police recommended his release, but the sheriff, an Erskine Caldwell sheriff with pistols bulging from his pockets, refused to let his prisoner go. That night, however, he reluctantly released Schuyler, telling him to get out of the state as fast as he could "hoof it on the highway." Schuyler left the state although he had not yet completed his investigations. In a few days, both he and Wilkins returned to New York.

In the meantime, Walter White had been busy at Washington. The then Secretary of War, Patrick J. Hurley, had challenged our investigation, and tried to whitewash the work of his department. White turned to the Senate where Senator Wagner, our tried friend, promised to push senatorial investigation on the treatment of the Negro in the Mississippi Flood Control work. President Hoover also appointed an investigating committee of four men—three of them Negroes —but as no appropriation was given the committee, it could do very little. One member, Robert R. Moton of Tuskegee, tendered a report that confirmed ours. It was not until the spring of 1933 that action came. In April the Senate began its investigations and in September a new Secretary of War, George H. Dern, announced that unskilled workers in the levee camps on the lower Mississippi, working on projects financed by the Public Works Administration in the South, would receive forty cents an hour and work a thirty-hour week. Those under working contractors would receive $14.40 for a week of 48 hours. Altogether the increase was $3.00 a week, $79,000 more for the entire area. These wages are not to be thought of in terms of today's expenditures by the Government, but rather as a step forward for the sharecropper who thus took his place in the nation's service, was paid a wage, and was protected while he earned it.

Our struggle to obtain for the Negro his share of the nation's country-wide work went on from year to year but without much success. Few men were employed at the Boulder Dam. The Tennessee Valley Authority used colored men only as unskilled labor. By constant prodding and with the help of friends in Congress, the right of the Negro to participate in defense work was not forgotten. Cultural government products—the Federal Theater, extracurricular school work—proved of much value as we saw it in New York. Canada Lee made *Stevedore* a great play, and the Lafayette in Harlem gave interesting productions of *Macbeth* and *Androcles and the Lion*. This educational and cultural work was undertaken to provide employment, and closed with the beginning of World War II.

When war was declared, the Association watched feverishly to see what would happen. The Negro was drafted in the service of his country. Would his country in turn offer employment to non-combatants in war industry, or would the old pattern continue? It did continue, and complaints poured in from all over the country. One branch after another furnished data. White men were given good jobs, Negroes unskilled jobs or none at all.

Drama entered the picture when A. Philip Randolph, president of the Sleeping Car Porters, and the most conspicuous Negro organizer in the labor world, proposed a March-on-Washington by way of protest. Thousands of Negroes were to march to the capital of the republic and demand their right to enter war industries. Walter White had the ear of the President, and had pleaded with him to give the Negro a chance in the industries. The President was aroused, and summoned White and Randolph to the White House. With the President were the secretaries of the Army and the Navy, as well as Sidney Hillman and William S. Knudsen. What did they want, the President inquired. What could the Government do? The answer was simple—the Negro worker wanted equality of opportunity with the white worker. Would Randolph call off the March-on-Washington? He agreed to do so, and the result of the conference was the issuance of Executive Order No. 8892. This order banned discrimination on account of race, creed, color, or national origin in industries holding government contracts and in training for jobs in war industry. The order set up the Committee on Fair Employment Practice, the FEPC.

The new decade had started with a battle against President Hoover and the Republican party concerning the nomination of John J. Parker of North Carolina to a vacancy on the Supreme Court of the United States. In 1928, the country had gone Republican and Hoover had carried the State of North Carolina. Party politics demanded recognition of this remarkable vote, and a Supreme Court judgeship was chosen as a noble reward. Parker was not a national figure, but he was a good lawyer and a good Republican. His name was sent to the Senate for confirmation.

The Association at once looked up Parker's record. It found that when running for Governor on the Republican ticket in 1920, he had approved the literacy test for voters, and had also approved the Grandfather Clause, which gave the vote to illiterates whose grandfathers had voted in 1866 —a clause which the Supreme Court declared unconstitutional in 1915. This had been Parker's stand ten years earlier. How did he feel now? Did he or did he not stand by this statement? The Association sent the judge a letter asking him just this. It was received but not answered.

Then a campaign began against his nomination. James Weldon Johnson, who was leaving the Association shortly to take a chair in creative literature at Fisk, was at the Institute of Pacific Relations, and the leadership of the NAACP fell on the acting secretary, Walter White. White began with a request to the President that he withdraw the nomination because of Parker's attitude on Negroes' rights. This only stiffened the President's determination to have his candidate accepted.

Next the Judiciary Committee of the Senate to which the nomination was referred, received our formal protest. Other forces were against Parker, notably organized labor, and since the Negroes' protest was considered unimportant, it was the last to be placed before the committee. But while other protestors were less vehement in their opposition, the Negro protest grew stronger. The branches, well-organized, thoroughly familiar with our work, knew what they were to do and did it faithfully, day after day. In an article in

Harper's, January 1931, Walter White says, "Negro protests began to pour into Washington in a steadily mounting
volume. Telegrams, long-distance telephone calls, letters,
petitions, and personal visits impressed upon Senators, particularly from northern and border states where the Negro
vote is potent, that their Negro constituents were very much
in earnest. . . . A few Senators were frankly skeptical of the
protests, believing that they were ephemeral and would soon
die down. Others resented the protests, being somewhat bewildered by the spectacle of the Negro stepping out of his
traditional role of a meek, uncomplaining creature who sub-
mitted without question to whatever was put upon him.
Others were alarmed at the extent of the movement and
apprehensively thought of approaching elections. Soon they
were beseeching the White House to withdraw the nomination of Judge Parker, and save them from the dilemma of
voting either against the Administration or against the wishes
of their constituents. To such requests the White House
turned a deaf ear."

It was a thrilling battle. Walter White's driving force, his
abiding belief in victory, brought him many influential allies
who at first were half indifferent, half amused. Newspaper
men in Washington put him at the end of their lines, giving
him the latest news. The enemy varied their tactics. They
denied the validity of the statement imputed to Parker.
Within twenty-four hours, photostatic copies of the ten-year-
old clipping were in the hands of the senators and the president. Sectional appeal was used on Democratic senators, but
the Association then whispered with good effect, "Do you
want to reward North Carolina for going Republican?" The
North Carolina Negroes were approached by the Republi-

cans, and persuasion and veiled threats employed to win their endorsement of Parker. In this the enemy was routed. Almost without exception the North Carolina Negroes took the Association's side. Those few who supported the Party had positions dependent upon politics for their continuance. "Only one Negro of standing," Walter White wrote, "gave active support to Parker, and his action brought down upon his head unequivocal condemnation from Negroes of all classes." White went on to tell of 188 prominent men and women who braved the white politicians and signed affidavits to Washington registering their opposition to the confirmation of Parker for the Supreme Court.

Delay was the next tactic. It was answered by mass-meetings. J. E. Spingarn, who had always favored political pressure, made one of his greatest speeches. Herbert Seligmann's publicity was magnificent. In the office we felt that the Negro world was back of us. Not only branch members but church members by the hundred, fraternal organizations, doctors, lawyers, teachers, elevator boys were telling their Senators not to ratify Parker's appointment.

At length, on April 21, the sub-committee of the judiciary to which the nomination had been referred reported ten to six against confirmation. That should have settled the matter, but the President tried to force the nomination through the Senate. The Association kept up its barrage, and the Negro press, a tower of strength from the beginning, wrote editorials calling for more action. Telegrams heaped higher and higher on Senators' tables. Admittedly the Negro had come back into politics, an independent no longer to be counted upon by the Republican party to do its bidding. The vote came at last. Visitors crowded the Senate chamber. Sixteen Senators

were paired. Of those voting, 39 voted for the acceptance of
John J. Parker's name, 41 against it. The nomination was
defeated.

Du Bois wrote in *The Crisis*, "The campaigning was con-
ducted with a snap, determination, and intelligence never
surpassed in colored America and very seldom in white."
In another part of his magazine he printed some fifty opinions of various papers of prominence in the United States,
north, south, east, and west. They are still interesting reading and vary from warm recommendation by the Springfield
Republican, to the implication by the New York *Times* that
there was something shameful in a United States Senator
allowing himself to be influenced by the threat of the Negro
vote. Reading them now, I find that surprise, varying from
mild to furious, was the dominating note. The *Christian
Science Monitor* called the Senate vote "the first national
demonstration of the Negro's power since Reconstruction
days."

During the campaign I had an amusing minute, when I
received a telephone call from a person named Mabel Wille-
brandt. At the moment, I did not remember that she was
an assistant attorney-general in charge of prohibition, but if
I did not place her at once, she certainly did not place me.
"Will you not use your influence in support of Judge
Parker?" she asked. I struggled to make clear my position
as chairman of the NAACP board. When I did, she hung
up, but the joke was on her. We took heart at the office. Our
opponents were certainly hard put to it when they called on
the NAACP chairman to support Parker.

The day following the Senate vote, the Association sent
out a press release to colored editors assuring them that the

defeat of Parker was only a beginning. Election Day was coming!

Then came the rewarding of friends—Capper of Kansas and Wagner of New York, the only Senator who had made Parker's denial of the ballot to the Negro a part of his argument. Second came the defeat of our enemies. Seven northern Senators who had voted for Parker came up for re-election in the autumn. Of these, six were Republicans, one a Democrat. The Association decided to center its work on the defeat of Henry J. Allen of Kansas and of Roscoe C. McCulloch of Ohio.

The Republican party machine has always been powerful in Ohio and very active at the capital, Columbus. The president of the Columbus branch and head of the Ohio conference of branches was C. E. Dickinson who worked unsparingly. The Republican party in Ohio had taken the Negro vote for granted, but now they learned its new independence.

As the campaign went on, McCulloch's chance began to look doubtful, and his Democratic opponent, Robert J. Bulkley, asked for a conference with our secretary. They met in Cleveland on September 20, and Bulkley proposed making a statement as to his attitude on the race question. He also expressed his readiness to answer questions. Later Dickinson issued a challenge to McCulloch to debate with Walter White on the subject of the Senator's vote to seat Parker. This challenge received wide publicity, and when it was turned down, Dickinson prophesied a Republican defeat.

A vigorous campaign was carried on in Kansas, as well as Ohio, and in the end McCulloch and Allen were both defeated by a substantial margin. The Negro vote alone did not do it, but from a study of the city vote, it was evident that the Republicans had lost heavily in certain Negro wards. In Toledo's Negro districts, the Democrat, Bulkley, polled more than three times as many votes as the Republican, Mc-Culloch. There were dramatic changes in Kansas, and a prominent newspaper man of the state telegraphed the Association, "Undoubtedly Allen would have won had he had every Negro vote as in previous years."

The name that Hoover next sent to the Senate to fill the vacancy in the Supreme Court was Owen J. Roberts of Philadelphia, a liberal on the race question and for many years a trustee of Lincoln University, Pennsylvania.

From January 1934, for six years, the Association made the passage of an Anti-Lynching Bill by Congress the first order of business. Since the post card which John Haynes Holmes received in 1911, showing a group of lynchers standing back of their victim, we had been publicizing this form of mob violence. Not only had we printed *Thirty Years of Lynching in the United States,* but we had secured a strong statement from President Wilson against lynching, and Franklin D. Roosevelt in 1933, at a conference of the Churches of Christ in America, had said over a nation-wide network, "Lynch law is murder, a deliberate and definite disobedience of the high command, 'Thou shalt not kill.' We do not excuse those in high places or low who condone lynch law." Under the secretaryship of James Weldon Johnson, we had tried for two years to pass the Dyer Anti-Lynching Bill. Now we were to enter upon a second battle for legislative action backed by a larger membership and led by a young secretary to whom this fight against mob violence, against injustice, humiliation, torture, had become a second duty.

"It's been dull here lately," a southern white man says, "we'll have to go out and lynch a nigger." Dr. Waller quoted this to me as overheard more than once by colored servants. I heard it quoted by one of my white New York friends whose work early in the century took him and his bride to Arkansas. It was said at a boarding-house table where he had dined for months and where he was introducing his young wife. "It's dull here," one of the diners said. "We must lynch a nigger." The husband let the words go by, but his wife turned on the speaker and poured out her anger at such inhuman talk. When the two went down to the next meal, they found the door locked.

It was this combination of cruelty and contempt that made the anti-lynching campaign a paramount issue. We had told the facts; now we demanded action. "Gentlemen," Walter White said before a Senate committee, "I have been talking recently with three eminent European scientists newly arrived in the United States. 'What is the first thing you remember hearing about in the United States?' I asked them. They all answered, 'Lynching!'" The Association made the decision that lynching must stop and that this could be done only by national legislation. Consequently a Bill was introduced in the Senate in 1934, drawn up by the Association's Legal Committee in consultation with a number of eminent Constitutional lawyers. It was revised from time to time, but without affecting its three basic provisions. These were:

First, that a lynching case should be tried in a Federal Court if after thirty days the state had taken no action to apprehend and punish the lyncher.

Walter White   259

Second, that if this Federal Court found that the Peace Officers of the state had been derelict in their duties, failing to protect their prisoners, such Officers should be punished by fine or imprisonment.

Third, that damages of not less than $2,000 and not more than $10,000 might be sought in action in the Federal Court, on behalf of the heirs of the victim, against the county in which the lynching occurred.

The NAACP Bill, with these three major points, was introduced by Senators Wagner of New York and Costigan of Colorado, both Democrats, and referred to the Senate Judiciary Committee. It was given a hearing in February at which nearly half of the fifty persons testifying were white Southerners. Its most dramatic moment was when Attorney General Preston Lane of Maryland testified to his inability to secure action against persons whom state investigators declared members of a mob that lynched a Negro, George Atwood. This was a particularly lurid and cruel exhibition of mob violence that lasted about an hour. No one could be found who participated in it although the crowd was roughly estimated at a thousand, and although the Governor sharply rebuked the local authorities. This case showed the imperative need of a change of venue. No one wants to testify against his neighbor, not so much because of affection as of fear.

Only someone who, like Walter White, has worked untiringly for the passage of a bill in Congress, can realize the many ways of allowing it to die. The public knows of the filibuster, but that is the last resort. All along the way, that ends with the President's signature, means are provided for getting rid of any needed but controversial legislation. Despite the prestige of its sponsors, our Bill did not come before the Senate until April 9, 1935. Among the first to debate it was Senator Smith of North Carolina, who gave the old, old argument that Negroes must be lynched in order to protect southern womanhood from brutes. But on the desk of every Senator was our literature showing that only 20 per cent of lynchings were for rape—or rather for the charge of rape; that fifty women had been lynched, and that charges ran from murder to "talking back."

The debate was extended and bitter. Those speaking for the Bill were Senators Costigan of Colorado, Capper of Kansas, Wagner of New York, Clark of Missouri, and Barbour of New Jersey. The opposition was led by Senators Black of Alabama, Connally of Texas, Borah of Idaho, and Smith of South Carolina. The opposition was determined not to let the Bill come to a vote. Senator Joseph T. Robinson of Arkansas moved for adjournment, but the vote was lost 34 to 33. Again, April 27 and 29, votes for adjournment were lost, but after a filibuster, on May 1 the motion to adjourn was carried, though not until the Southern Commission on Interracial Cooperation of Georgia had sent its endorsement of the measure. It was heartening that at one time or another, three southern Senators, Bachman of Tennessee and Logan and Barclay of Kentucky, voted against adjournment.

Effort might have been expected to cease at this point, but to the Association and to its secretary, this was only a first step. Strong support was next given to a resolution introduced by Senator Van Nuys of Indiana to investigate the fourteen lynchings that occurred between May 1935, and the end of the year. During the early part of the year, before the Bill's defeat, five lynchings had occurred. Afterward, however, when the potential lynchers found that federal intervention had been defeated, the number rose to fourteen, almost three times as many during the first five months. It was these fourteen lynchings—still recent in men's minds—that Senator Van Nuys proposed to investigate. Moreover, President Roosevelt had at one time expressed his approval of a lynching investigation.

The resolution carried with it an appropriation of $7,500. The Audit and Control Committee consisted of Senator Tydings of Maryland, Townsend of Delaware, Bachman of Tennessee, and Byrnes of South Carolina. Its chairman, Senator Byrnes, never called his committee together though a number of members of the Senate urged him to do so. So senatorial investigation proved impossible.

It was deemed wisest to have the Bill next introduced in the House and by Representative Joseph A. Gavagan of New York. It was promptly referred to the Judiciary Committee whose chairman was Hatton W. Sumners of Texas. He refused to hold any hearings or to take the Bill out of committee.

But Congressman Gavagan was not easily discouraged. He represented the Twenty-first Congressional District of New York where many Negroes resided. Here was a chance to do a good turn by sponsoring humane legislation. He proceeded to place a petition on the speaker's desk calling for the discharge of the committee for his Bill. This petition required the signatures of 218 Representatives, a majority of the House. Representative Hatton W. Sumners of Texas, when half the signatures had been quickly obtained, introduced about the weakest of the 60 other anti-lynching bills that had been buried in committee. This bill was quickly turned down, the 218 signatures secured, and Gavagan's Bill came to the floor.

The House cannot filibuster, and each side was limited to six hours' debate. Walter White wrote in his annual report, "In the beginning the Southerners kept their arguments on a relatively high plane, discussing the question of constitutionality and other matters. But as it became apparent that the Bill would pass, the speeches of the opposition became more bitter and loaded down with the usual anti-Negro sentiments. . . . Congressman Gavagan remained on the floor at the head of his supporters and engineered his Bill by brilliant parliamentary strategy. He yielded no points and permitted no amendments."

Victory was made certain when a member arose in the House and read a press dispatch that read, "At Duck Hill, Mississippi, two colored men on suspicion of having murdered a storekeeper, have been taken out of jail, chained to trees, and tortured with blow-torches. After this they were hanged." This story of immediate lawlessness had its effect. When the vote was taken, the Bill was carried 277 to 119.

In 1938, the Bill came a second time before the Senate, and the debate was bitter. Again it was filibustered out of existence. An effort was made to bring it back in 1940, but the war was too near and New Deal legislation too importunate to allow it to come to the floor. Its day was over.

This summary of unsuccessful legislation may seem uninteresting now that the subject is no longer before the public, but it served as a basis for six years of continuous and successful propaganda. In its intelligent and persistent placing of facts before the public, it vied with the Suffrage and Prohibition movements. Never for a day was the subject allowed to rest. At whatever point the Bill may have reached, someone was speaking for it; some society endorsed it; some newspaper discussed it in letter or editorial. Hundreds of organizations—religious, fraternal, philanthropic, social—men's societies and women's societies endorsed it. Metro-Goldwyn released its film, *Fury*. The Writers' League Against Lynching wrote and spoke on this shame of America. I remember an afternoon when, after reveling in an exhibition from Guatemala, gay, a riot of color, I went to a dim, quiet room to hear Pearl Buck voice her horror both at the suffering of the hunted Negro and at the indifference with which white America views it. Pearl Buck has never failed us, nor has Dorothy Canfield, who began her championship of the Negro cause almost with her first novel. A long line of authors, some of them Southerners, have told of the Negro's suffering under mob violence.

The Bill against lynching was dropped in the Senate, but not until it had united the Negroes of America. Differences were forgotten. They had a battle to fight and they were constantly informed as to the position of their friends and their enemies. They knew and rejoiced that five southern Representatives, Maury Maverick of Texas, Lyle H. Boren, R. P. Hill, Jed J. Johnson, and Jack Nichols of Oklahoma, had voted for their Bill. They knew that Senator Borah of Idaho had steadily helped defeat lynching legislation, and they used every effort to help defeat his aspirations to the presidency. Feeling was strong in Harlem when voters had to choose between Gavagan and a man of their own race, but the stern command went out to vote for Gavagan. The bottom would drop out of their political campaign if they failed to reward their friends.

Much publicity was given our work by the northern papers, especially the New York *World*, but the support that meant the most came from the South. Old and highly esteemed newspapers, the Richmond *Times Dispatch* with Virginius Dabney as its editor, the Louisville *Courier-Journal*, and the Greensboro *Daily News* openly supported the Bill. The New Orleans *Item-Tribune* was not opposed nor did the Birmingham papers show hostility. The most striking editorial of the year came from the Danville Virginia *Register* immediately following the Duck Hill lynching. Julian Harris, son of Joel Chandler Harris, and his brilliant wife, in the face of advertisers' boycotts, loss of a large percentage of readers, threats of violence, favored the Anti-Lynching Bill and fought the Ku Klux Klan when the Governor of the State was a Klansman.

Support by whites was sporadic; by Negroes it was well-nigh universal. Everywhere the Bill was endorsed and money sent to put it through. Churches, large and small, held meetings and their ministers urged their congregations to send letters to their Congressmen and money to the Association that was carrying on the fight. Doctors—the profession of physicians attracts a superior class of men—added work for the Anti-Lynching Bill to their many other tasks of healing. Lawyers worked for it; educators, businessmen. People in the poorer paid ranks of labor, housemaids, elevator boys, pushed on the battle for recognition of the Negro's right to due process of the law. Above all, the colored press was untiring. A news letter from the NAACP might arrive at what seemed an impossible time, but a box would be made and the news set in, and hang the expense! A war against lynching was on.

The law-abiding element in the South was active, and its efforts, sometimes heroic, were shown in many preventions of lynching. In one year, 1935, our annual report showed nineteen lynchings prevented. One argument used with the mobs was that, if they did not disperse, a federal anti-lynching bill would be passed that would destroy states' rights! In the last hearing before the Senate, two Southerners testified as to their knowledge of lynchings—one a research student, the second an Episcopal minister. Senator Connally of Texas, who had been demanding first-hand information, had the opportunity of hearing the clergyman tell of his hopeless efforts to stop a mob and of the two victims' hanging by clumsy and inexpert hands. That hearing is interesting for an omission. The Senator from Texas heckled the various men brought before the Committee, among them Walter White and Arthur Spingarn, but remained silent when William Hastie, a Negro, who succeeded Arthur Spingarn as head of the Association's Legal Committee, replied to questions regarding the constitutionality of the Bill. After Senator Wiley of Wisconsin and Senator Van Nuys of Indiana had put many questions and received Hastie's answers, the presiding officer asked Senator Connally if he had anything to say. Connally answered, "I have no questions."

"You have won your case," a friend told me in 1940. He was familiar with the history of lynching, and I had given him the number for 1939—two. Though this is in a large measure true, nevertheless, it rankles when, on the assumption that free speech means unlimited debate, it is possible to defeat a measure that has passed the House and has enough potential votes to pass the Senate. The filibuster means that a minority has the right to defeat the will of the majority. This rankles still more today when we are pushing forward our form of government as a model for the world. But ours *was* a victory—the greatest victory the Association had known —we united the Negroes of the United States.

The Association makes two conditions upon which it enters a case: (1) Does the case involve color discrimination? (2) Is some fundamental right of citizenship involved?

All our cases involve the right of the individual as a citizen. Sometimes they concern his protection when accused. Thus in 1936 in Mississippi, and in 1940 in Florida, decisions of the lower courts were reversed since the convictions were obtained under physical torture. Chief Justice Hughes declared, "The rack and torture chamber may not be substituted for the witness stand." A third case of this character in Oklahoma was lost since the evidence of torture did not satisfy the majority of the court. This is one of two cases that the Association has not won. The second case concerned a real estate restrictive covenant and was dismissed for want of jurisdiction.

Equal educational facilities for colored have occupied the Legal Committee. Such work is undertaken occasionally in the North in cities where segregated schools still exist, or when they appear in some new town. But the bulk of this work is in the South. As I found on my early journeys, taxes are levied on the basis of population and the money distributed on the basis of caste.

In one of its publications, the Legal Committee tells of its "fight to compel the states where segregated schools are mandatory to provide equal facilities for education. There have been many cases in state and federal courts for the purpose of equalizing educational opportunities such as equal school terms, bus transportation for pupils, high school facilities, teachers' salaries and other items." The most extensive and successful of these efforts has been the equalizing of colored teachers' salaries with white.

Our first teachers' salary case, won in 1937, was brought by William Gibbs, Jr., against the Board of Education of Montgomery County, Maryland. William Gibbs filed a petition to compel the board to establish salary schedules without regard to race. While a public school teacher, Gibbs was also acting as a principal and was paid in all $612 a year. White teachers with the same qualifications and essentially the same duties were paid $1,125 a year as teachers and $1,475 as principals. The case ended in the equalization of salaries in Montgomery County.

This differential was fairly typical of southern educational appropriations for Negroes. Primary school teachers were paid unbelievably low salaries. Naturally, the teachers generously co-operated with us. We have never estimated the total amount of money the Negro now earns in excess of his former salary, but it is in the hundreds of thousands. Some of the large southern cities, notably Birmingham, New Orleans, Columbia, South Carolina, and Richmond, have equalized salaries. Up to 1946, cases have been filed in twelve of the southern states. It is a slow process but it brings results, not only to the teachers but to the pupils from first primary to college. In the college we find teachers with degrees from our best northern universities and from Europe. This has always been true, but the numbers have enormously increased. Go to Columbia University Summer School and learn of the increase in number of colored teachers from the states in which salaries have been equalized. Visit the rural districts and notice that the primary grades, some of them at least, are taught by women familiar with modern methods, and that the children look happy, not perplexed.

A second legal battle involved the education of colored students in state graduate schools. Donald G. Murray, Amherst graduate and a resident of Baltimore, filed a petition in 1935 against the University of Maryland, a tax-supported institution, to compel its officers to consider his application as a first-year student in the Law School. The Baltimore City Court rendered a decision favorable to Murray. The University petitioned that the Negro be denied entrance to its Law School; that if he were admitted, the enrollment would fall off; that the University had white women among its students. This petition was denied, and Murray entered the Law School. He graduated in June 1938, and the Attorney General who had opposed his admission handed him his diploma. To the credit of Maryland, Negroes are attending this Law School today.

Another one of our education cases went to the United States Supreme Court, and in 1938 a decision was rendered that a Negro may not be denied admission to a state university solely because of his color. This should have settled the matter, but Negroes have not yet entered southern white state colleges except in Maryland and Missouri—and Missouri hardly belongs to the South. Instead, money is raised— an inadequate amount—to send the student to a northern college, or effort is made to give the colored man such graduate instruction as he desires in his own state institution. Recently, southern governors have met to consider the advisability of regional post-graduate schools.

The Negro's right to vote in the United States was affirmed in the Fifteenth Amendment to the Constitution. Nevertheless, after the Government withdrew its troops from the South in 1877, the colored citizen was never safe in his political rights. He was disfranchised by state laws and by terrorism. When Populism, the South's one popular movement, was merged with the Democratic party, the Solid South was again politically established. The Republican party had dwindled, and at an election the Democratic party always won.

Believing that the right to vote is fundamental to all advancement, the Association attacked the primary, for the primary, at which the candidate was really elected, was for whites only.

Dr. L. A. Nixon, a Negro of the State of Texas, attempted to vote in the Democratic primary. Though eligible in every particular except color, he was refused. No Negro, he was told, might vote in a primary in the State of Texas. Dr. Nixon filed a suit for damages. This, in 1927, came before the Supreme Court of the United States, was argued by Arthur B. Spingarn, and was won. Justice Holmes declared that "color cannot be made the basis of a statutory classification."

After this decision, the State of Texas passed a statute empowering the State Democratic Committee to set up its own limitations on voting at its primaries. The Democratic Committee did this and excluded Negroes. Dr. Nixon tried again to vote and was refused. Again the case came before the

Supreme Court, was argued by J. Alston Atkins of Houston, Texas, and again was decided in the Negro's favor. Justice Cardozo maintained that the situation was as before. This was the second Texas Primary Case, 1932.

The third case was argued in 1944 by William H. Hastie and Thurgood Marshall, the Association's special counsel. It was started by Dr. L. E. Smith in the local Federal Court in Houston. Again the case was decided in favor of the Negro. Justice Roberts declared, "The United States is a constitutional democracy. Its organic law grants to all citizens a right to participate in the choice of elected officials without restriction by any state because of race. This grant to the people of the opportunity for choice is not to be nullified by a state through casting its electoral process in a form which permits a private organization to practice racial discrimination in the election. Constitutional rights would be of little value if they could be thus indirectly denied."

This last decision seems to have been accepted by legal southern opinion, and has greatly affected Negroes in all the southern states. In primary registrations and elections of 1946, they turned out by the thousands and materially affected the results. For months before the primaries, our branches held classes in voting, and the men and women who went to the polls understood clearly what was required of them. So far as we have been able to learn, they voted for reform candidates.

The latest great legal triumph of the NAACP is the case of *Irene Morgan* v. *Commonwealth of Virginia*. It concerns bus travel, one of the most annoying forms of segregation. A statute of the State of Virginia forbade the seating of colored passengers with white. Mrs. Morgan was arrested and fined for violating this statute. The Association took the ground that the decision of the State of Virginia was unconstitutional as being violative of the Commerce Clause of the Constitution. The Supreme Court of the United States held that the Virginia statute as applied to Mrs. Morgan was a burden on Interstate Commerce and was therefore unconstitutional. This case was argued by William H. Hastie and Thurgood Marshall. Decision was handed down in June 1946. This constituted the twenty-first case before the United States Supreme Court won by the National Association for the Advancement of Colored People. An effort will at once be made by the Association to make the decision applicable to railroad travel.

The Legal Committee, headed since 1939 by William H. Hastie, is made up of many eminent lawyers of both races. Famous members have been Moorfield Storey, Clarence Darrow, Louis Marshall, Felix Frankfurter, Francis Biddle, Frank Murphy, Arthur Garfield Hays, Morris L. Ernst, and James Marshall. The conduct of the work, however, has increasingly been in the hands of our resident staff. The chairman of the Legal Committee, Arthur B. Spingarn who, until 1936 had the whole burden on his shoulders, obtained adequate assistance with the engagement of Charles H. Houston as our special counsel. Before Houston came William T. Andrews who served for a year. After two years Houston retired to take up private practice, and Thurgood Marshall succeeded him. Since Hastie's appointment to the Virgin Islands as Governor, Charles H. Houston has become chairman of the Legal Committee. Our work has grown to such proportions that the staff was enlarged, including the addition of Mrs. Marian Wynn Perry. Now in 1946, we have four salaried lawyers giving full time to legal defense and education.

To recapitulate, of the twenty-three cases that the Association has brought before the Supreme Court, all have been won but two: a restrictive covenant case where the Court refused to take jurisdiction and a criminal case involving a confession extracted by torture. Of the cases won, the most recent struck down a state law requiring the segregation of Negroes on interstate buses. Of the other twenty, five concerned voting, three segregation ordinances, one restrictive covenants, ten criminal cases, and one the equalization of educational opportunities.

This is an inadequate attempt to describe the national legal work of the Association since 1930. It doesn't include the eighteen successful extradition cases where the fugitive was held on the ground that he would not receive justice in his native state. Local cases have been won in and out of court by our branches all over the country. We believe we have gained for the Negro a greater measure of security in the United States.

After a period of preparation, in December 1941, the United States entered World War II. Negroes were drafted with white on a basis of equality in the face of danger and suffering, but not on equality of opportunity and advancement. Some signs were favorable. President Roosevelt, always ready to appoint the ablest Negro he could find, made William H. Hastie, now Governor of the Virgin Islands, a civilian aide to the Secretary of War. A second appointment was that of Benjamin O. Davis, Sr., to Brigadier General.

All officers, white and colored, were trained in the same camps, and assigned in alphabetical order to hutments and classes. This was a victory. No friction occurred, and the Army saved money. Every branch of the service was open to Negroes: Army and Navy, Aviation, Marines, Signal Corps, Coast Guard, WACS, and later WAVES. For the first time Negro nurses were used in numbers.

The Navy had been adamant in its determination to use Negroes only in the mess. With the pressure of war, it opened other forms of service, and in the Merchant Marine, "Jim Crow was dumped overboard." All of the 4,000 odd merchant vessels in the fleet of Liberty and Victory ships were manned by colored and white who slept, ate, and worked together—Americans bent on winning the war. Four of the ships had Negro captains. Credit for all this belonged to the War Shipping Administration, the ship owners, and the CIO National Maritime Union.

These welcome signs presaged no general changes in the War Department's attitude. The Army did not intend to break with the past. It trained Negro soldiers in separate camps, and failed to protect the uniform if worn by a man whose face was black. "You ought to be ashamed of yourself," a white woman said to a Negro soldier in uniform. "You should be in overalls," and spat in his face. This is not typical but what is typical is that nothing was done about it. *The Crisis* reported:

There were beatings, shootings, riots and killings all over the South where most of the Negro troops were in training. Bus drivers, civilian police, and military police had a field day beating and killing Negroes in uniform.

Negro soldiers were segregated in buses, at motion pictures, in shops, at counters in drugstores. One would suppose the Negro did not belong to the classification *homo*. The height of stupidity was reached when the Red Cross first refused blood from Negro donors, but later accepted it and segregated it. This was done although the American Medical Association and the American Association of Physical Anthropologists officially declared there was no basis for such segregation.

Early in 1943, William H. Hastie resigned his position, unable to effect any change in Army policy. His immediate complaint was the segregation in the Air Force, a procedure which ended in training less than a thousand colored aviators. The few hundred who at length reached Europe gave intelligent and daring service.

Discrimination, the too frequent treatment of the newly drafted Negro as inferior simply because of his color, was unfortunate and cruel and affected Negro morale. These young soldiers, though often ill-educated, knew the object of this war, that it was being fought to rid the world of a man who had taught his people to believe in the supremacy of a particular race—a race that of course was his own. This was Nazism. Millions of people in Germany were being killed because they were not Nazis. Some of the most distinguished men in the world were driven into exile. Others were murdered. But America was going to stop this. Negro Americans were called from their tasks to risk their lives that these outrages might cease. Then they went to their various camps to be set apart as Hitler set apart the Jews.

Under these circumstances, how well did the colored troops fight? The question was debated in Congress in June

1945. Senator Eastland of Mississippi, in a lengthy speech, enumerated his complaints against the colored soldier. From conversations with generals whom he did not name, he arrived at the conclusion that Negro soldiers were no good, that they had "not initiative, no sense of responsibility, very low intelligence, and were a failure."

He was answered by Senators Robert F. Wagner and James M. Mead of New York. Senator Wagner read into the record some of the awards given Negroes. He counted the sixty-five stars awarded the Ninety-second Division; the four Air Medals and the seven Legions of Merit. He told of favorable opinions of generals, giving their names: Generals Patton, Simpson, Clark, and last, Eisenhower. Some days later, Senator Mead spoke. He said that in 1943 he had visited practically every battlefield where our troops were. His account of the colored troops did not jibe with Senator Eastland's. He cited the Navy's high praise of the men at Pearl Harbor, and told of heroism in North Africa and Italy. These speeches were written into the *Congressional Record* of July 12, 1945

In the House, Representative Helen Gahagan Douglas of California paid her tribute to the Negro troops, those in service battalions and those in combat. It was a lengthy rebuttal of Senator Eastland's talk, later printed in a thirty-six-page pamphlet.

The Navy had held the Negro to the Mess Department, and it was significant of Negro courage that Dorrie Miller of the Mess, one of the heroes of Pearl Harbor, after dragging his wounded captain to safety, manned a gun and killed many of the enemy. Reluctantly at first, then with appreciation of their value, the Navy began to use colored men—use them and promote them.

Among the Association's early friends was the late Francis Batchelder, a public accountant who generously gave many hours to the auditing of the Association and *Crisis* books. Writing from Eniwetok Island, his son shows his father's spirit. After describing his own duties as ensign, he continues:

> Lieutenant Dennis Donald Nelson, a Negro officer, is my commanding officer. We feel that we have made history since, as far as we know, this is the first time in the history of the United States Navy that a Negro officer has commanded white officers. Mr. Nelson has several University degrees, used to teach sociology, and has written at length on that subject.

Ensign Batchelder goes on to describe his superior officer's fine presence, his manners "those of a perfect gentleman," and adds that there are about forty colored officers commissioned in the Navy.

There has been persistent criticism of the Negro infantry. Captain Wellever of the Ninety-second Division, writing in *Harpers'*, May 1945, considers the use of Negro troops a failure. He puts the blame squarely on the Army and its discriminatory policy, a policy tending to destroy qualities that a soldier needs. This is an extreme statement but one can realize the difference in the spirit of the Ninety-second Division in 1918 and in 1944. In World War I, it was integrated with the French troops under sympathetic applauding French commanders; in World War II, it was set apart, separated from the whites, and was often under commanders who did not hold his troops in respect. It was the spirit of 1918 that the Germans had to fear.

However, the Negro infantry got its chance at last. When

our troops were hard pressed by the Germans, in the spring of 1945, the United States First and Seventh Armies dropped caste and offered to train volunteers from service units. Thousands of colored men volunteered and after a short six weeks of rifle training entered the combat divisions in platoons. It was war; they were needed. They became a part of a mixed force and they did well. "The platoon quickly proved its metal as a fighting force and won enthusiastic approval from commanders and other troops," a Wisconsin Lieutenant wrote of his men; and Brigadier General Charles Lanhan said, "I have never seen any soldiers who performed better in combat than you."

And yet—a service man, talking on his return with his friends tells of the Battle of the Bulge almost with pleasure. There had been so many exciting things to do beside his regular task of driving a truckload of ammunition to the front lines. Then suddenly, "But the thing that burns me up is that when I get home to the relocation center they hand me a ticket and say, 'You colored boys go to House 25.' Then they hand the white guy with me a slip and say, 'You go over to House 26.' And to think us fellows ate together, fought together, and slept together in the same fox-hole!—What did we fight this war for anyhow?"

The war poured down work upon the Association. The Legal Department was continually concerned with soldiers' cases, sometimes of men proved innocent, sometimes of men guilty but deserving clemency. There was work to do at home and abroad. Accredited correspondent of the New York *Post*, inoculated for familiar and unfamiliar diseases, Walter White, donning the United States uniform, flew across the Atlantic. He investigated conditions in England where large numbers of colored troops were stationed. The English were friendly, but friction developed as the white American soldier created it. Negroes were liked in England as they had been in France. Walter White found the men at the top—he had a long interview with Eisenhower—opposed to race discrimination, but less important officers showed prejudice. Moreover, the Army had ordered segregation in housing and recreation. Natural contacts that would have smoothed away differences were thus tacitly forbidden. The Red Cross always had two clubhouses though at times it was needlessly expensive. If the Negro clubhouse was ready first, white soldiers might go to it and, liking it, continue to go there. For the white man North or South, in my observation, is ready to take anything from the Negro—a good meal, a concert, a play—if the Negro offers it. When it comes to reciprocating—that is another matter. The Negro soldier entering a white club would be arrested.

White heard the same old stories of insolence and buffoonery. He gathered facts for publication and then flew from England to Africa where he met Félix Eboué.

Félix Eboué was Colonial Governor of Chad, one of the five provinces of French Equatorial Africa. After the French had surrendered to Germany and the British retreated to Dunkirk, when Hitler held Scandinavia, Holland, Belgium, and much of Poland, the Vichy Government came to Eboué and demanded that he join them. Instead, Eboué threw in his lot with De Gaulle. By so doing, he kept communication open to Brazil and to the Near East. White's admiration for this African Governor was profound. Eboué was loyal to France, and he held high hopes that, the war over, the policy of the French Colonial Government might be liberalized. "It is not enough," he told White, "to put more money into the pockets of the native. We must end the robbing of the natives by big planters and companies who are determined to continue colonial exploitation." Eboué died before the war was over.

Our secretary went to Algiers and to the Italian theater of war. Here he found fraternization between Italian and Negro, and saw the colored soldier at the front. One day, with two war correspondents, one from the Pittsburgh *Courier* and the other from the Baltimore *Afro-American*, he lost his way and the three men found themselves in the thick of a battle. The Negro soldiers seemed deeply grateful that their press should have sent correspondents across the seas. But "What the hell are you doing here?" one boy asked as he came up to Walter White. "What are you doing here?" White countered. "I'm here because the Draft Board said so, but you don't have to be here." Shrapnel, bullets, hellish deafening sounds came upon them from all sides and from the skies, but they got away unharmed.

When he reached home, Walter White put his new knowledge into a book, *A Rising Wind*, and then started for the Pacific to see and to hear and to tell the world what he saw and heard.

It was then the National Association for the Advancement of Colored People became a living power of sympathy and understanding that was felt around the world. "Why, yes," one soldier would say to another. "I remember the NAACP. When I was a kid, it had drives and Mom would go out to get members and leave us with a cold dinner. But, Christ, the Association is *here!* Here on this god-forsaken island that you can't find on the map." Its secretary looked into the cruel charges of mutiny in Guam, and the men were shortly released from prison and returned to duty. He was invited by the authorities to defend a soldier who was up for trial the third time. Invited to represent a colored boy!

"For what were you court-martialed the first time?" White asked the prisoner, a fine looking youth, northern born and bred.

"I sat down in a bus on a seat that wasn't for colored."

"What happened then?"

"They arrested me and put me in solitary confinement for five days on bread and water."

"And what was the charge the second time?"

"I went into a white restaurant and asked to be served food."

"What happened then?"

"The same sentence, Sir. Solitary confinement on bread and water for five days."

He told that to Walter White, secretary of the NAACP, and Walter White told it afterward on the radio, on the Columbia Broadcasting System, told it to everybody!

In New York, memberships poured in by the thousands from overseas, memberships and contributions from whites as well as Negroes. "I am sending you one month's pay," a white soldier wrote. "I never knew such injustice existed. We didn't understand!" That was the dominant word from the whites. From the Negroes, "We want to help; we know we have a friend."

It was then that the NAACP became an international organization. At the January annual meeting, I listened as the treasurer's report was read for the year 1945. Money was coming from all over the world: from Guam to India, from India to England; from England to California. It was coming from the returned soldier and from the soldier left to sweat it out more months. From the war worker at home as well as abroad. From old friends and new. The report ended, "From all sources, memberships, contributions, subscriptions, $400,000."

Oswald Garrison Villard sat next to me. "I can't believe it," he whispered. I reminded him of the time when after he had given us our rent, I assured him we could get along upon twenty-five dollars a day! The membership secretary reported 530,000 members in regular branches, college chapters, youth councils. "And all dues-paying," the treasurer said to herself. "All able to show their receipts from the national office."

Half a million members of the National Association for the Advancement of Colored Peoplè! William English Walling ought to hear this. He would rejoice while explaining to us how it happened. Charles Edward Russell ought to hear these reports, especially the part regarding the soldier. He loved to point out the patriotism of the Negro in all our wars. Bishop Alexander Walters ought to hear it. But we are not all dead. Du Bois is here, very much alive, and sometimes John Haynes Holmes drops in to see us. Du Bois, Holmes, Villard, and myself, four of the five incorporators can answer "Present."

It is pleasant to recall the beginning of a movement, but I suspect the beginning is the easiest time. Everything is ahead, hope is high, and the problem has not yet presented its perplexities. Difficulties come with the years; but they have been overcome, and here we are, January 1946, with a comfortable balance tucked away in government bonds and savings accounts; with two floors of offices in the beautiful Wendell

Willkie Building opposite the south end of the New York Public Library. We have a board of forty trusted directors, many of them experts in legal knowledge and in experience of minority group problems. Among them is Eleanor Roosevelt. I think of her side by side with Jane Addams, once one of our board members.

Our staff numbers 60, with 25 senior and junior executives. Our Legal and Educational Committee has four salaried lawyers. We have a permanent bureau at Washington with a new secretary in charge of labor affairs and another of our veterans' bureau. Our official organ, *The Crisis*, continues to circulate widely. Our 1,100 branches meet regularly and hold occasional regional conferences, and our executive secretary, Walter White, young in thought and action, obeys Emerson's command, "Hitch your wagon to a star," and drives at the star's speed. No matter how difficult the task, he never admits the possibility of defeat.

So we move into the troubled year.

CHAPTER VIII

THE WALLS CAME TUMBLING DOWN

THIS book was interrupted by illness, and I found myself bewildered when in 1945 I resumed it. The NAACP was making history every year, and I might choose only a few important incidents. This was not easy. But when I looked over the field of Negro advancement, comparing present achievements with conditions existing at the beginning of this century, I was nonplussed. Such a recital given in detail would swamp my story, and yet a word is needed. However inadequately, I must try to point out some of the things that I see and that I read of in this new Negro world.

When at the beginning of the century I wrote of the Negro in New York, I had to hunt to find him. Today he, or rather she, is close at hand. She shops at the grocer or the drugstore where I shop. When I take a Madison Avenue bus to go downtown, about a quarter of its occupants are Negroes, and when I go to Fifth Avenue, some buses will have a larger proportion. Their errands take them where my errands take me. And why not? One out of every fifteen persons in New York is a Negro. It was one out of fifty a generation ago. Some of the people I see are on their way to work, but others find that New York gives them a superfluity which they use as white people use theirs. They buy what the newspapers and the hucksters on the radio and the shop windows invite them to buy. These shoppers come from all over greater New York. Miles of blocks in Brooklyn are occupied by them. They are in Queens and in the little towns out of Brooklyn on the Island, and many come from New Jersey.

"Never was the Negro so disliked," a New York friend tells me. "Here in this apartment where we employed Negroes, our service has changed to whites who do a little better, not much but a little. Negroes have lost their good manners and their ability to do good work."

This is a severe indictment, and sounds very familiar to an old inhabitant like myself. The loss of good manners has been said of every nationality that has come into our harbor, and while the colored man came by train, he too is a migrant. Given freedom, some greet the crowd with both elbows. I, myself, always encounter kindness. Shakily entering a bus, I am offered a seat by the young woman nearest me, whatever her color. The charge of poor work may disappear when we have a new basis for personal service.

I take the bus to the campus of Columbia University with its manifold buildings. Here I see many hundreds of colored students. Some have the accent of the South, and I notice the accent again in a white student. "I liked your paper," a small delicate-looking southern girl says to her dark-faced companion. "You see," she goes on admiringly, "you're the smartest student in the class." This same brightest scholar, I learn later, makes a point of inviting some Negro far from home to her own home in New York. "I want you to dine with my husband and me on Thursday," she says to a bronze-colored young man from Texas. He accepts with alacrity. Having heard that he did newspaper work, she asks him the name of the paper. He tells her. "Do you know," she says thoughtfully, "I thought I knew all the Texas colored papers, but I don't remember that one." "Well, you see," he answers smiling, "I'm not colored!"

On my way home, I stop at the March-on-Washington Movement Bookstore on Seventh Avenue near 125th Street. I find a large, attractive stock of books, the majority of them written by Negroes. Here are the best sellers: Richard Wright whose *Black Boy* made history, and Frank Yerby's *Foxes of Harrow*, rival of *Gone with the Wind*. Zora Hurston is here with her inimitable folklore, and Chester Hines with *If He Hollers, Let Him Go*. Many books tell instructive facts in a highly entertaining manner. Roi Ottley's *New World A-Coming* is an example. I understand that in 1946, twenty-eight publishers of good standing had Negro titles on their spring lists.

I noticed a number of magazines, some on the Negro in Africa. One magazine excellent in its physical make-up and with interesting reading is *Ebony*. It is about the size of *Life*, and its photography vies with that of the popular magazine. Here, too, I find the *Negro Digest*, in form like the *Reader's Digest*. To anyone desirous of learning about the race today, it is indispensable. Picking up a number at random, I am impressed with the sources from which the digests are made: *Metronome, The Ladies' Home Journal, Read, The Saturday Evening Post, Stage Pictorial, Commonweal, Hollywood Quarterly, Reader's Digest, Survey Graphic, Sunday Visitor.*

At the rear of the shop is the room where celebrities have been entertained, notably Ann Petry of *The Street.*

Sociological surveys of a colored quarter in town or city are now made by Negro sociologists, the best-known, Charles S. Johnson of Fisk University. I recall with amusement the days when I was invited to speak on the Negro before church and club groups. Today such groups turn to headquarters, inviting a Negro himself who presents his own sociological data.

As I leave the book shop, the Hotel Theresa with its frontage of a block stretches out before me. Until a few years ago, this two million dollar hotel accommodated only whites; then, employing a colored manager, the Hotel accepted the Negro. It has been of unspeakable benefit to the traveler, for hotels, though violating the law, still practice segregation in New York.

"You must see Lillian Smith's *Strange Fruit,*" a friend tells me. "It's a powerful play." "Don't waste your time on it," another says. "It's acted by amateurs, except for Juano Hernandez who years ago acted in Annie Nathan Meyer's exciting play, *Black Souls,* at the Provincetown Theatre." Of course I go. A play with a mixed cast on Broadway is an event in itself. I found it not as good as the book, but it tells its story and has great moments. One is when its heroine, played by Jane White, is deserted by her lover, and walks, blind and dumb, toward her cabin. Her little nephew runs to take her hand and leads her up the three steps into her home. Sometimes I wish I might forget her tragic, symbolic figure. The play has a sinister ending, the last figure on the stage an imbecile white boy.

Of course I saw *Deep Are the Roots,* our second play with

a mixed cast. Its blonde ingenue, Barbara Bel Geddes, was one of the winter's "finds." Its lover from the North does not as usually depicted change his opinions regarding the Negro when he meets his betrothed's father, a southern Senator. Rosamond Johnson said of *Deep Are the Roots*, "I could lean back comfortably, sure that the northern white man would say everything that I wanted said."

The notable play, to me, both for its acting and its text was *On Whitman Avenue*. Canada Lee of *Native Son* and Will Geer of *Tobacco Road* were the leading men and were supported by two excellent small boy actors. I was glad to see an old friend, Abbie Mitchell. Granted its premise, that in the absence of her father and mother, the daughter would rent a floor of their house to a Negro family, the play moved to an inescapable conclusion. Canada Lee said in an interview (I quote from memory) "It is the white family that is broken by the problem of segregation; the colored family remains intact."

Robeson's *Othello* was the theatrical event of the 1944-45 season. Many actors have portrayed *Othello* on Broadway. Edwin Booth played it, though he preferred Iago. Salvini was intense in his passion and hard as stone when convinced of Desdemona's guilt. I missed the Robeson performance, but learned that it was rich in beauty, a noble portraiture of Shakespeare's most tragic hero. Whenever I see or hear Robeson, I feel in the presence of a controlled, deeply sympathetic personality. The obstacle of language that holds most of us tongue-tied, he overcomes with ease. One evening I heard him sing in English, French, German, Russian, and Chinese. I wish he might represent us in Europe at the world's councils.

According to George Jean Nathan writing on the stage in *Esquire,* October 1945, "Discrimination against whites in favor of Negroes is a matter of some concern." He swings through Broadway finding Negro favorites in every form of dramatic art, singing, dancing, or acting. Frederick O'Neal was awarded the Derwent Prize for the best performance of a supporting player; Alice Childress, pitted against a host of white women, was chosen in the same category. The season of 1943-44 "exhibited all of twenty-nine plays and shows containing colored players."

Those New York visitors interested in sculpture and painting will find the Negro represented in all the galleries exhibiting contemporaneous art. Among the sculptors, Barthé still stands at the head though Selma Burke is a close second. The July 22nd issue of *Life* devoted an article to Negro art of today. Booker T. Washington's bust by Richmond Barthé now stands on its pedestal at New York University's Hall of Fame.

I think of three singers before the public today: Marian Anderson, Dorothy Maynor, and Carol Brice, the last two discovered by Koussevitzky. Marian Anderson is known throughout the world. One cannot overestimate the good will that she has brought to men through her noble voice and no less noble personality. I can best illustrate this by a story in *True Confessions.* She tells of a little girl of thirteen who waits to speak to her at the stage door. "Tell me, Miss Anderson," she says, "is there anything I can do to bring about understanding between your people and mine?"

"I was touched and thrilled," Miss Anderson says. "Ask your grade teacher in school if she will invite a Negro girl your own age to correspond with you. If each of you will tell about yourself, how you live and what your daily problems are, even if it only brings about a better understanding between you two girls, that will have accomplished something." Another girl, Phillipa Schuyler, appeared in June 1946, at the Lewisohn Stadium playing her own composition with the Philharmonic Symphony Orchestra. Two years before, this orchestra played her "Manhattan Nocturne." She is an attractive child, a genius, and a hard worker.

Carl Parish, formerly director of the department of music at Fisk University, writing in the *Saturday Review of Literature*, Jan. 26, 1946, gives an interesting account of the contribution of the Negro to music today. Among other notables, he speaks of Todd Duncan who "has recently opened the way for Negro opera singers through his several appearances in leading roles at the New York City Center." Parish, who is a white man, ends with this prediction, "There are places in our land today where nothing on earth save this force (music) alone, could bring the two races together into one mixed, unsegregated body of listeners, temporarily unmindful of the barriers that have been set up between them."

The radio for years has brought Negro music old and new to its millions of listeners. Its prize propaganda broadcast was given by Station WMCA in its program "New World A-Coming." Its many commentators from New York to Atlanta tell stories of the Negro's achievements, while they hurl their wrath against the lyncher.

Coronet, April 1946, features Louis T. Wright and the extraordinary progress made by the Negro in medicine. Dr. Wright, Harvard Medical School graduate, first won for himself the right to work at Harlem Hospital, and next, through his efforts and those of a few friends, succeeded in securing positions for Negroes on its medical staff until now one quarter of the doctors at Harlem Hospital are colored. He hates all favoritism, and demands that an applicant be chosen solely on his merits. Dr. William A. Hinton's test for syphilis is now accounted the best. Lt. Col. Poindexter of the United States Army has done outstanding work on the control of malaria. The Negro is, of course, received in all northern medical schools, and the segregated medical schools of Meharry, at Nashville, and Howard, at Washington, compare favorably with the best schools of the country. Mordecai Johnson, president of Howard, has made that University, born in politics, an institution now untrammeled, able to secure the best in equipment and in teaching force.

The higher standard of education in Negro colleges is noticeable in the South, especially in those colleges supported by the states. I would see a great advance in education if I went as far South as I did thirty years ago. But of course, this is true of all education. A new departure is the placing of Negroes on the faculties of northern colleges. James Weldon Johnson was a pioneer, lecturing at New York University. At Smith College, one of its graduates, Adelaide Cromwell Hill (What lovely curls she had when a little girl!) is appointed an instructor in the Department of Sociology. Smith has always been fair on the Negro question since Carrie Lee in 1914, thanks to her quiet persistence, was taken into one of its dormitories. Mrs. Hill's recent appointment, we are told in the college paper, is "the recognition of a distinguished alumna of the college and one of the most promising sociology majors the department has turned out in recent years. It is to be considered as offered regardless of race." Her grandfather, John W. Cromwell, one of Washington's distinguished Negroes of the last century, would have been very happy to have read this.

Vassar College, slow to admit Negro students, called a Negro, Sterling Brown of Howard University, to its English department in 1944. He came as exchange professor, taught successfully for a year, and was greatly missed by students and teachers when he returned to Washington. Professor Brown occupied an apartment in a two-family house, but unlike the tenants "On Whitman Avenue," was received without pother by the occupants of the first floor. Other colleges have Negroes on their faculties, at Harvard and Yale in the Medical Schools. Antioch College, Ohio, has appointed Walter F. Anderson as head of the department of music. For some time in New York we have had colored professors at New York University, City College, and Brooklyn College.

A second and much larger group of workers which, among the whites, goes into business, is still insignificant with the colored. Life insurance companies have for years been of importance in the Negro world, their growth having been fostered by white prejudice. Small enterprises so common once in America among white as well as colored, are in an extremely precarious situation. The chain store always wins. The co-operative, that training ground in business management, has small success in the United States, save among foreign born whites. Co-operation demands sacrifice today for the good of tomorrow. Still the co-operative movement is gaining, and the Negro is becoming aware of its meaning and its value. The great gain in business has been the entrance of the Negro into white shops and offices in positions he never had before.

Where one sees a great advance, so great as to be revolutionary, is in labor. No longer is the Negro on its outskirts, hated as a strikebreaker. He has become a part of the labor world. There are about 1,000,000 Negroes in the AFL and 750,000 in the CIO as of 1946. Both organizations plan a campaign in 1947 in the South and both will work for Negro membership. It would be hard to overemphasize the importance of this to the colored worker. His work will be more stable, he will be better paid, and a higher standard will be demanded of him. He will find himself a part of the working-class movement, not underbidding, but a fellow worker with the white. Fannie Cook in her entertaining novel, *Mrs. Palmer's Honey*, describes the effect of union membership on her colored heroine and on Honey's brother. The girl learned to think clearly, and the boy lost his sullen hate. Good humor returned to both as they laughed at caste with their white brothers. "The union is a stabilizing influence," the Rev. O. Clay Maxwell of Mt. Olivet tells me. Members must attend meetings or pay a fine. They acquire a sense of responsibility and learn of conditions outside their little group. Some become organizers. Frank Crossthwaite, organizer for the Ladies Garment Workers' Union, a friend of old days, drops in to tell me of the work he is doing and of its success. Enthusiasm like this is contagious. The Negro worker in industry is at last getting his chance.

I leave labor to go to the radio and listen to the Joe Louis fight. Of course he wins, and how satisfying it is to know that he is of good character, not boastful, never indulging in foul play, a good sport. Jackie Robinson playing in professional baseball is another heartening event. Like Jesse Owens, the Negro dashes his way into sport, and soon we shall not think of his race in our interest in him as an individual.

This morning's mail brings a communication from the *Churchman* (Episcopalian) describing "a program for providing incentive to clergymen throughout the United States to use their pulpits to combat religious and racial bias." The incentive is the offering of prizes for the best sermons on interracial subjects furnished by the *Churchman*. The sermons chosen will be given publicity. That so staid a denomination should offer so popular an appeal shows its belief in the immediate need of Christian teaching against racial prejudice. The Federation of Churches of Christ in America is giving much of its time and fervor to combating such prejudice. The Catholic Church is showing a determination to help by receiving more Negroes into the priesthood. But the most remarkable and far-reaching action of a religious organization is the stand of the Convention of the National Young Women's Christian Association in a recent pronouncement condemning all racial discrimination within the Association and urging the early cessation of all segregation.

A young movement, distinctly Christian in its form of attack, is the Congress of Racial Equality, familiarly known as Core. The great majority of its members are young people joined together in an organization to bring about racial equality. Their method is non-violent direct action. Operating in Syracuse, Oberlin, Detroit, Cleveland, Chicago, Columbus, Flint, Indianapolis, and San Francisco, their quiet work has succeeded when appeals to the civil law have failed. They never threaten, never launch diatribes, but try to persuade by argument and by quiet persistent action. Any campaign is thought out, planned in detail, and must be carried through in obedience to the leader's orders.

As an example, a restaurant discriminated against colored. The manager was approached and asked to serve Negroes. When argument failed, direct action began. Some twenty young people of both races went into the restaurant together and asked for service. The Negroes were told that they could not be served. They remained in their seats and the white companions with them refused to take the food offered them. Other white and colored came in, stood in line, and were refused counter service. So Core members remained for hours, some talking, some quietly reading, all behaving with the utmost decorum. The manager called in the police who refused to make an arrest since there was no disturbance. Hours went on. Other diners, interested in the outcome, remained at their seats. At length a woman not in Core left her place to invite a colored girl standing in line to sit at her table. The room broke into applause, and the manager gave the order to serve the colored. The restaurant continues to serve Negroes and has not lost trade. "What are you?" an inquiring policeman asked, "Communists?" "No, Christians."

Once a man is won over by these methods, Core finds, he becomes a friend and is won over for good. Swimming pools where segregation has been practiced have been opened to Negroes by the good nature of white and black members of Core.

One can see a very important result from these tactics; the white man or woman learns what the Negro is up against. He gets just as tired as the black man when he stands in line for hours. He, too, will find egg shells in his hash when service is reluctantly given. He will learn what it is like to be unwanted. Strong with courage and humility, it is amazing how often he wins. "We have no failures," George Houser, young Methodist preacher and one of Core's leaders, says, and then adds, "We never regard a job as finished until we have won."

Of changes in the South, I know no more than any other reader. In the winter of 1943-44 I was at Fisk University spending much of my time in the library, well known for its Negro collection. I delayed studying local conditions until I found it necessary to return to New York. I met a small group of students from Fisk and Scarrett, and deeply appreciated their friendly work among white and colored. I heard Dorothy Maynor sing in the city's auditorium and was pleased at the rapt attention of the white youth of the city. Among southern students good will is growing. Again and again, I meet with forward thinking men and women from the South. The post card John Haynes Holmes brought to the NAACP office and which started our lynching campaign could not exist today, much less go through the mails. Lynchers do not advertise themselves any longer. Governor Ellis Arnall, determined to put the Klan and the lyncher out of existence, left the State House in Atlanta, Georgia, on Jan. 1, 1947, but though a reactionary may succeed him the state has moved forward too fast to allow anyone for long to drag it back.

Virginius Dabney of the Richmond *Times Dispatch*, asked in *The Saturday Review of Literature*, April 13, 1946, *Is the South That Bad?*: "No section of America gets half as much attention in the public print as the South. How explain this fact? Why is the South the most discussed, the most debated, and the most denounced section of the United States?" The writer goes on to tell of the progress made in race relations, of the South's support of Franklin D. Roosevelt, of the new men running for office who stand for the best interests of colored and white alike. His plaint is that his section is represented at its worst, while little attention is given to its unquestioned advancement.

I sympathize with the editor of the *Times Dispatch,* but I am sure he can answer his own question. News of constructive work is rarely dramatic. Given time and talent for its preparation, it attracts popular interest as we realize when we find it in a magazine. But news of crime and violence is in itself drama, is easily handled and, with well-chosen headlines, sell the news-sheet. As long as lynchings, now few in number, continue, they will be featured. I suggest that Virginius Dabney turn the tables and call the country's attention to crime in New York. We do not lynch, our courts are orderly, but our crowded tenements thrust youth into the street where gangsters with bright but perverted minds teach theft and murder. Let some correspondent from the South, in vituperative language, describe the criminal aspects of the largest and richest city of the world. New York needs to hear this from outside, for its self-criticism is becoming feeble.

That night at the Civic Club when Taylor Gordon and Rosamond Johnson sang and played, Joshua fought the battle of Jericho until at length the walls came tumbling down. But the Walls of Jericho were rebuilt here in America—walls of prejudice, of injustice, of arrogance. At the end of these forty years of which I have written, are the trumpets sounding loud enough, and have the walls begun to fall? Certainly a breach has appeared through which many thousands have marched, a few with the genius to tell of their former restricted life. But those to whom the belief in white supremacy is a religion, hurry to close the opening. "These are exceptions," they say, "like trained dogs or the learned pig. The Negro can imitate the white, but he cannot create." "Higher education merely spoils a plough hand or a housemaid."

This last sentence is from W. B. Smith whose *The Color Line* I have already quoted. In florid language he repeated loose assertions, statements from little known documents, and from a few men of science. "We know the Negro," he said. The white Southerner reiterated this, and the listening Northerner, knowing few Negroes, usually nodded assent. Northern teachers in southern schools, social workers in northern cities, pointing out the Negro's ability, were discounted as prejudiced. Not until Binet devised his scale of intelligence tests was measured observation made possible, and World War I provided such observation on a large scale. The tests at first were inclined to ignore environment. As an example, an ignorant Negro sharecropper was asked to explain the position in a photograph of the ball and net on a tennis court!

But as time has gone on, and as sociologists have come to be regarded increasingly with respect ("Sociology is political economy for women," I heard a German professor hiss), the Negro has entered into his own. But slowly. In 1923, C. C. Bingham in *A Study of American Intelligence*, on the basis of Army psychologists' tests, asserted that beyond any doubt the intelligence of the white man was superior to that of the Negro. Seven years later, writing in the *Psychological Review*, he repudiated this statement declaring that his interpretation of the Army tests was all wrong and his comparative racial studies "without foundation." In the meantime, tests of white and colored children in Northern schools, as well as tests in World War II, have shown that coming from an environment as favorable as that of the white, the Negro is capable of the same intellectual attainment. Today's scientific opinion is clearly expressed by Ethel J. Alpenfils, anthropologist, Bureau for Intercultural Education, when she says in the *Catholic Review*, "In all important physical traits man is everywhere exactly the same. Important means brains, heart, lungs, nervous system."

This is the breach in Jericho's Walls. Whites can no longer lean back, like Smith of Tulane, secure in biological superiority and confident that in a short time the Negro will fulfill the prophecy of Walter Wilcox of Cornell and die of "disease, vice, and profound discouragement." The Negro is very much alive and is proving the truth of his new biological status by moving fast into the civilization, such as it is, of the white world.

What will happen? Nothing catastrophic. Despite science, the inhabitants of Jericho will think pretty much the same as before. But the Negro each year stands more securely in the United States. He has quietly registered his citizenship throughout much of the South. He understands our laws and our ways. American born, of the same cultural background as the white, he believes in upholding our standard of democracy at home as well as abroad. More and more the two races will meet on terms of equality. Sometimes it will be planned. In New England this summer, 1946, children from Shelton Bishop's Episcopal Church, from Representative A. Clayton Powell's Abyssinian Baptist Church, from Grace Congregational Church, and probably others, are sending children of their congregations to visit children of friendly congregations in Vermont, New Hampshire, Massachusetts, and Connecticut. These interracial visits were started in 1945 and proved a great success. The City of Quincy, Massachusetts, this year entertains young people of fifteen and sixteen, arranging many good times and also inter-racial study and discussion. Girls, like the one who spoke to Marian Anderson, will have the chance to put into action their desire to help. These planned opportunities may seem artificial, but the racial barrier of caste, built to give oppor-tunity only to the white, must be attacked in many ways.

In the meantime, those of us who "knew it all along" and felt something like contempt for others who sneered or adapted a Pecksniffian sympathy, can recall a "credo" that appeared a generation ago. The Negro, W. E. Burghardt Du Bois, born and educated in Massachusetts, teacher at Atlanta University, representative of America abroad, wrote:

"I believe that all men, black and brown and white, are brothers, varying through time and opportunity, in form and gift and feature, but differing in no essential particular, and alike in soul and the possibility of infinite development." *

And the anthropologist whom I have quoted closes the ques-tion when she says:

"Science affirms the great religious teaching, the Brother-hood of Man."

* From *Darkwater* by W. E. B. Du Bois (New York: Harcourt, Brace & World, 1920; reprinted by Schocken Books, New York, 1969).

APPENDIX

SPINGARN MEDAL WINNERS 1947–1969

32. Dr. Percy L. Julian, research chemist, 1947
33. Channing H. Tobias, defender of fundamental liberties, 1948
34. Ralph J. Bunche, international civil servant, 1949
35. Charles Hamilton Houston, chairman, NAACP legal committee, 1950
36. Mabel Keaton Staupers, leader in Negro nursing, 1951
37. Harry T. Moore, NAACP leader in Florida, 1952
38. Paul R. Williams, architect, 1953
39. Theodore K. Lawless, physician, 1954
40. Carl Murphy, publisher and civic leader, 1955
41. Jack Roosevelt Robinson, athlete, 1956
42. Martin Luther King, Jr., clergyman, 1957
43. Mrs. Daisy Bates and the Little Rock Nine, upholders of democratic ideals, 1958
44. Edward Kennedy (Duke) Ellington, musician, 1959
45. Langston Hughes, poet, 1960
46. Kenneth B. Clark, psychologist, 1961
47. Robert C. Weaver, "open occupancy" housing advocate, 1962
48. Medgar Wiley Evers, NAACP leader in Mississippi, 1963
49. Roy Wilkins, executive director, NAACP, 1964
50. Leontyne Price, Metropolitan Opera soprano, 1965
51. John H. Johnson, publisher, 1966
52. Edward W. Brooke III, U.S. senator, 1967
53. Sammy Davis, Jr., entertainer, 1968
54. Clarence M. Mitchell, Jr., civil rights leader, 1969

INDEX

Abolition, 5, 20, 170
Actors, Negro, 29, 30, 192, 250, 286-8
Addams, Jane, 282
Africa, 214
Afro-American, the, 279
Alexander, Will, 66, 180
Allen, Henry J., 256
Allyn School, 231
American Magazine, 113
Anderson, Marian, 288, 299
Anderson, Walter F., 291
Anti-Bias Bill, 220
Anti-lynching Bill, *see* lynching
Armstrong, General, 6, 67, 77
Arnall, Governor Ellis, 295
Artists, Negro, 118-22, 192, 288
Asbury Park Case, 108
Ashley, William J., 9
Astral tenement, 8, 11, 49
Atkins, J. Alston, 270
Atlanta Conference NAACP, 53-60, 177-80
Atlanta Constitution, 62, 178
Atlanta Race Commission, 233
Atlanta University, 53, 54, 77, 107, 148, 178, 183, 299
Atlantic Monthly, 54
Attucks, Crispus, 22
Atwood, George, 259

Bagnall, Robert W., 176, 241
Bahaist movement, 125-6
Baker, Ray Stannard, 73
Baldridge, Roy, 217
Baldwin, Roger, 205
Baldwin, W. H., 76
Ballou, General C. C., 135, 144

Baltimore, Corporal, 137
Barber, Max, 58
Barnett, Ida Wells, 106
Barrett, Jane Porter, 123
Batchelder, Francis, 276
Bates, Ruby, 235-6
Beaseley, Delia, 214
Beecher, Henry Ward, 5, 221
Bell, Thomas J., 24, 82
Benson, William, 78
Bentley, Charles E., 101, 105
Bernays, Edward, 178
Besant, Annie, 132
Bethune, Mary McLeod, 77, 228
Bird, Augusta, 240
Birth of a Nation, 127-30
Bishop, Hutchins, 110
Blascoer, Frances, 110, 111, 147
Boardman, Helen, 247
Bontemps, Arna, 188
Boston Conference, NAACP, 125
Boutté, Captain Matthew, 138
Braithwaite, William Stanley, 189
Bratton, U. S., 155, 158
Breiner, Leon, 202, 205
Bridge Street Church, 27
Brooklyn, Connecticut, 4
Brooklyn, N. Y., 16, 21, 27, 59, 121, 180
Brooks, Dr. William, 25, 26, 110
Brown, Charlotte Hawkins, 77, 229
Brown, John, 101
Brown, Richard Lonsdale, 119-21
Brown, Sterling N., 291
Brush, George de Forrest, 118
Bryan, William Jennings, 203
Buck, Pearl, 263
Bulkley, Robert J., 256, 257

Bulkley, Dr. W. L., 103
Burleigh, Charles, 5
Burleigh, Harry T., 27, 28
Burns, William, 114
Byrnes, Senator, 261

Calhoun colored school, 66-79, 83
Canfield, Dorothy, 263
Cardozo, Dr. F. N., 111
Carter, Lester, 234-6
Carver, George Washington, 77
Century Magazine, 6
Chain gang, 58
Charity Organization Society, 49, 105, 124
Chesnutt, Charles, 19, 214, 238
Chesnutt, Edward, 69, 71
Chesnutt, Helen, 238, 239, 240, 241
Chicago Conference, NAACP, 125, 126
Children's Aid Society, 38, 39, 41
Children's Court, 37
Christian Science Monitor, 255
Christian, Virginia, 122-3
Church, Robert, 247
Civic Club, 189, 193-8, 296
Civil Rights Law, 194
Clark University, Atlanta, 56, 65, 178
Cleveland Conference, NAACP, 167-71, 238
Coatesville, Pennsylvania lynching, 113-5
Cody, Mr., 122
Cole, Bob, 28, 189
Cole, Lorenza Jordan, 215-20
Connelly, Marc, 30
Consumers' League, 110, 179
Cook, George W., 110
Cook, Myrtle Foster, 227
Cook, Will Marion, 28
Core (Congress of Racial Equality), 293-5
Cosmopolitan Club Dinner, 43-7
Costigan-Wagner anti-lynching bill, 257-66

Crandall, Prudence, 4-5
Crawford, Anthony, 150-1, 171
Crisis, the, 107, 108, 111, 144, 149, 172, 176, 183, 191, 255, 273, 282
Crispus Attucks, 22
Crogman, Dr., 56, 65
Cromwell, Mary E., 41, 42
Crosby, Ernest Howard, 11
Cullen, Countee, 190, 193
Curley, Mayor James W., 128

Dabney, Virginius, 264, 295-6
Dancers, Negro, 192, 288
Dancy, John C., 207, 209
Darrow, Clarence, 198-213, 271
Davenport, Frances G., 132
Davis, Brigadier-General Benjamin O., 272
Delleas, the, 240
Denison, Colonel Franklin A., 142
Dern, George H., 249
Deutsch, Babette, 193
Devol, Dr. Edmund, 44
Dickinson, C. E., 256
Dill, Augustus Granville, 108, 195
Dillingham, Mabel, 67, 68
Discrimination, racial, 20, 138-40, 144, 200, 216, 220, 228-9, 245-50, 267-9, 273-4, 277, 278, 280, 293-5
Diton, Mr. and Mrs. Carl, 215
Domestic Service, Negroes in, 14, 30
Douglas, Aaron, 192
Douglas, Helen Gahagan, 275
Douglass, Frederick, 3, 7, 16
Draper, Ruth, 39
Du Bois, W. E. Burghardt, 8, 47, 53, 54, 55, 56, 65, 100, 101, 102, 103, 107, 108, 111, 126, 131, 144, 176, 183, 193, 195, 240, 241, 255, 281, 299
Dudley, Sam, 29, 30
Dunbar, Paul Laurence, 187
Durham, Plato, 179
Dvorak's *New World Symphony*, 28
Dyer anti-lynching bill, 236-8, 257

Eagan, John J., 179
Eagels, Jeanne, 208
Eastland, Senator, 275
Eastman, Max, 87
Eaton, Isabel, 22
Eboué, Félix, 287-9
Education, the Negro in, 5, 20, 55, 57, 59-60, 66-78, 84, 101, 103, 104, 130, 170, 178, 230, 266-9, 290-1, 297
Edwards, Harry Stilward, 6
Eleazer, Mr., 233, 236
Elliott, John Lovejoy, 113
Emerson, Helena, 36
Employment, Negro in, 12, 13-16
Europe, James Reese, 141

Fair Employment Practice Committee, 251
Farmers' Conference, Tuskegee, Ala., 74
Farrand, Livingston, 104
Fauset, Jessie, 192
Favrot, Leo M., 169-71
Federal Council of Churches, 140
Ferris, William, 44
Field Work, NAACP, 221-36
Finot, Jean, 131
Fisher, Harrison, 227
Fisher, Rudolph, 192
Fisk University, 112, 192, 217, 252, 295
Fort Valley School, 226
Frankfurter, Felix, 110, 271

Gammon Theological School, 178
Garland Fund, 205
Garrison, William Lloyd, 107, 114
Gavagan anti-lynching bill, 261-3
Gibbs, William, Jr., 267
Gilpin, Charles, 30, 192
Gordon, Taylor, 194, 217
Grandfather Clause Case, 116-7, 252
Greene, Paul, 30
Greenpoint Settlement, 8, 10, 12, 34, 41, 44, 49, 226
Greenwich House, 12, 13, 33

Griffith, David Wark, 127-9
Grimke, Archibald, 107, 125, 168
Gross, George, 227
Gruening, Martha, 111, 114, 217

Haiti, American occupation of, 181-3
Half a Man, 14
Hallowell, Emily, 71
Hampton Institute, 6, 53, 67, 70, 140
Harding, Ann, 208
Harding, President Warren G., 182
Harlem, 16, 33, 41, 184, 188, 192
Harris, Joel Chandler, 6
Harris, Julian, 264
Hastie, William H., 109, 265, 270-2
Hayes, Roland, 27
Haynes, George, 112
Hayward, Colonel, 141
Henderson, G. W., 192
Henry Street Settlement, 110
Hershaw, W. H., 100
Heyward, Du Bose, 30
Hill, Adelaide Cromwell, 290
Hill, Leslie Pinckney, 185
Hillman, Sidney, 251
Hogan, Ernest, 29
Holmes, Justice, 161
Holmes, John Haynes, 107, 112, 113, 133, 281, 295
Holsey, Albon W., 184
Holt, Hamilton, 44, 45
Hoover, President Herbert, 249, 251, 257
Hope Day Nursery, 39
Horton, Judge, 234-6
Housing, 12, 21, 32-7, 56, 115, 199, 208
Houston, Charles H., 109, 271
Houston, Texas, Riots, 137, 142
Howard Colored Orphan Asylum, 6
Howard University, 110, 120, 134, 201, 290
Hughes, Chief Justice, 266

Hughes, Langston, 52, 191
Hull House, 126
Hunt, Henry, 226
Hunton, Addie W., 58, 59, 139, 183
Hunton, Eunice, 240
Hurst, Bishop John, 110, 171

Independent, the, 44, 73, 100, 102
Interracial Committee, Atlanta, 178-80

Jacksonville, Florida, 195
Johnson, Charles S., 286
Johnson, Grace Nail, 242
Johnson, Dr. Guy, 230
Johnson, James Weldon, 28, 47, 147, 148, 149, 171, 176-243, 252, 290
Johnson, Jed J., 263
Johnson, Kathryn, 139
Johnson, Mordecai, 290
Johnson, Rosamond, 189, 194, 195, 287, 296
Jonas, Rosalie M., 39
Jones (of Piney Woods), 77
Jones, Scipio Africanus, 158-62

Katy Ferguson Home, 26
Kelley, Florence, 110, 179
Kenneday, Paul, 110
Kirchwey, George W., 194
Ku Klux Klan, 128, 177, 200, 201, 242, 264, 295

Labor, the Negro in, 245, 250, 251, 291-2
Ladies Garment Workers, 27, 292
Lakewood, New Jersey, Case, 108
Lampkin, Daisy E., 176, 221
Lane, Preston, 259
L'Ouverture, Toussaint, 182
Leach, Mrs. Henry Goddard, 158
League of Nations, 183
Lee, Canada, 250, 287, 108-11
Legal Committee, NAACP, 258, 265, 266, 271, 282

Légitime, M. and Mlle., 131
Liberator, the, 107
Liebowitz, Samuel, 233
Lincoln Settlement, 111
Lincoln University, 19, 257
Litany of Atlanta, 65
Locke, Alain, 187
London, England, 131
London, Jack, 85
Los Angeles Conference, NAACP, 214
Loud, Joseph Prince, 110
Louis, Joe, 292
Louisville Segregation Case, 116, 148
Loving, Pierre, 193
Lowell, Josephine Shaw, 11
Lucas, Dr., 227
Lynching, 104, 106, 113-15, 130, 149-55, 170, 173, 177, 195, 257-66, 295-6
Lyons, Maritcha, 20

McClendon, Rose, 192
McCulloch, Roscoe C., 256
McKay, Claude, 185
McWilliams, Carey, 166
Maclean, Mary, 113, 114, 120, 125
MacVane, Silas, 9
Maley, William, 27, 79-82
Manning, Joseph, 87
March-on-Washington Movement, 251, 285
Marshall, Louis, 109, 162, 271
Marshall, Thurgood, 270, 271
Martin, Isadore, 110
Martineau, Judge John E., 160
Masses, the, 87
Maxwell, William, 20
May, Samuel J., 4
Mead, Senator James M., 275
Medicine, the Negro in, 289
Messenger, the, 188
Meyer, Annie Nathan, 286
Migration of Negro to the North, 21, 208, 215
Milholland, John E., 33, 34, 63, 79, 80, 110, 131, 132

Millard, Laura Williams, 240
Miller and Lyle, 28
Miller, Dorrie, 275
Miller, Frank, 223
Miller, Rev. Fraser, 44
Mills, Florence, 30
Miscegenation, 16, 17, 19
Mississippi Flood Control, 245-9
Mitchell, Abbie, 287
Moffat, Adeline, 22
Morris Brown College, 178
Morton-Jones, Dr. V., 111, 121
Moryck, Brenda, 220, 241
Moskovitz, Henry, 103
Motion pictures, the Negro in, 127-30, 193
Moton, Robert Russa, 143, 249
Murphy, Colonel, 158, 159
Murphy, Judge Frank, 204, 205, 212, 271
Musicians, Negro, 29, 189-92, 288-9, 291 (*see* Spirituals)

Nail, John B., 16, 242
Nash, Roy, 111, 147, 150
Nation, the, 182
National Association of Colored Women, 123-4, 177
National Conference on Lynching, 170
National Negro Business League, 60, 184
National Negro Committee, 105, 124
Nelson, Lt. Dennis Donald, 276
Nerney, May Childs, 111, 147
Newbold, Superintendent, 230
New-Negro movement, 185-93
New York City, status of Negro in, 12-16, 24, 63, 220, 283-7
New York Evening Post, 60, 101, 109, 113
New York Times, 177, 255
New York World, 264
Niagara Movement, 100, 104, 110
Nixon, Dr. L. A., 269
Nock, Albert J., 113, 190
Norwood, Judge, 46

Odum, Dr. Howard, 229
Ogden, Robert, 53
O'Neal, Emmet, 153
O'Neill, Eugene, 30, 193
Opera, the Negro in, 192
Opportunity, 188
O'Reilly, Leonora, 11
Outlook, the, 11, 12
Ovington, Mrs. C. K. (sister-in-law), 220

Pace, Harry, 55
Padmore, George, 183
Page, Thomas Nelson, 6
Pan-African Congress, 183-4
Parade, silent protest, 180
Parrish, Carl, 289
Parker, Judge John J., 251-7
"Passing," 18
Patterson, Heywood, 234-6
Paulding, James K., 11
Payton, Philip, 16, 60
Perry, Julian, 204
Phelps-Stokes Fund, 140
Phipps, Henry, 33, 34, 48
Pickens, William, 176, 221
Pillsbury, Albert E., 105
Pittsburgh Courier, the, 246, 279
Plymouth Church, 5, 6, 7
Postles, Grace, 218-9
Powell, Adam Clayton, Jr., 125, 298
Pratt Institute, 8
Price, Victoria, 235-6
Progressive Farmers and Household Union, 154
Public Works Administration, the Negro in, 250

Race traits, 10-11, 37, 226-7
Radcliffe College, 7-9, 19
Rai, Lajput, 193
Rainsford, William, 27
Randolph, A. Philip, 251
Randolph, Richetta, 109, 241
Ray, Cornelia, 20
Red Cross, 139, 278
Restrictive Covenant Cases, 266

Riots, race, 63-6, 102, 126, 137, 154-65, 172, 180, 201-2
Riverbank, 239
Roberts, Owen J., 257
Robeson, Paul, 193, 287
Robinson, Bill, 30, 192
Rollins College, 228
Roosevelt, Eleanor, 282
Roosevelt, Franklin D., 251, 261, 272, 296
Roosevelt, Theodore, 25, 61, 155
Roseborough, Viola, 74
Russell, Charles Edward, 103, 105, 106, 110, 208, 222, 281
Rynder, Isaiah, 5

Sachs, Walter C., 107
St. Augustine's Church, 44
St. Benedict the Moor, 40
St. Cyprian's Episcopal Church, 41
St. George's Church, 27
St. Mark's M. E. Church, 24, 25, 110
St. Philip's Church, 40, 110
Sanial, Lucien, 47
San Juan Hill, 35, 36, 40, 43, 49, 50, 56, 71
Sawkins, Major Alfred, 141
Schiff, Jacob, 115
Schuyler, George, 246-9
Schuyler, Phillipa, 289
Scott, Emmett J., 136
Scottsboro Case, 231-6
Seager, Henry, 13
Segregation, 21, 22, 56, 58, 101, 111, 115-6, 198-213, 266, 270, 274, 277, 287
Seligmann, Herbert, 108, 111, 176, 178, 241, 254
Sharecropper system, 68, 74, 158, 245, 297
Shaw, Anna Howard, 153
Shaw, Mrs. Quincy, 22
Shaw House (Robert Gould Shaw), 22
Sheldon, Edward, 17
Shillady, John R., 147-75

Simkhovitch, Dr., 13
Simkhovitch, Mary Kingsbury, 13, 39
Sims, Rev. George H., 39, 40
Sinclair, William, 110, 130, 131
Sleet, Jessie, 124
Smith College, 290
Smith, Gerrit, 26
Smith, Dr. L. E., 270
Smith, W. B., 16
Social Reform Club, 11-13
Social workers, colored, 123
Socialism, 87
Somerville, Dr., 214
Southerners against slavery, 8, 71, 74, 263
Spahr, Charles, 11, 12, 14
Spargo, John, 44
Spaulding, Mr. and Mrs., 207, 209
Spiller, 131
Spingarn, Arthur B., 109, 110, 179, 199, 204, 208, 265, 271
Spingarn, J. E., 110, 117, 134, 136, 148, 168, 222, 254
Spingarn Medal, 117-8, 135, 168, 214
Spirituals, Negro, 27, 28, 51, 71, 193-5, 228
Sports, the Negro in, 292-3
Springfield, Mass. Conference, NAACP, 218
Steffens, Lincoln, 223
Storey, Moorfield, 23, 105, 109, 116, 129, 148-9, 161, 170, 237, 271
Stover, Charles, 11
Stowe, Harriet Beecher, 3
Studin, Charles H., 109, 110
Sweet Segregation Case, 198-213

Talbert, Mary B., 154, 177
Teachers' salary cases, 267-8
Tenements, Negro, 30-5, 42, 48
Texas Primary Cases, 269-70
Thomas, Neval, 168
Thomson, Beatrice, 227
Thorne, Charlotte R., 67, 68, 70, 73, 74

Toms, Robert M., 200, 208, 212
Torrence, Ridgely, 30
Torrey, Beth, 231
Torture cases, 266
Towns, Professor, 58
Toynbee, Arnold, 9
Tridon, Andre, 44
Trotter, Monroe, 23, 106
Turner, Dr., 200-2
Turner, Frank M., 149
Turner, Mary, 152
Tuskegee Institute, 12, 53, 74, 77, 80, 143
Tuskegee apartments, 34, 35

Underground railroad, 4
Union Baptist Church, 39, 40, 41, 51
Unions, Negro, 27, 154, 163, 164
Unitarian Church, 6
University cases, 268-9
Urban League, 26, 112, 208, 244

Van Ness Place, 216
Van Vechten, Carl, 47
Vassar College, 291
Villard, Oswald Garrison, 44, 45, 62, 103, 105, 107, 109, 110, 112, 114, 119, 127, 133, 147, 281
Vote, the Negro, 57, 104, 107, 256, 269-70

Wagner, Robert F., 256, 259, 275
Wald, Lillian, 110
Walker, Zack, 113
Wallace, James, 15, 60
Waller, Dr. Owen M., 17, 43, 44, 101
Walling, William English, 100, 101, 103, 104, 110, 157, 281
Walling, Anna Strunsky, 102

Walters, Bishop Alexander, 103, 105, 281
Walton, Elizabeth, 112
Walton Free Kindergarten, 36, 39, 41
Waring, Laura Wheeler, 241
Washington, Booker T., 6, 12, 16, 22, 25, 54, 60, 61, 67, 74, 76, 105
Wellever, Captain, 276
Wells, H. G., 183
White Brute, The, 88-98
White, Jane, 286
White, Walter, 64, 148, 149, 156, 157, 176, 186, 195, 199, 203, 204, 208, 241, 244-282
Wilberforce University, 202, 209
Wile, Dr. Ira S., 194
Wilkins, Roy, 246, 249
Williams, Bert, 28, 29
Williams, Charles H., 140, 143
Wilson, Butler R., 23
Wilson, Mrs. Butler R., 129
Wilmer, Rev. C. B., 179
Winter, Ella, 223
Wise, Rabbi Stephen S., 113
Wood, Holingsworth, 112
Woofter, Professor, 230
World War I, 133-46, 169, 297
World War II, 250, 272-80, 298
Wright, Dr. Louis T., 289
Writers, Negro, 185-92, 214, 230, 285-6

Yergan, Max, 241
Young, Colonel Charles, 134
Young Men's Christian Association, 22, 23, 24, 76, 82, 139
Young Women's Christian Association, 293